BLACK WIDOW

KISS OR KILL

W9-AYG-323

BLACK WIDOW: KISS OR KILL. Contains material originally published in magazine form as BLACK WIDOW #6-8 and IRON MAN: KISS AND KILL #1. First printing 2011. ISBN# 978-0-7851-4701-5. Published by MARVEL WORLDWIDE, INC., a subsidiary of MARVEL ENTERTAINMENT, LLC. OFFICE OF PUBLICATION: 135 West 50th Street, New York, NY 10020. Copyright © 2010 and 2011 Marvel Characters, Inc. All rights reserved. $12.99 per copy in the U.S. and $13.99 in Canada (GST #R127032852); Canadian Agreement #40668537. All characters featured in this issue and the distinctive names and likenesses thereof, and all related indicia are trademarks of Marvel Characters, Inc. No similarity between any of the names, characters, persons, and/or institutions in this magazine with those of any living or dead person or institution is intended, and any such similarity which may exist is purely coincidental. **Printed in the U.S.A.** ALAN FINE, EVP - Office of the President, Marvel Worldwide, Inc. and EVP & CMO Marvel Characters B.V.; DAN BUCKLEY, Publisher & President - Print, Animation & Digital Divisions; JOE QUESADA, Chief Creative Officer; JIM SOKOLOWSKI, Chief Operating Officer; DAVID BOGART, SVP of Business Affairs & Talent Management; TOM BREVOORT, SVP of Publishing; C.B. CEBULSKI, SVP of Creator & Content Development; DAVID GABRIEL, SVP of Publishing Sales & Circulation; MICHAEL PASCIULLO, SVP of Brand Planning & Communications; JIM O'KEEFE, VP of Operations & Logistics; DAN CARR, Executive Director of Publishing Technology; JUSTIN F. GABRIE, Director of Publishing & Editorial Operations; SUSAN CRESPI, Editorial Operations Manager; ALEX MORALES, Publishing Operations Manager; STAN LEE, Chairman Emeritus. For information regarding advertising in Marvel Comics or on Marvel.com, please contact John Dokes, SVP Integrated Sales and Marketing, at jdokes@marvel.com. For Marvel subscription inquiries, please call 800-217-9158. **Manufactured between 6/23/2011 and 7/12/2011 by QUAD/GRAPHICS, DUBUQUE, IA, USA.**

0 9 8 7 6 5 4 3 2 1

WRITER
DUANE SWIERCZYNSKI
PENCILER
MANUEL GARCIA
INKERS
LORENZO RUGGIERO (#1 & #3)
& BIT (#2)
COLORIST
JIM CHARALAPIDIS
LETTERER
BLAMBOT'S NATE PIEKOS
COVER ART
TRAVEL FOREMAN & JUNE CHUNG
ASSISTANT EDITOR
CHARLIE BECKERMAN
EDITOR
RALPH MACCHIO

"IRON WIDOW" FROM
IRON MAN: KISS AND KILL

WRITER
JOE AHEARNE
ARTIST
BRIAN CHING
COLORIST
MICHAEL ATIYEH
LETTERER
DAVE SHARPE
COVER ART
BRIAN CHING & CHRIS SOTOMAYOR
EDITOR
MICHAEL HORWITZ

COLLECTION EDITOR
JENNIFER GRÜNWALD
EDITORIAL ASSISTANTS
JAMES EMMETT & JOE HOCHSTEIN
ASSISTANT EDITORS
ALEX STARBUCK & NELSON RIBEIRO
EDITOR, SPECIAL PROJECTS
MARK D. BEAZLEY
SENIOR EDITOR, SPECIAL PROJECTS
JEFF YOUNGQUIST
SENIOR VICE PRESIDENT OF SALES
DAVID GABRIEL
SVP OF BRAND PLANNING & COMMUNICATIONS
MICHAEL PASCIULLO
BOOK DESIGN
JEFF POWELL

EDITOR IN CHIEF **AXEL ALONSO**
CHIEF CREATIVE OFFICER **JOE QUESADA**
PUBLISHER **DAN BUCKLEY**
EXECUTIVE PRODUCER **ALAN FINE**

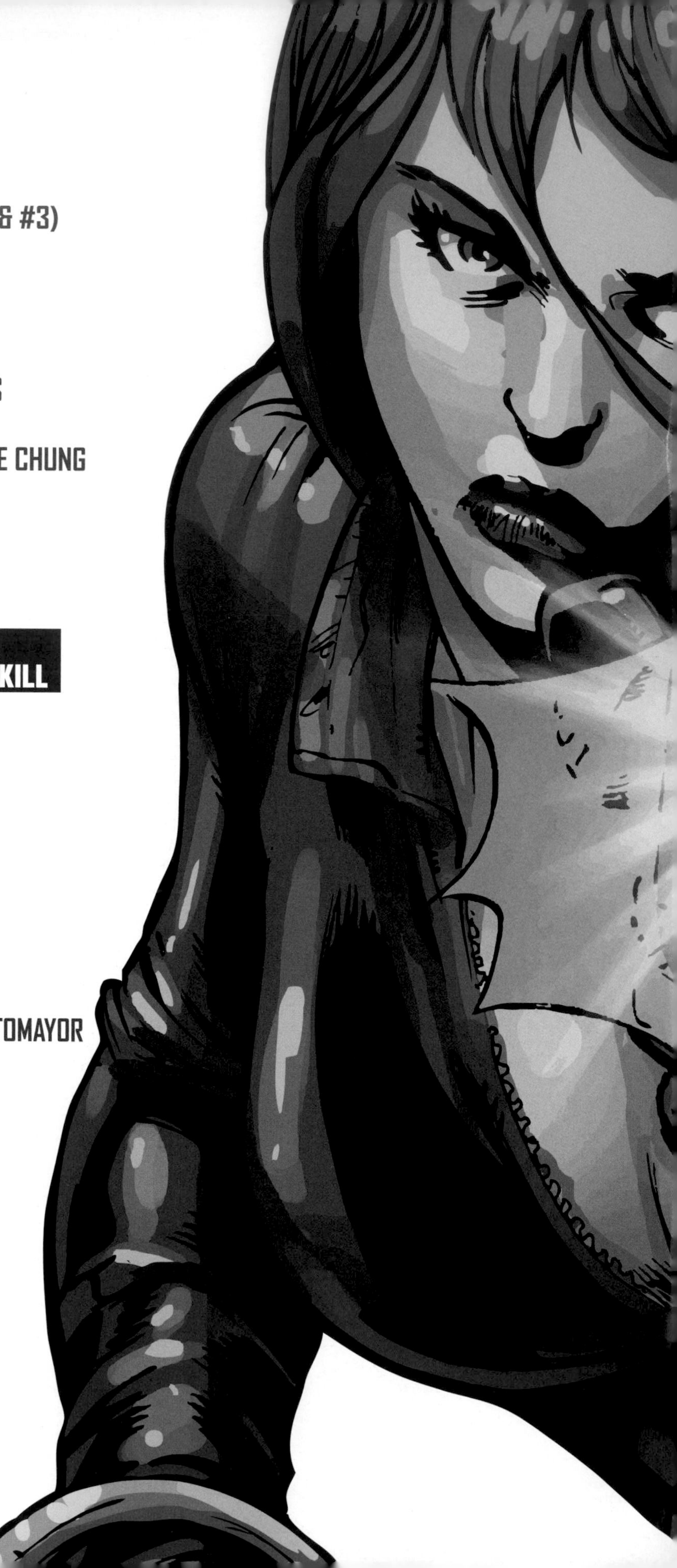

6

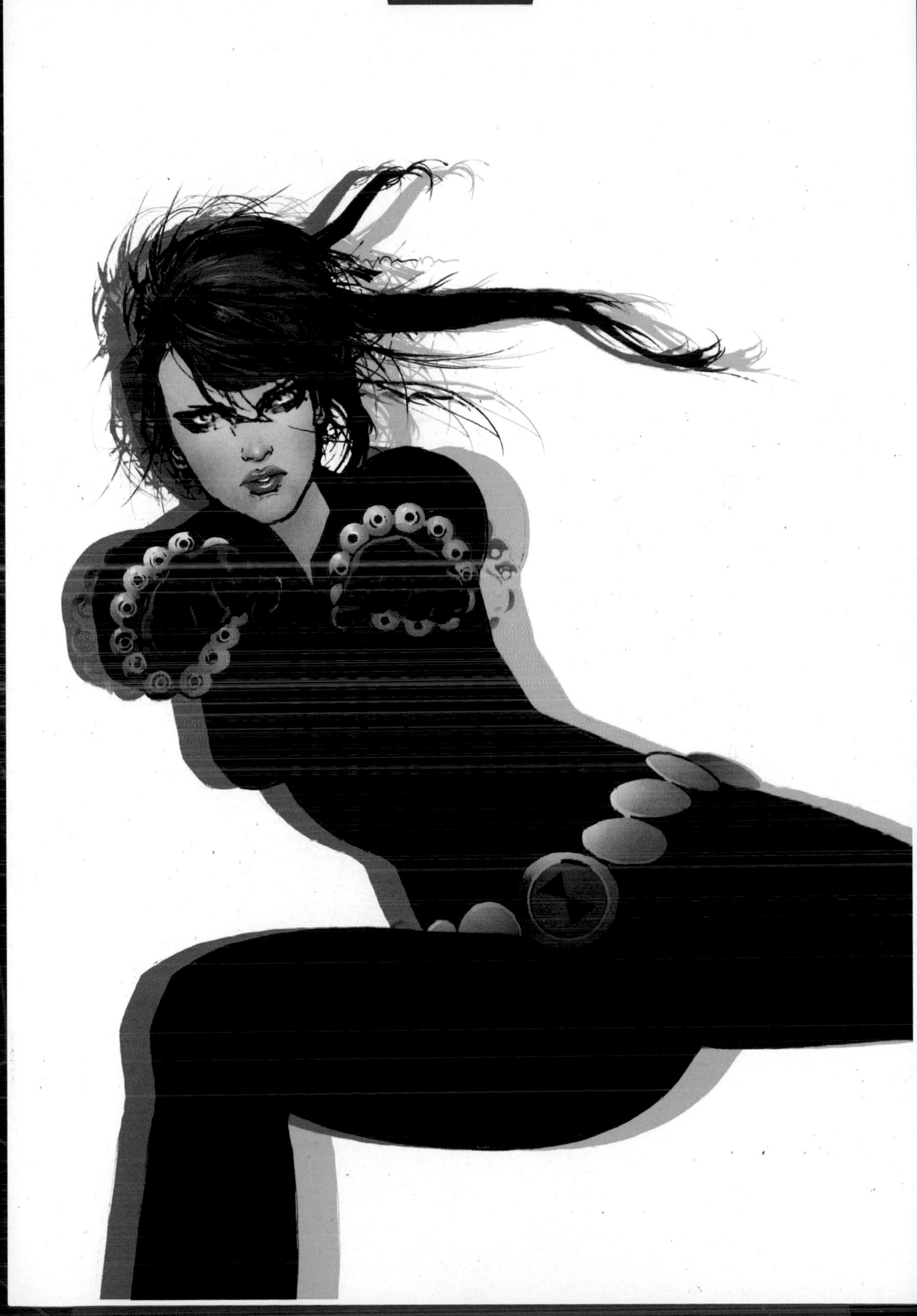

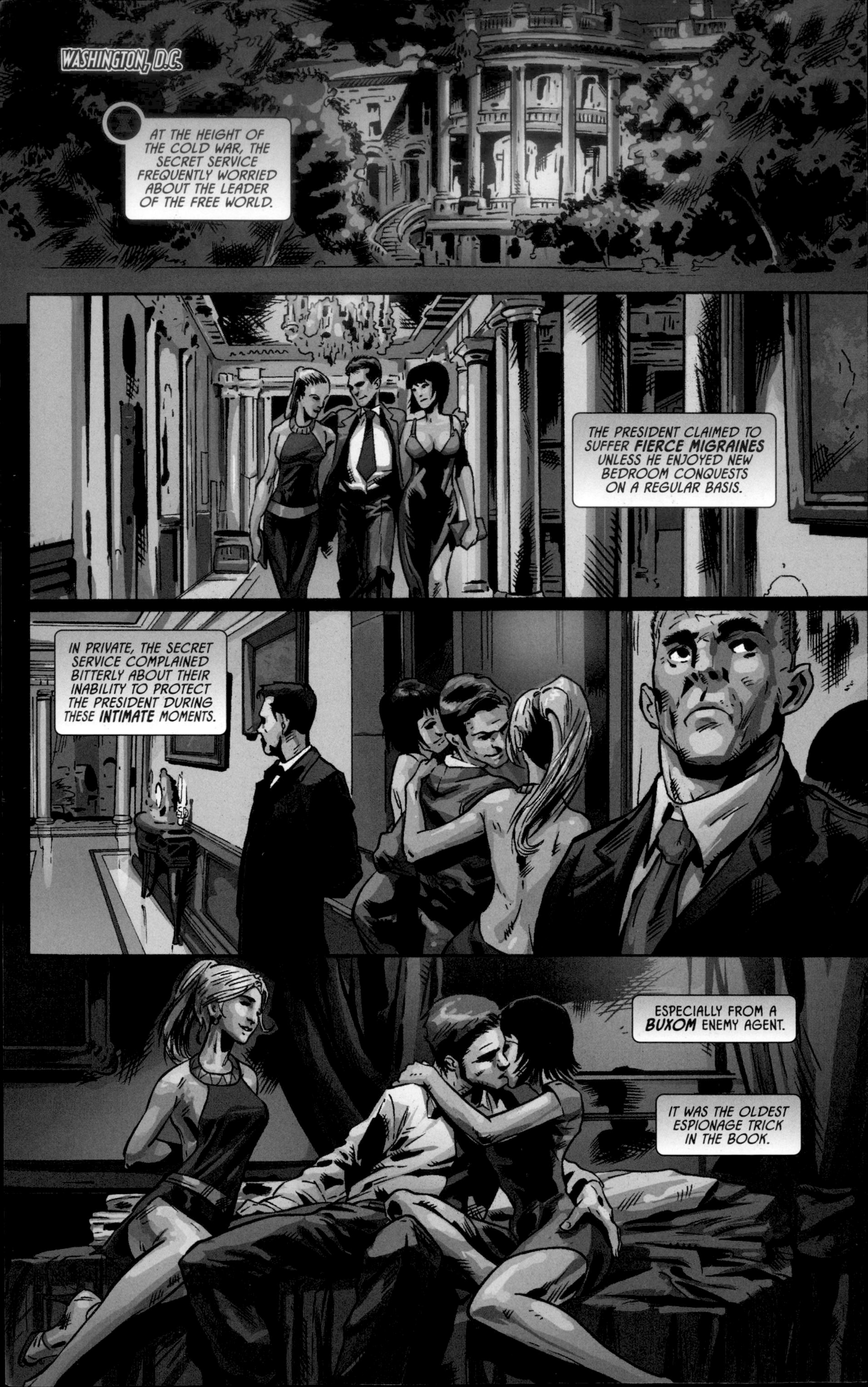
WASHINGTON, D.C.
AT THE HEIGHT OF THE COLD WAR, THE SECRET SERVICE FREQUENTLY WORRIED ABOUT THE LEADER OF THE FREE WORLD.
THE PRESIDENT CLAIMED TO SUFFER FIERCE MIGRAINES UNLESS HE ENJOYED NEW BEDROOM CONQUESTS ON A REGULAR BASIS.
IN PRIVATE, THE SECRET SERVICE COMPLAINED BITTERLY ABOUT THEIR INABILITY TO PROTECT THE PRESIDENT DURING THESE INTIMATE MOMENTS.
ESPECIALLY FROM A BUXOM ENEMY AGENT.
IT WAS THE OLDEST ESPIONAGE TRICK IN THE BOOK.

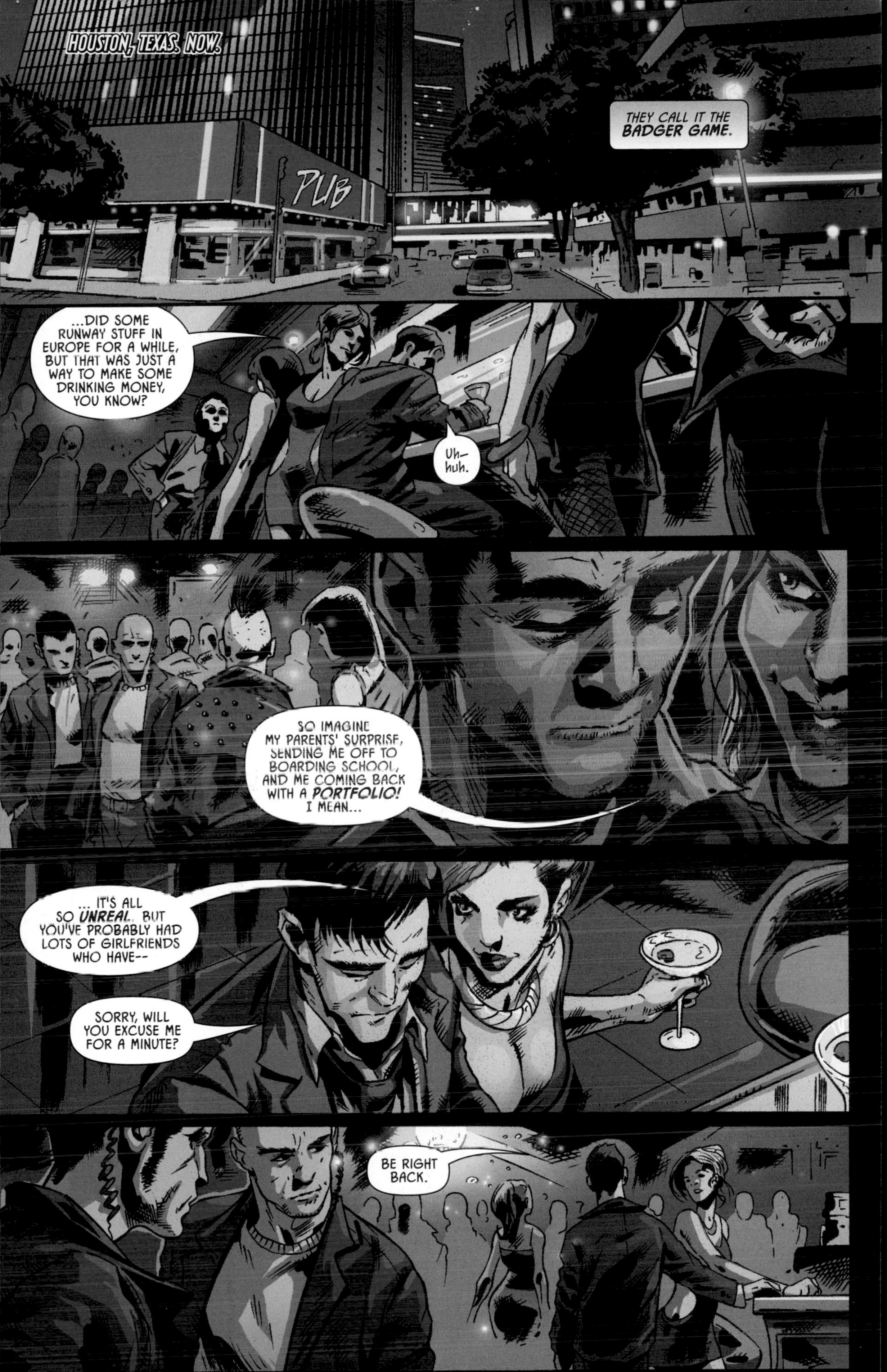
HOUSTON, TEXAS. NOW.
THEY CALL IT THE BADGER GAME.
...DID SOME RUNWAY STUFF IN EUROPE FOR A WHILE, BUT THAT WAS JUST A WAY TO MAKE SOME DRINKING MONEY, YOU KNOW?
Uh-huh.
SO IMAGINE MY PARENTS' SURPRISE, SENDING ME OFF TO BOARDING SCHOOL, AND ME COMING BACK WITH A PORTFOLIO! I MEAN...
... IT'S ALL SO UNREAL. BUT YOU'VE PROBABLY HAD LOTS OF GIRLFRIENDS WHO HAVE--
SORRY, WILL YOU EXCUSE ME FOR A MINUTE?
BE RIGHT BACK.

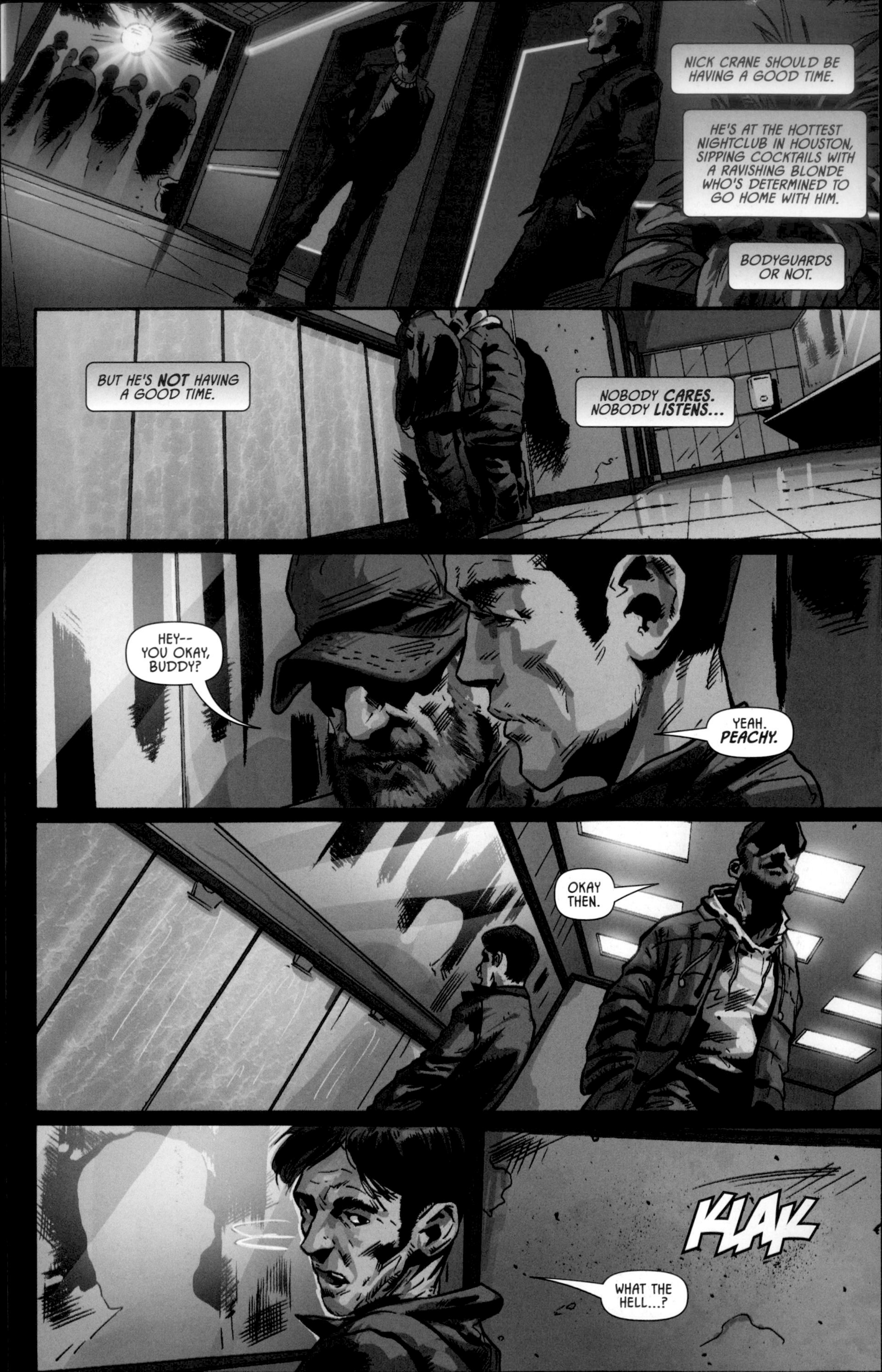
NICK CRANE SHOULD BE HAVING A GOOD TIME.
HE'S AT THE HOTTEST NIGHTCLUB IN HOUSTON, SIPPING COCKTAILS WITH A RAVISHING BLONDE WHO'S DETERMINED TO GO HOME WITH HIM.
BODYGUARDS OR NOT.
BUT HE'S NOT HAVING A GOOD TIME.
NOBODY CARES. NOBODY LISTENS...
HEY-- YOU OKAY, BUDDY?
YEAH. PEACHY.
OKAY THEN.
KLAK
WHAT THE HELL...?

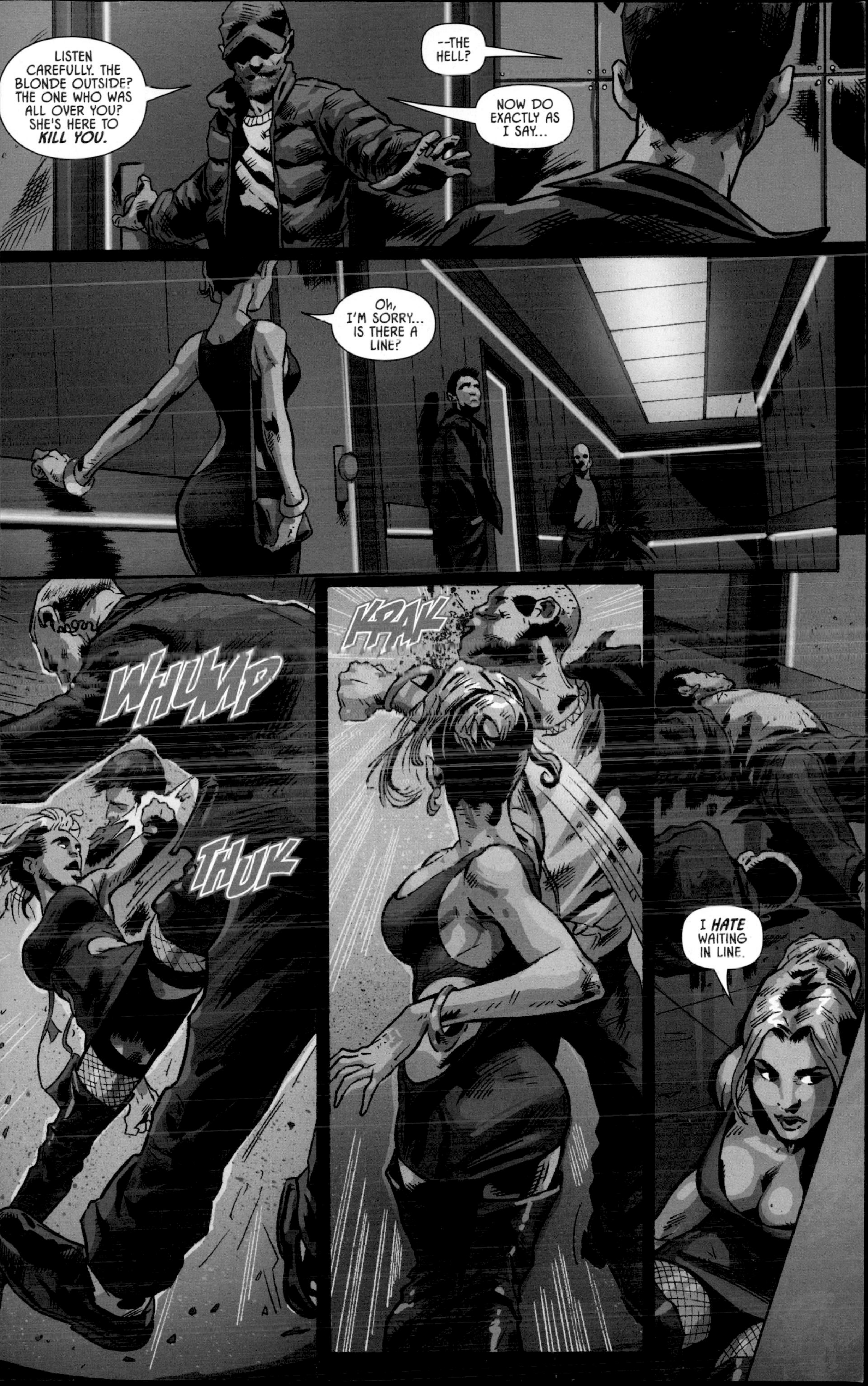
LISTEN CAREFULLY. THE BLONDE OUTSIDE? THE ONE WHO WAS ALL OVER YOU? SHE'S HERE TO KILL YOU.
--THE HELL?
NOW DO EXACTLY AS I SAY...
Oh, I'M SORRY... IS THERE A LINE?
WHUMP
THUK
KRAK
I HATE WAITING IN LINE.

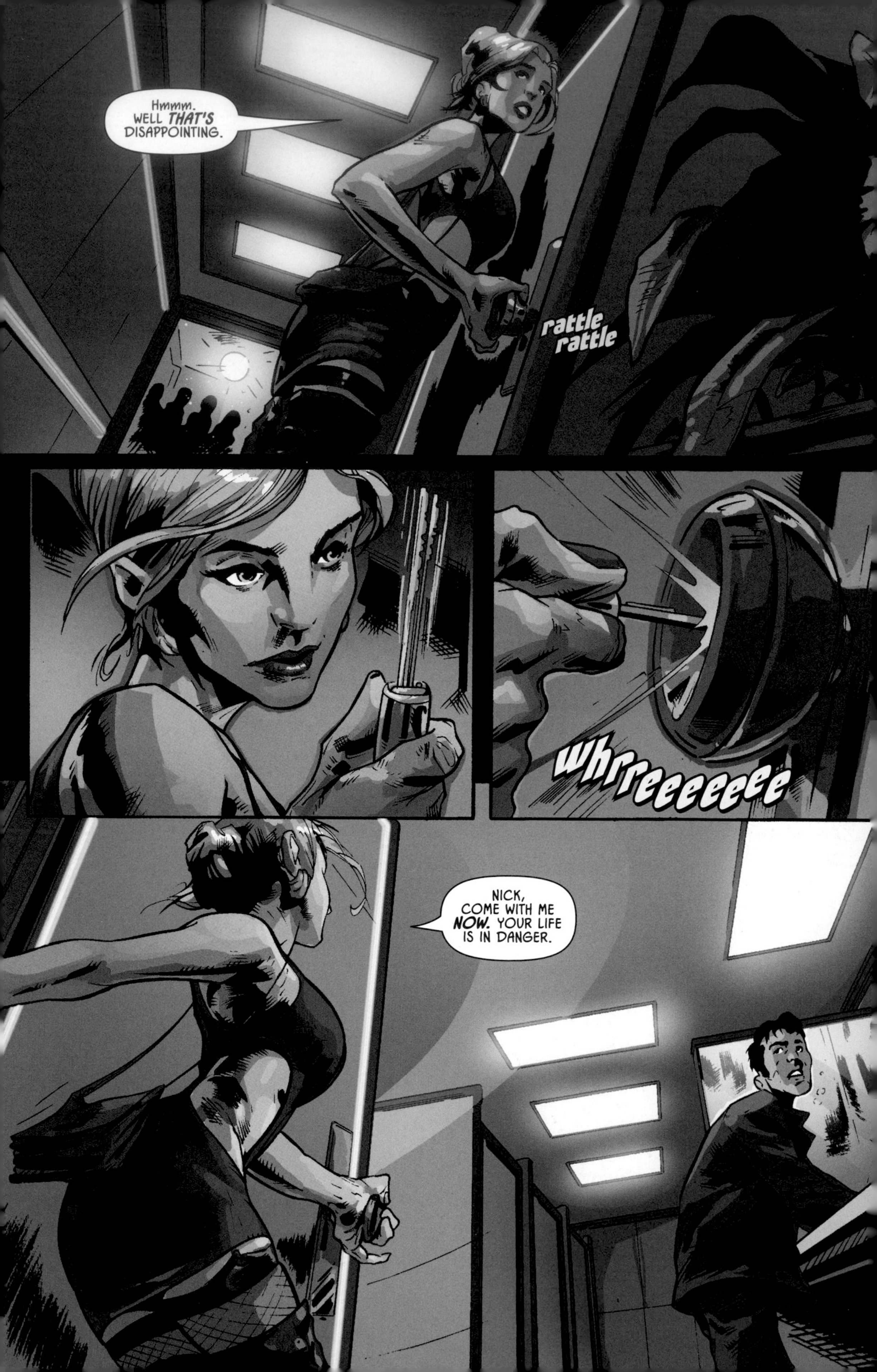
Hmmm. WELL THAT'S DISAPPOINTING.
rattle rattle
whrreeeeeeee
NICK, COME WITH ME NOW. YOUR LIFE IS IN DANGER.

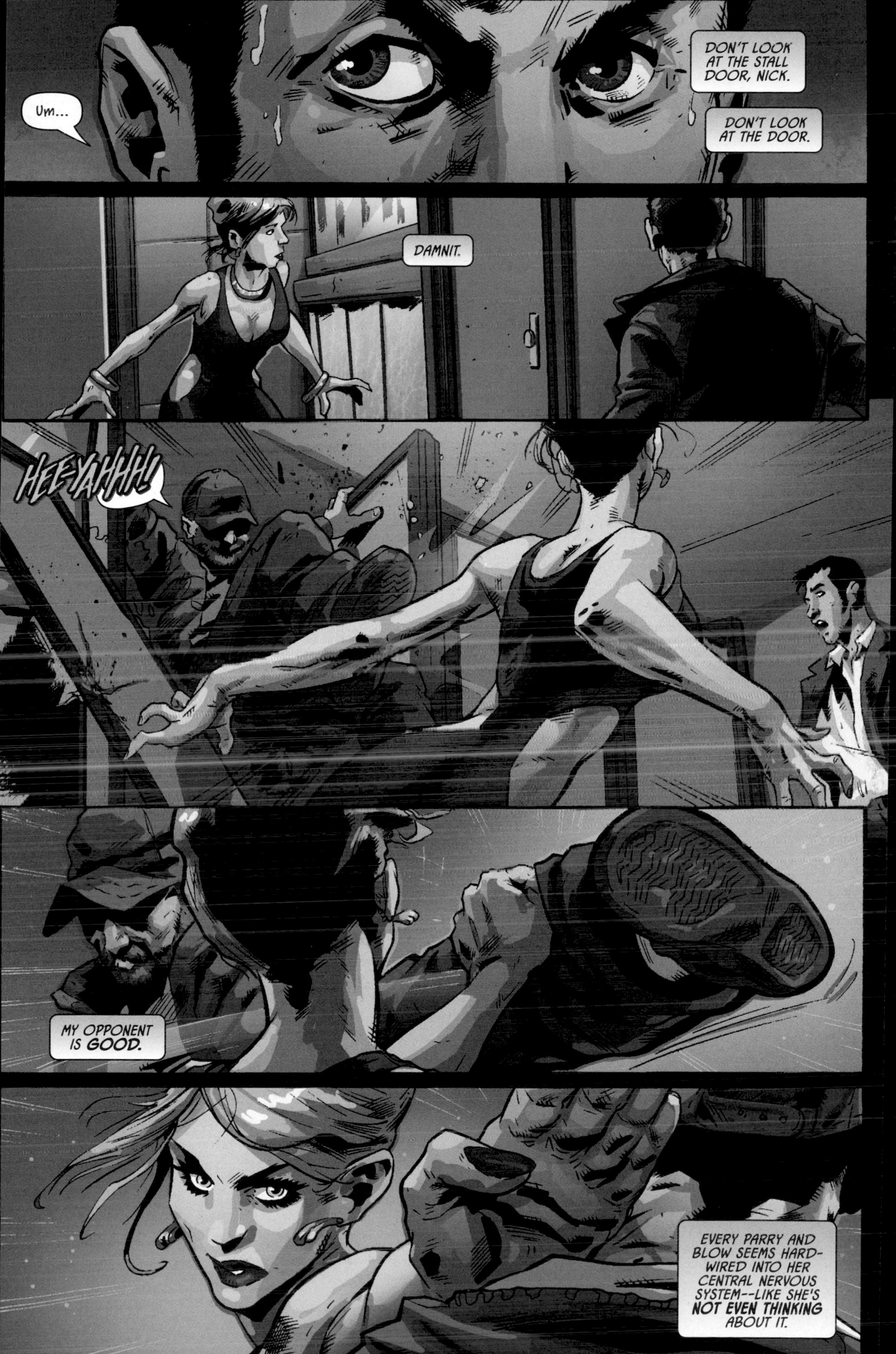

Um...
DON'T LOOK AT THE STALL DOOR, NICK.
DON'T LOOK AT THE DOOR.
DAMNIT.
HEE-YAHHH!
MY OPPONENT IS **GOOD.**
EVERY PARRY AND BLOW SEEMS HARD-WIRED INTO HER CENTRAL NERVOUS SYSTEM--LIKE SHE'S **NOT EVEN THINKING** ABOUT IT.

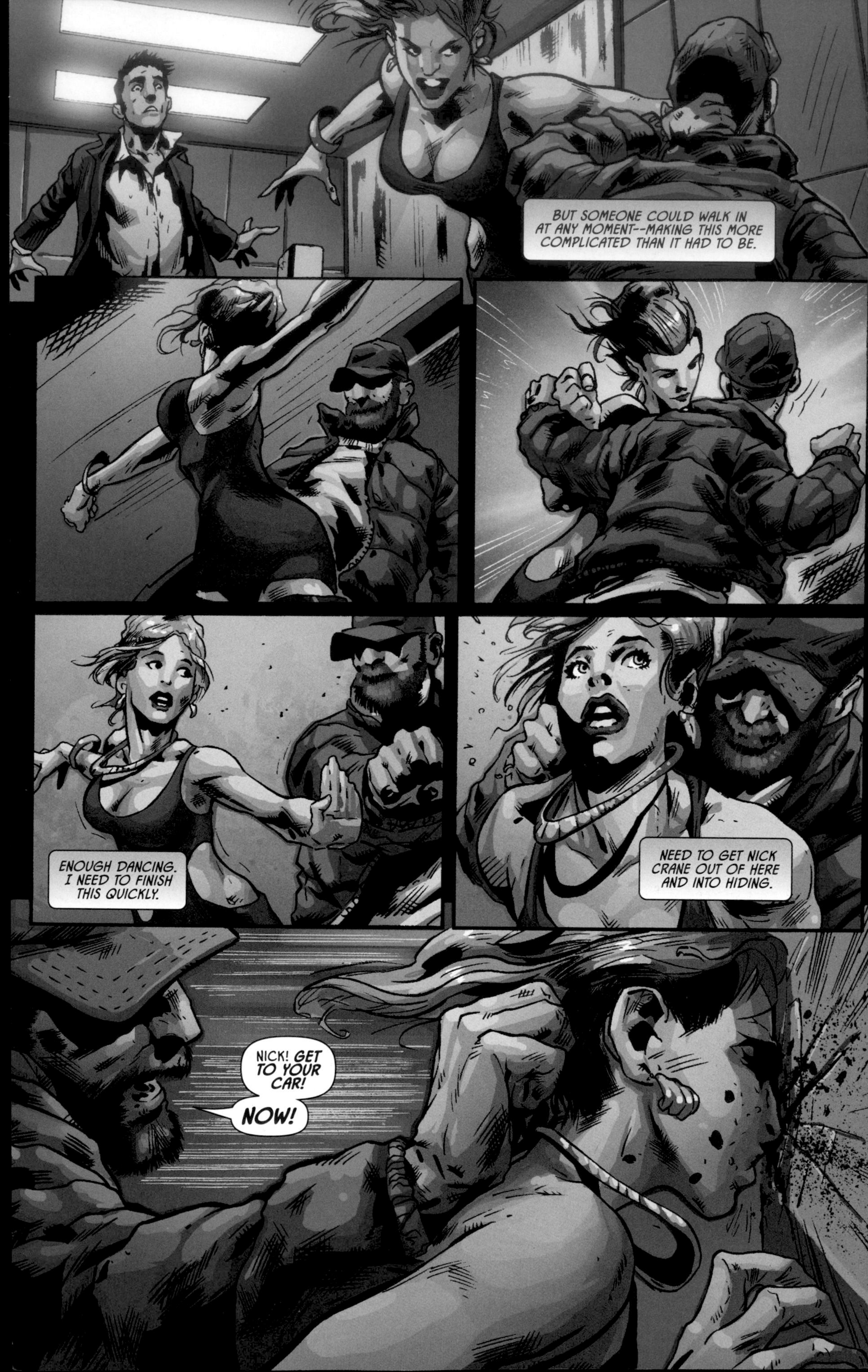
BUT SOMEONE COULD WALK IN AT ANY MOMENT--MAKING THIS MORE COMPLICATED THAN IT HAD TO BE.
ENOUGH DANCING. I NEED TO FINISH THIS QUICKLY.
NEED TO GET NICK CRANE OUT OF HERE AND INTO HIDING.
NICK! GET TO YOUR CAR!
NOW!

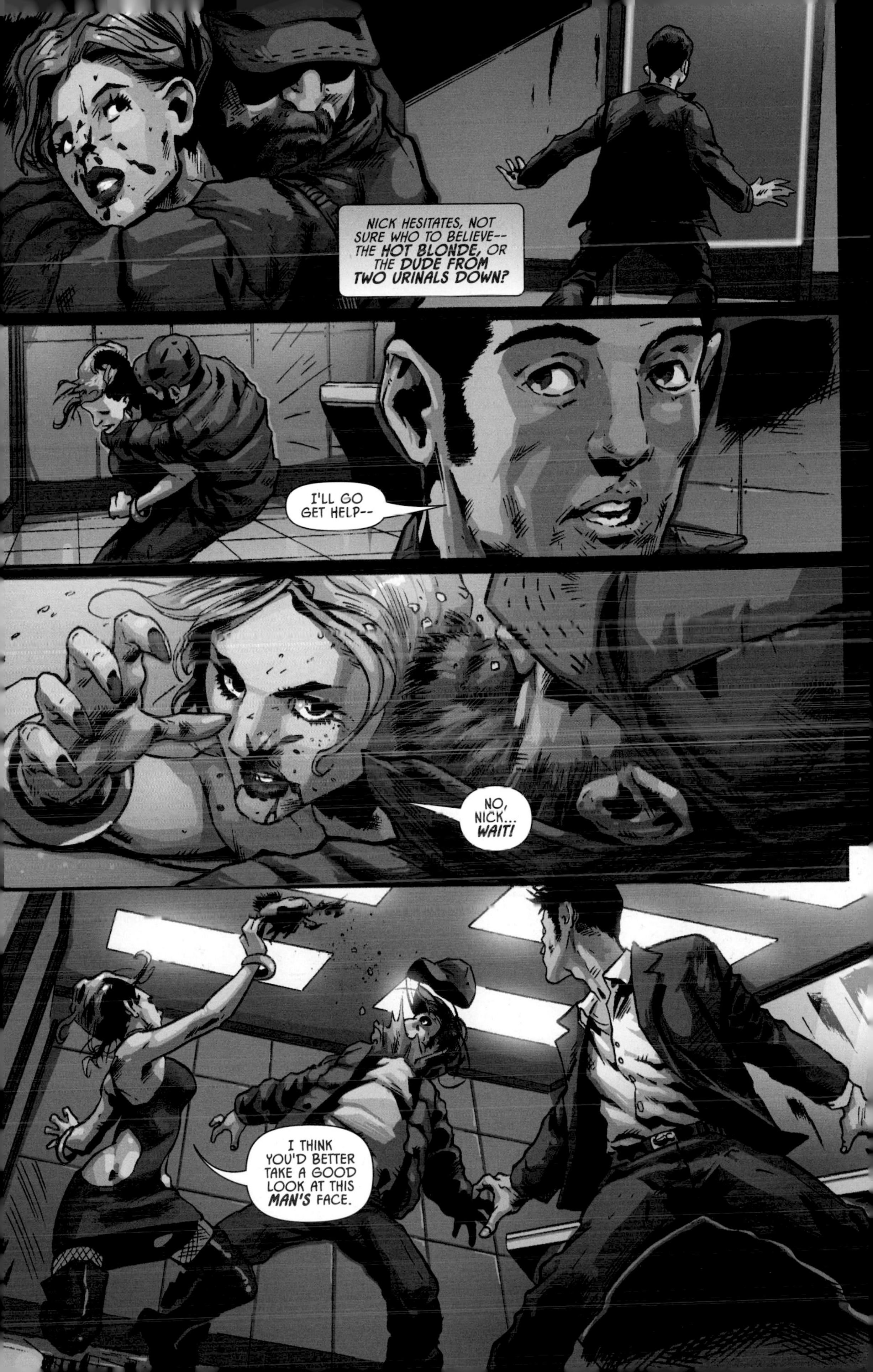
NICK HESITATES, NOT SURE WHO TO BELIEVE-- THE HOT BLONDE, OR THE DUDE FROM TWO URINALS DOWN?
I'LL GO GET HELP--
NO, NICK... WAIT!
I THINK YOU'D BETTER TAKE A GOOD LOOK AT THIS MAN'S FACE.

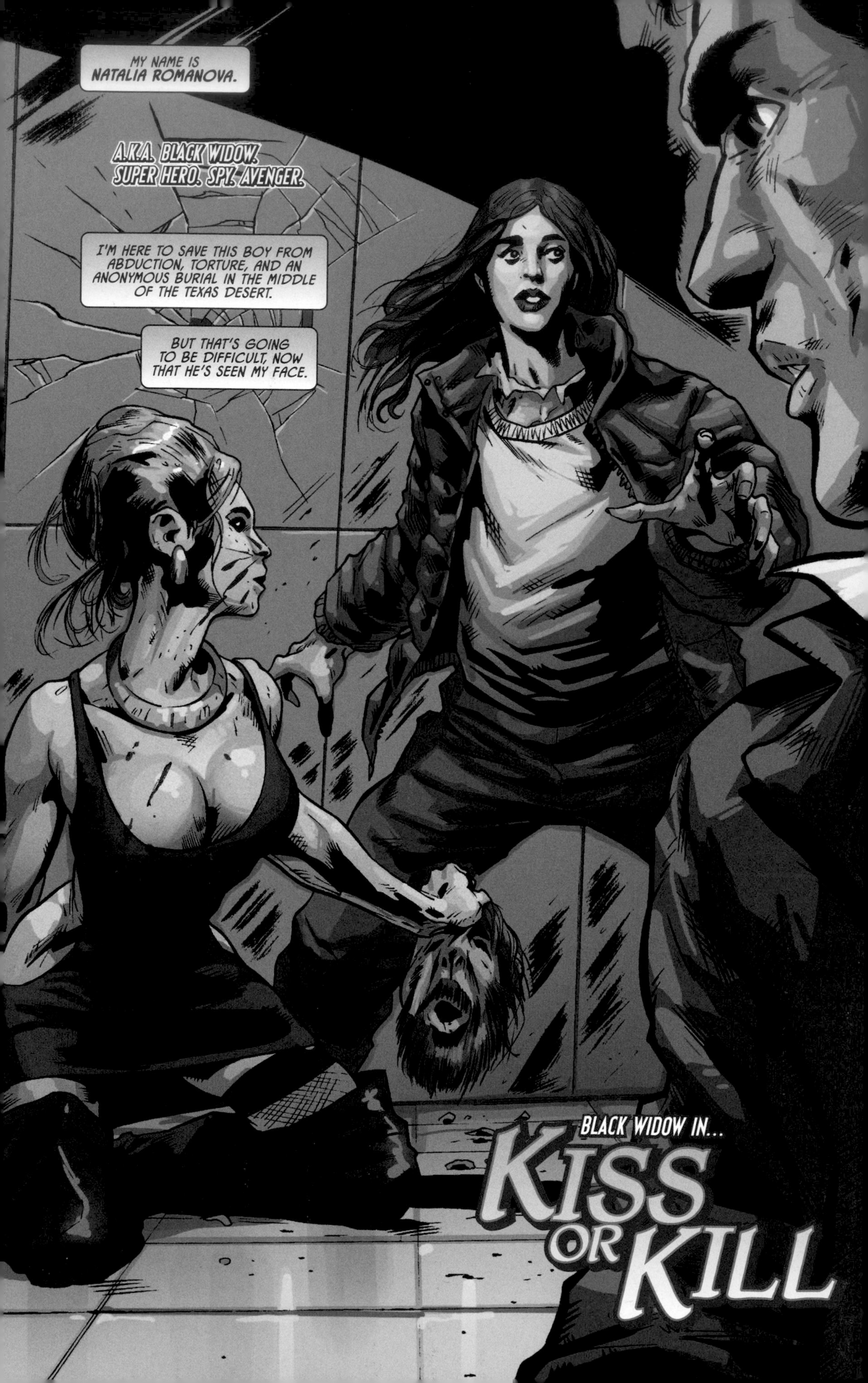
MY NAME IS NATALIA ROMANOVA.
A.K.A. BLACK WIDOW. SUPER HERO. SPY. AVENGER.
I'M HERE TO SAVE THIS BOY FROM ABDUCTION, TORTURE, AND AN ANONYMOUS BURIAL IN THE MIDDLE OF THE TEXAS DESERT.
BUT THAT'S GOING TO BE DIFFICULT, NOW THAT HE'S SEEN MY FACE.
BLACK WIDOW IN...
KISS OR KILL

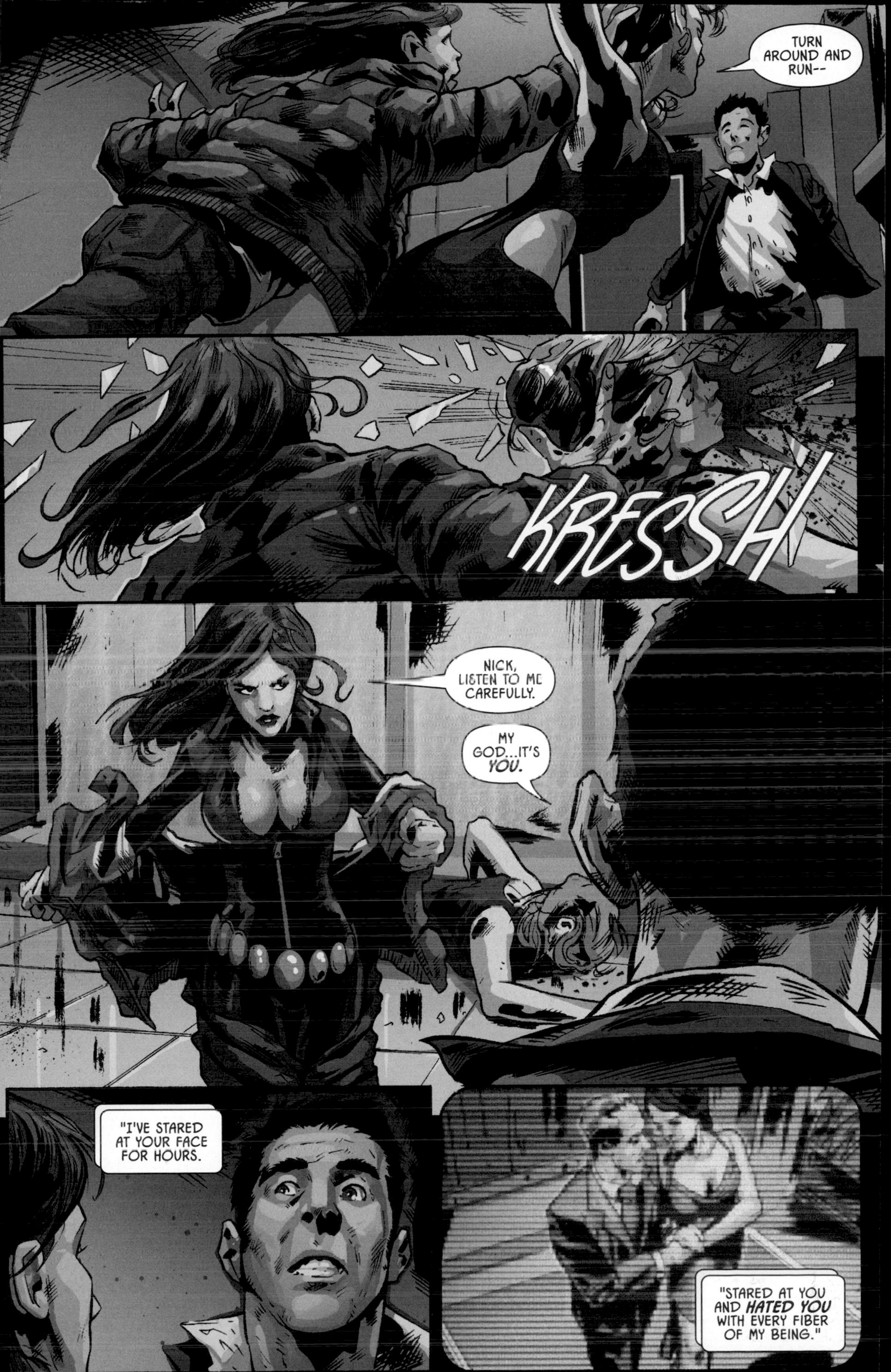
TURN AROUND AND RUN--
KRESSH
NICK, LISTEN TO ME CAREFULLY.
MY GOD...IT'S YOU.
"I'VE STARED AT YOUR FACE FOR HOURS.
"STARED AT YOU AND HATED YOU WITH EVERY FIBER OF MY BEING."

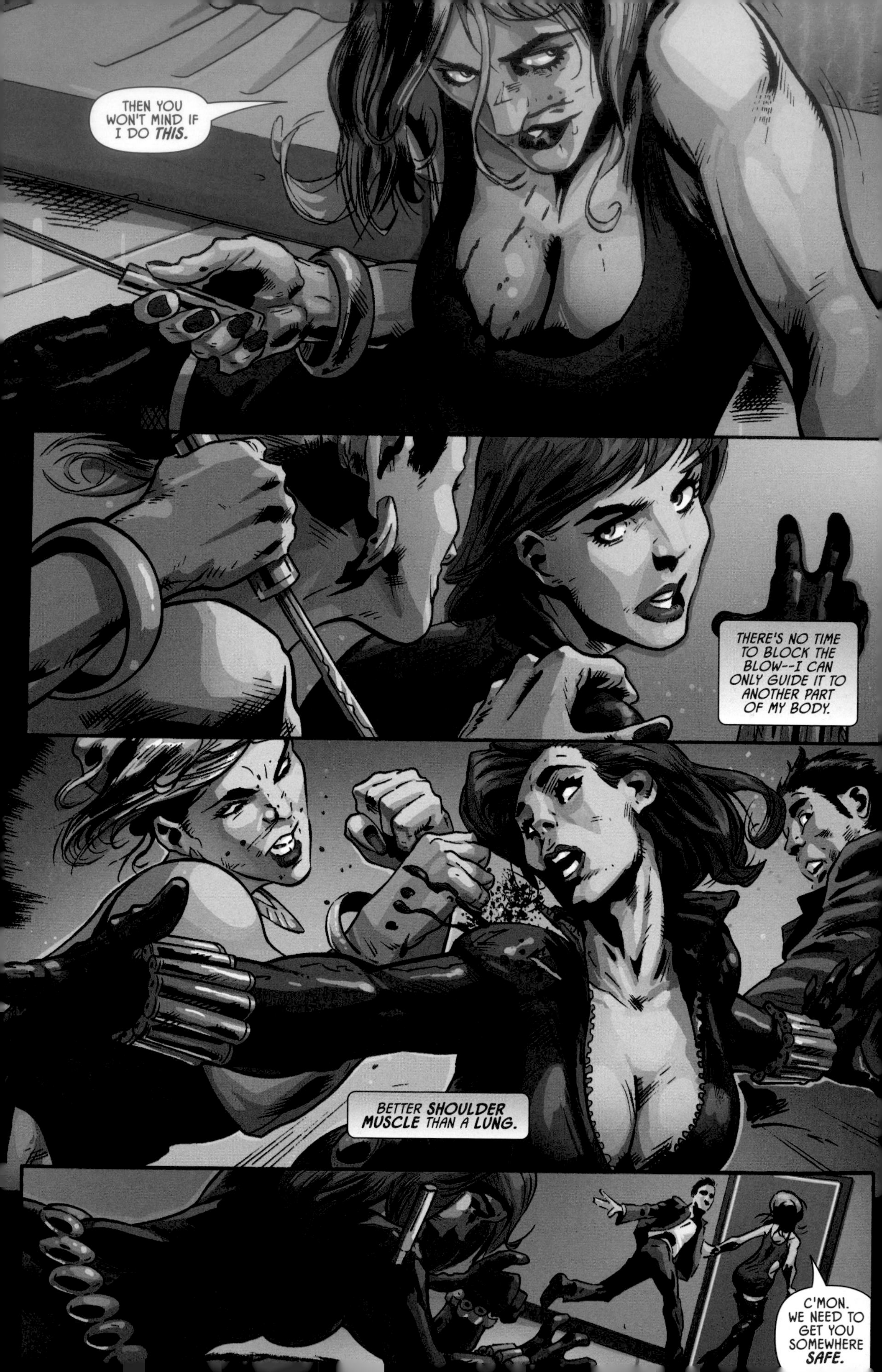

THEN YOU WON'T MIND IF I DO *THIS.*
THERE'S NO TIME TO BLOCK THE BLOW--I CAN ONLY GUIDE IT TO ANOTHER PART OF MY BODY.
BETTER **SHOULDER MUSCLE** THAN A **LUNG.**
C'MON. WE NEED TO GET YOU SOMEWHERE *SAFE.*

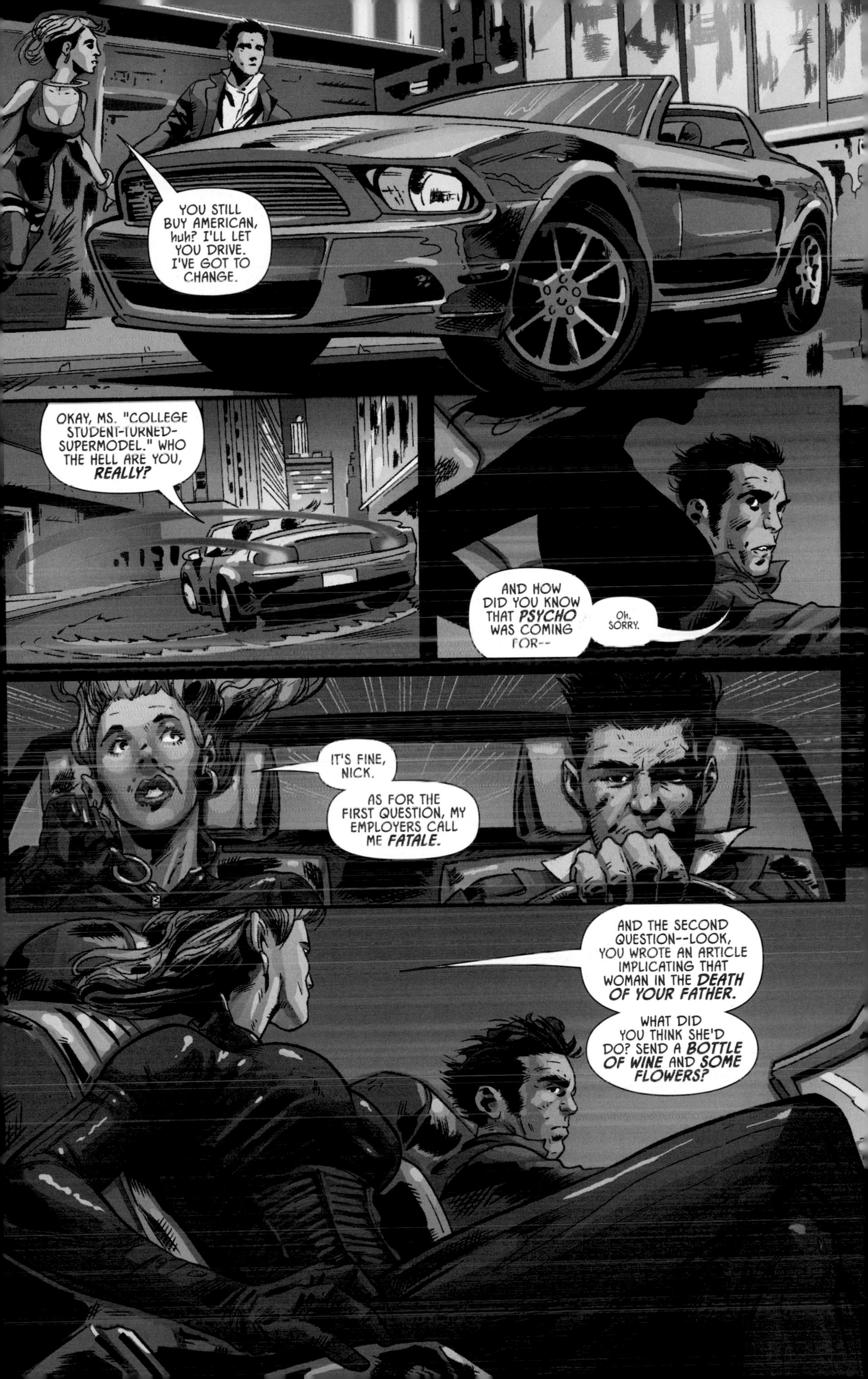
YOU STILL BUY AMERICAN, huh? I'LL LET YOU DRIVE. I'VE GOT TO CHANGE.
OKAY, MS. "COLLEGE STUDENT-TURNED-SUPERMODEL." WHO THE HELL ARE YOU, REALLY?
AND HOW DID YOU KNOW THAT PSYCHO WAS COMING FOR--
Oh. SORRY.
IT'S FINE, NICK.
AS FOR THE FIRST QUESTION, MY EMPLOYERS CALL ME FATALE.
AND THE SECOND QUESTION--LOOK, YOU WROTE AN ARTICLE IMPLICATING THAT WOMAN IN THE DEATH OF YOUR FATHER.
WHAT DID YOU THINK SHE'D DO? SEND A BOTTLE OF WINE AND SOME FLOWERS?

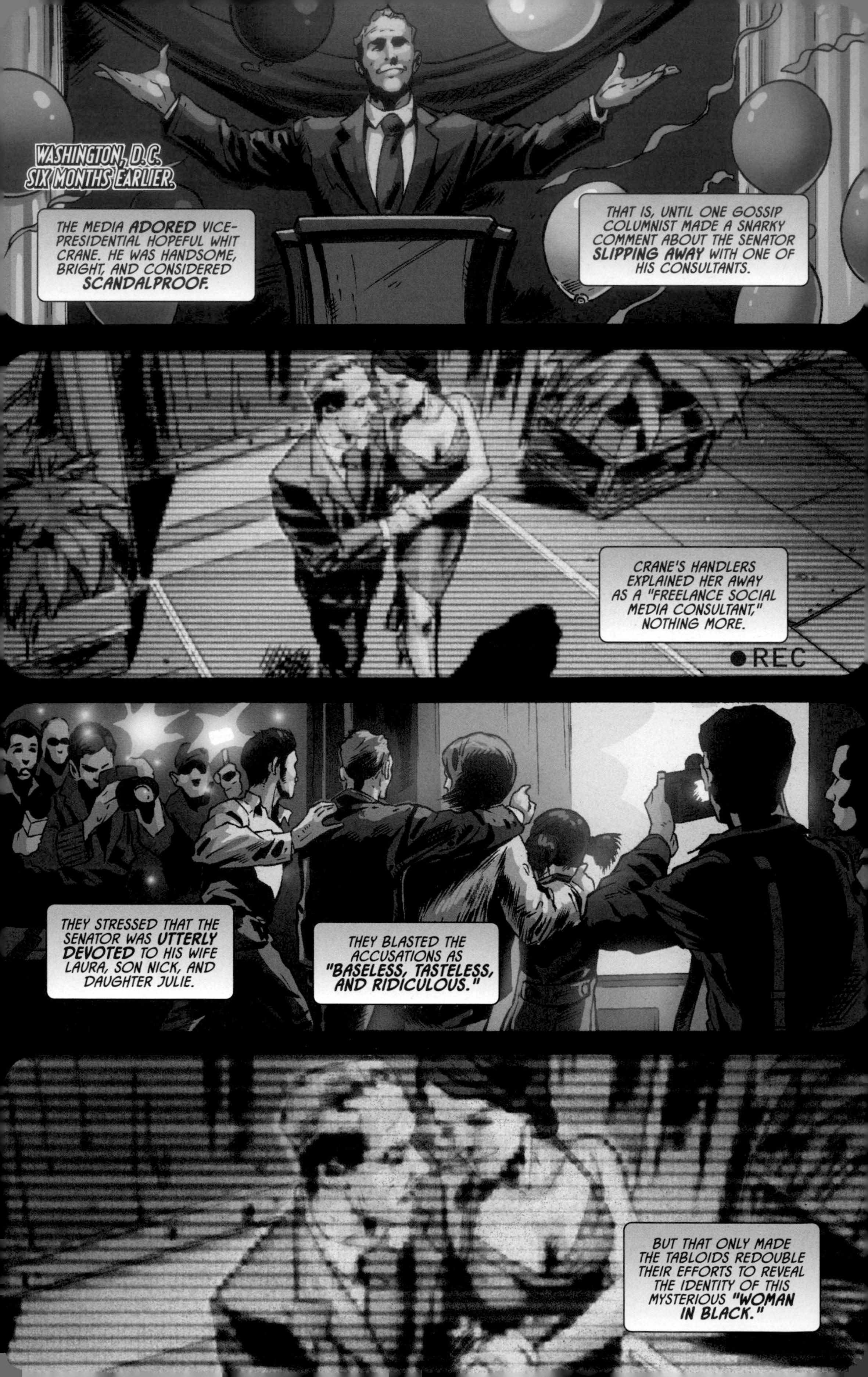
WASHINGTON, D.C. SIX MONTHS EARLIER.
THE MEDIA ADORED VICE-PRESIDENTIAL HOPEFUL WHIT CRANE. HE WAS HANDSOME, BRIGHT, AND CONSIDERED SCANDALPROOF.
THAT IS, UNTIL ONE GOSSIP COLUMNIST MADE A SNARKY COMMENT ABOUT THE SENATOR SLIPPING AWAY WITH ONE OF HIS CONSULTANTS.
CRANE'S HANDLERS EXPLAINED HER AWAY AS A "FREELANCE SOCIAL MEDIA CONSULTANT," NOTHING MORE.
REC
THEY STRESSED THAT THE SENATOR WAS UTTERLY DEVOTED TO HIS WIFE LAURA, SON NICK, AND DAUGHTER JULIE.
THEY BLASTED THE ACCUSATIONS AS "BASELESS, TASTELESS, AND RIDICULOUS."
BUT THAT ONLY MADE THE TABLOIDS REDOUBLE THEIR EFFORTS TO REVEAL THE IDENTITY OF THIS MYSTERIOUS "WOMAN IN BLACK."

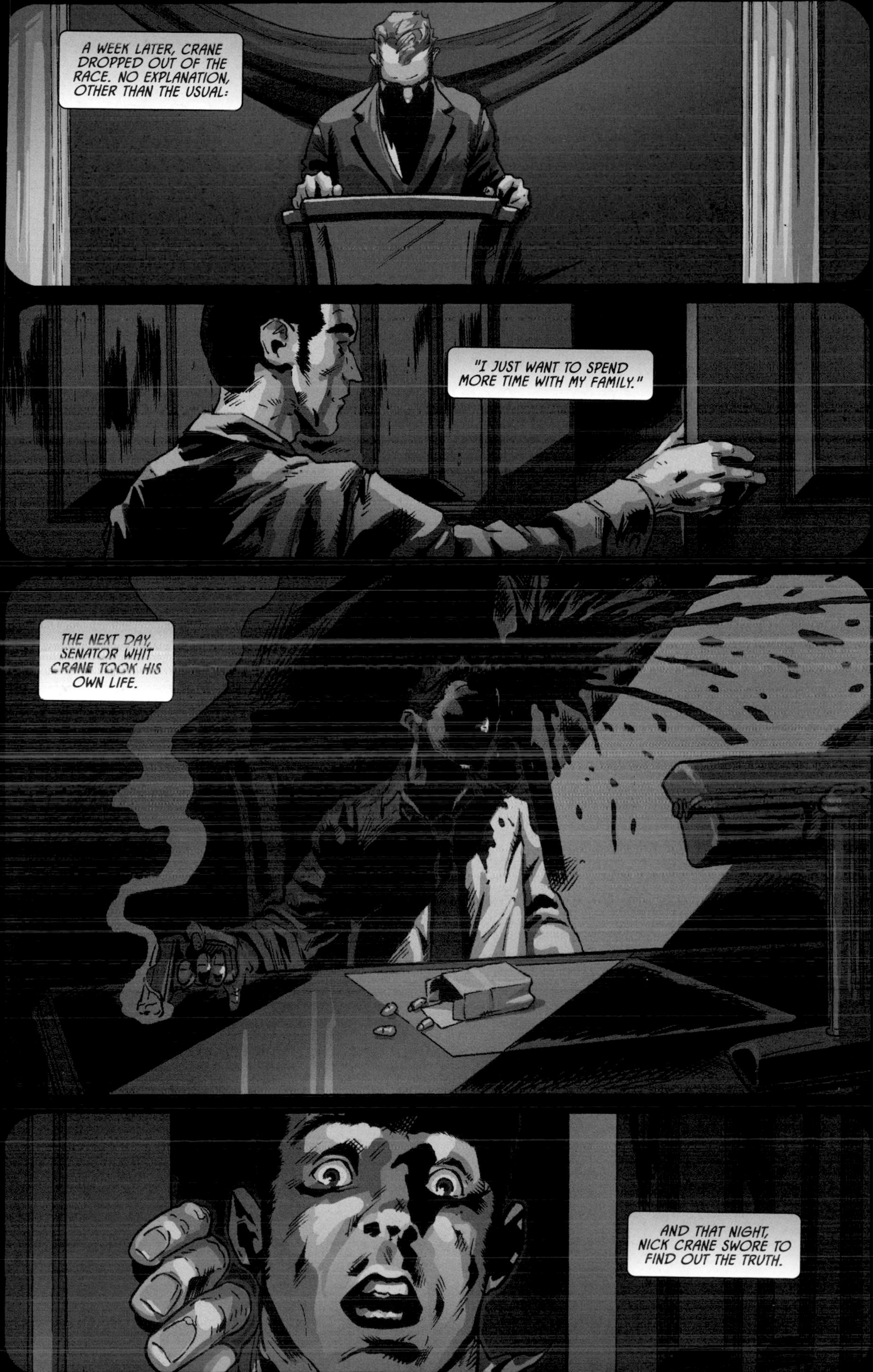
A WEEK LATER, CRANE DROPPED OUT OF THE RACE. NO EXPLANATION, OTHER THAN THE USUAL:
"I JUST WANT TO SPEND MORE TIME WITH MY FAMILY."
THE NEXT DAY, SENATOR WHIT CRANE TOOK HIS OWN LIFE.
AND THAT NIGHT, NICK CRANE SWORE TO FIND OUT THE TRUTH.

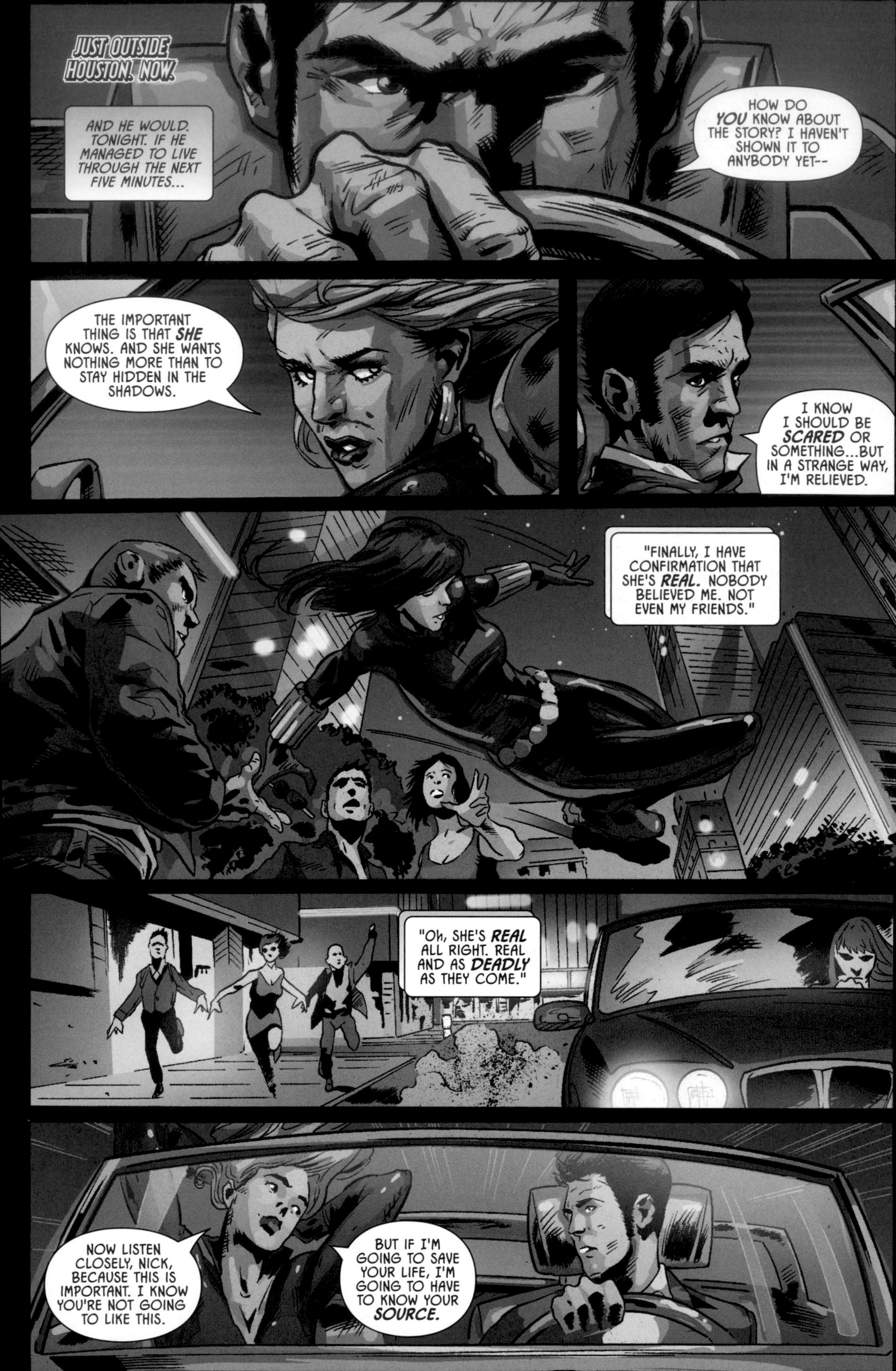
JUST OUTSIDE HOUSTON. NOW.
AND HE WOULD. TONIGHT. IF HE MANAGED TO LIVE THROUGH THE NEXT FIVE MINUTES...
HOW DO YOU KNOW ABOUT THE STORY? I HAVEN'T SHOWN IT TO ANYBODY YET--
THE IMPORTANT THING IS THAT SHE KNOWS. AND SHE WANTS NOTHING MORE THAN TO STAY HIDDEN IN THE SHADOWS.
I KNOW I SHOULD BE SCARED OR SOMETHING...BUT IN A STRANGE WAY, I'M RELIEVED.
"FINALLY, I HAVE CONFIRMATION THAT SHE'S REAL. NOBODY BELIEVED ME. NOT EVEN MY FRIENDS."
"Oh, SHE'S REAL ALL RIGHT. REAL AND AS DEADLY AS THEY COME."
NOW LISTEN CLOSELY, NICK, BECAUSE THIS IS IMPORTANT. I KNOW YOU'RE NOT GOING TO LIKE THIS.
BUT IF I'M GOING TO SAVE YOUR LIFE, I'M GOING TO HAVE TO KNOW YOUR SOURCE.

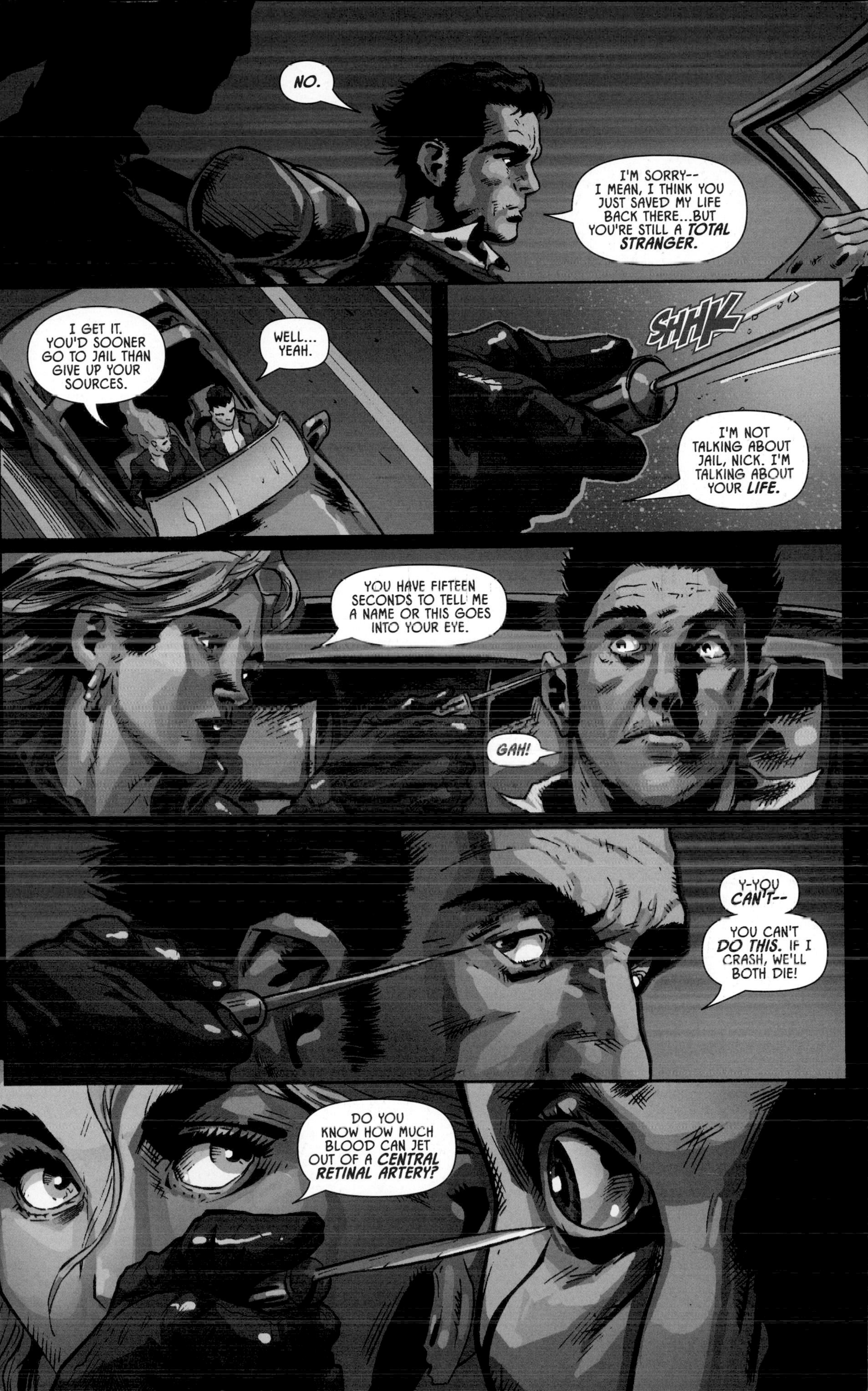
NO.
I'M SORRY-- I MEAN, I THINK YOU JUST SAVED MY LIFE BACK THERE...BUT YOU'RE STILL A TOTAL STRANGER.
I GET IT. YOU'D SOONER GO TO JAIL THAN GIVE UP YOUR SOURCES.
WELL... YEAH.
SHHK
I'M NOT TALKING ABOUT JAIL, NICK. I'M TALKING ABOUT YOUR LIFE.
YOU HAVE FIFTEEN SECONDS TO TELL ME A NAME OR THIS GOES INTO YOUR EYE.
GAH!
Y-YOU CAN'T--
YOU CAN'T DO THIS. IF I CRASH, WE'LL BOTH DIE!
DO YOU KNOW HOW MUCH BLOOD CAN JET OUT OF A CENTRAL RETINAL ARTERY?

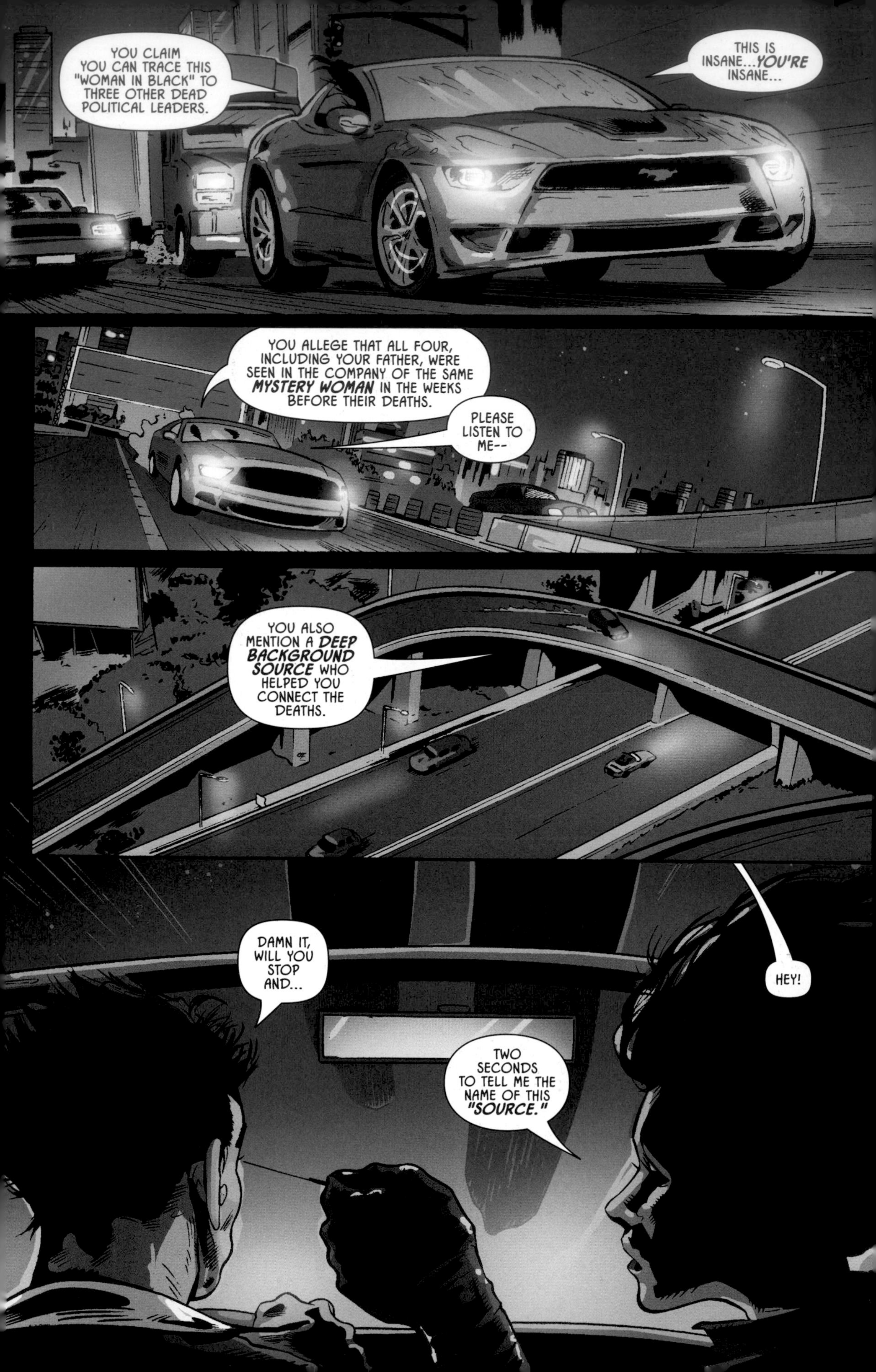
YOU CLAIM YOU CAN TRACE THIS "WOMAN IN BLACK" TO THREE OTHER DEAD POLITICAL LEADERS.
THIS IS INSANE...YOU'RE INSANE...
YOU ALLEGE THAT ALL FOUR, INCLUDING YOUR FATHER, WERE SEEN IN THE COMPANY OF THE SAME MYSTERY WOMAN IN THE WEEKS BEFORE THEIR DEATHS.
PLEASE LISTEN TO ME--
YOU ALSO MENTION A DEEP BACKGROUND SOURCE WHO HELPED YOU CONNECT THE DEATHS.
DAMN IT, WILL YOU STOP AND...
HEY!
TWO SECONDS TO TELL ME THE NAME OF THIS "SOURCE."

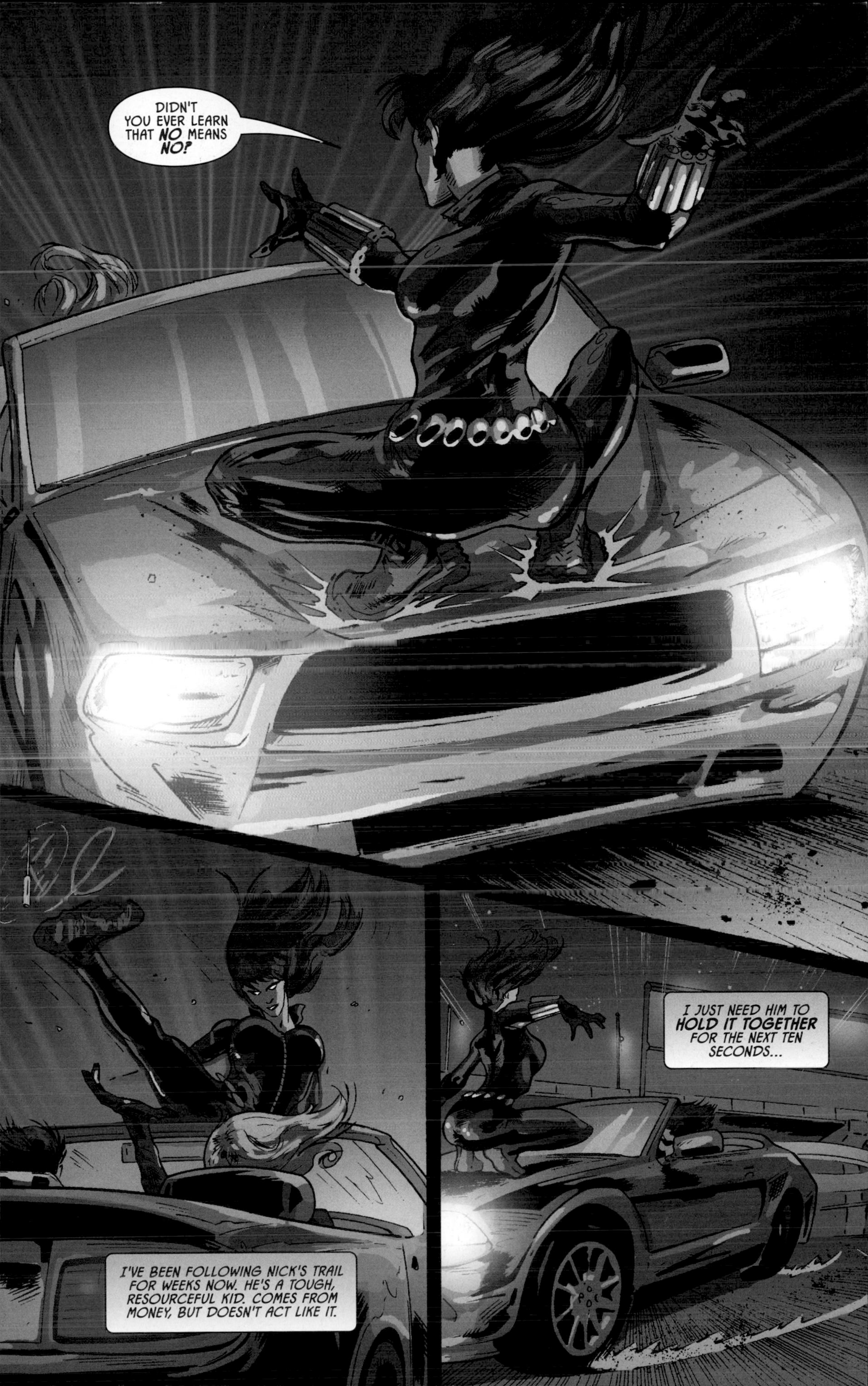
DIDN'T YOU EVER LEARN THAT NO MEANS NO?
I'VE BEEN FOLLOWING NICK'S TRAIL FOR WEEKS NOW. HE'S A TOUGH, RESOURCEFUL KID. COMES FROM MONEY, BUT DOESN'T ACT LIKE IT.
I JUST NEED HIM TO HOLD IT TOGETHER FOR THE NEXT TEN SECONDS...

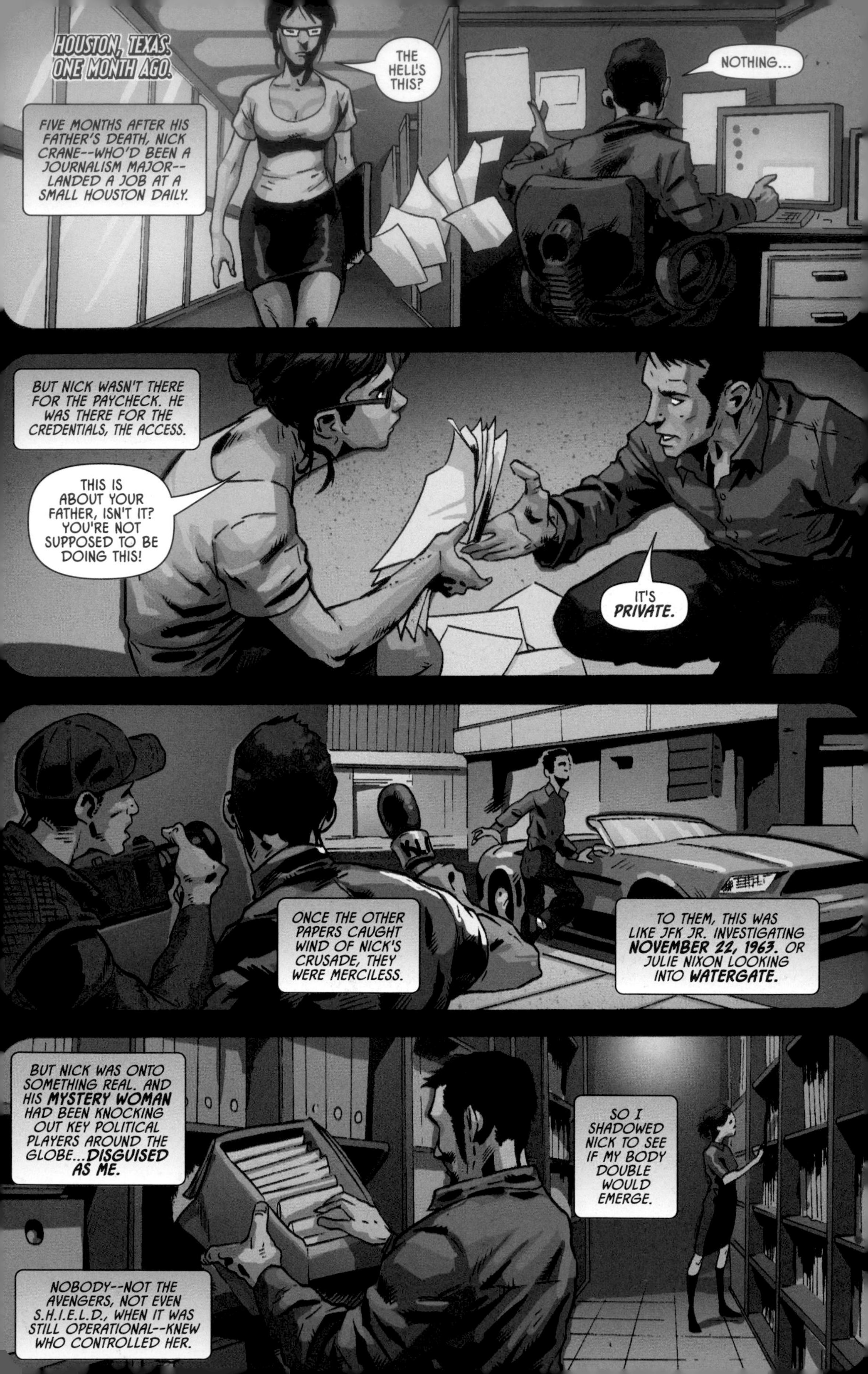
HOUSTON, TEXAS. ONE MONTH AGO.
FIVE MONTHS AFTER HIS FATHER'S DEATH, NICK CRANE--WHO'D BEEN A JOURNALISM MAJOR--LANDED A JOB AT A SMALL HOUSTON DAILY.
THE HELL'S THIS?
NOTHING...
BUT NICK WASN'T THERE FOR THE PAYCHECK. HE WAS THERE FOR THE CREDENTIALS, THE ACCESS.
THIS IS ABOUT YOUR FATHER, ISN'T IT? YOU'RE NOT SUPPOSED TO BE DOING THIS!
IT'S PRIVATE.
ONCE THE OTHER PAPERS CAUGHT WIND OF NICK'S CRUSADE, THEY WERE MERCILESS.
TO THEM, THIS WAS LIKE JFK JR. INVESTIGATING NOVEMBER 22, 1963. OR JULIE NIXON LOOKING INTO WATERGATE.
BUT NICK WAS ONTO SOMETHING REAL. AND HIS MYSTERY WOMAN HAD BEEN KNOCKING OUT KEY POLITICAL PLAYERS AROUND THE GLOBE...DISGUISED AS ME.
SO I SHADOWED NICK TO SEE IF MY BODY DOUBLE WOULD EMERGE.
NOBODY--NOT THE AVENGERS, NOT EVEN S.H.I.E.L.D., WHEN IT WAS STILL OPERATIONAL--KNEW WHO CONTROLLED HER.

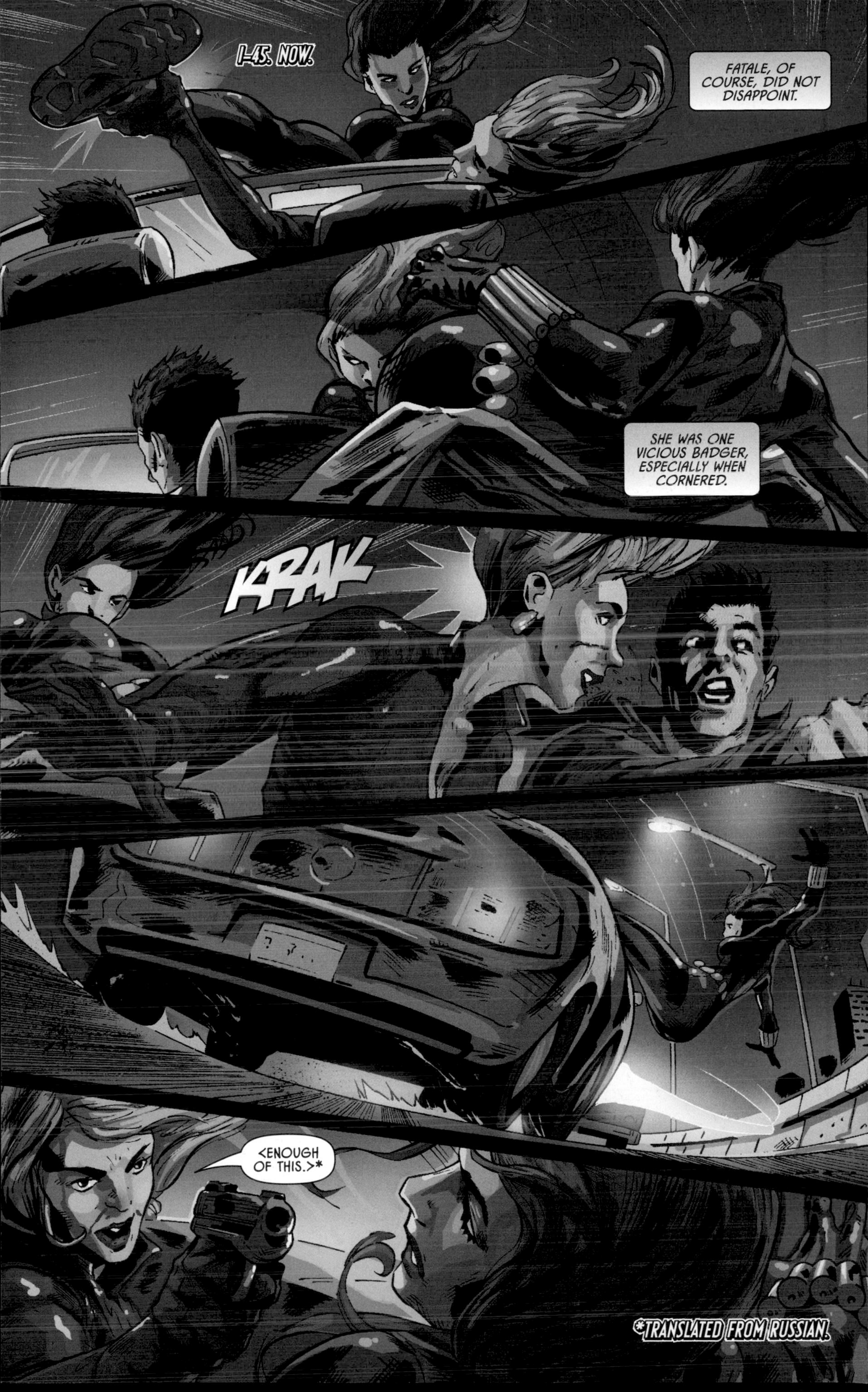
I-45. NOW.
FATALE, OF COURSE, DID NOT DISAPPOINT.
SHE WAS ONE VICIOUS BADGER, ESPECIALLY WHEN CORNERED.
KRAK
<ENOUGH OF THIS.>*
*TRANSLATED FROM RUSSIAN.

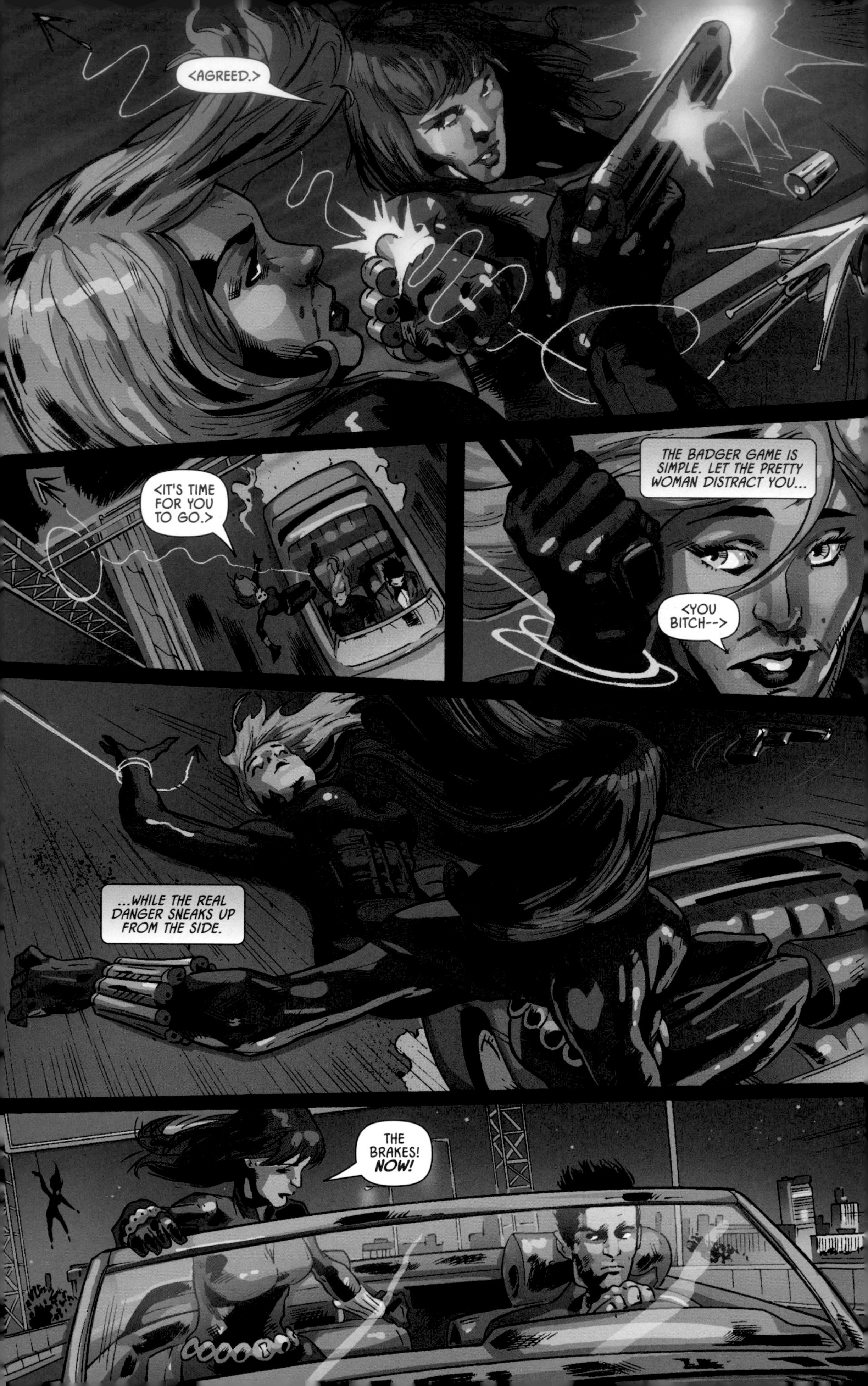
<AGREED.>
<IT'S TIME FOR YOU TO GO.>
THE BADGER GAME IS SIMPLE. LET THE PRETTY WOMAN DISTRACT YOU...
<YOU BITCH-->
...WHILE THE REAL DANGER SNEAKS UP FROM THE SIDE.
THE BRAKES! NOW!

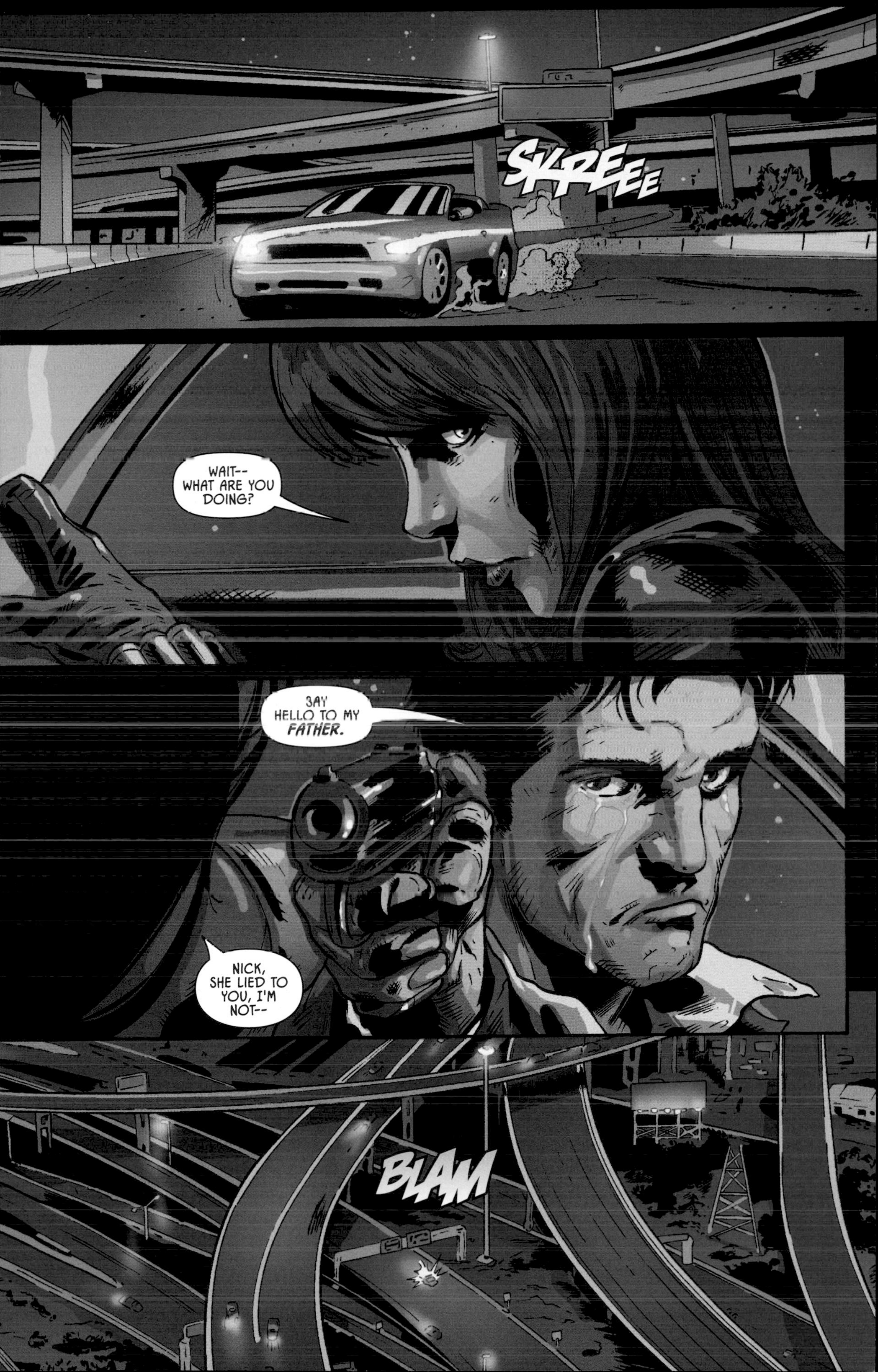
SKREEEE
WAIT-- WHAT ARE YOU DOING?
SAY HELLO TO MY FATHER.
NICK, SHE LIED TO YOU, I'M NOT--
BLAM

7

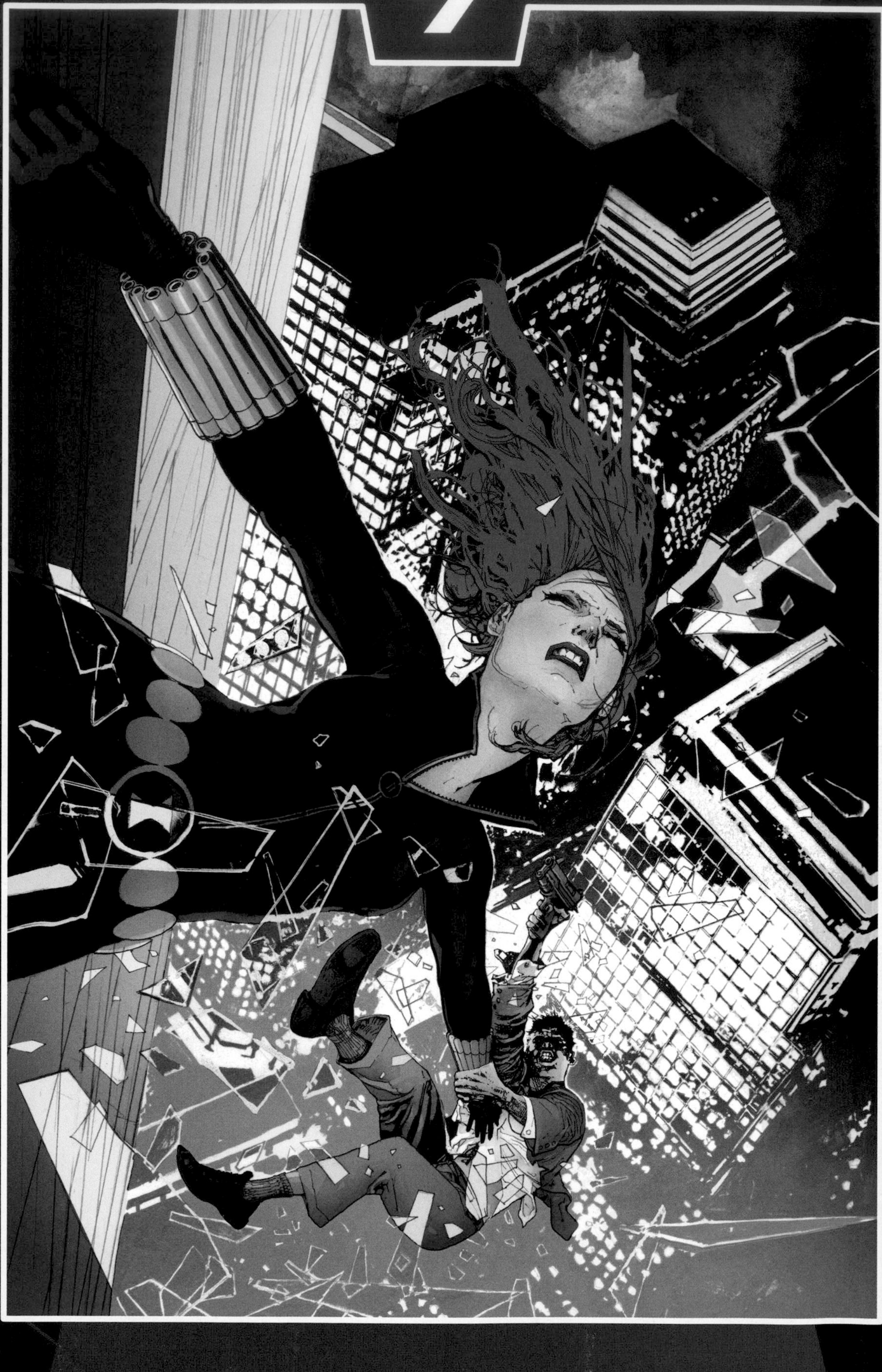

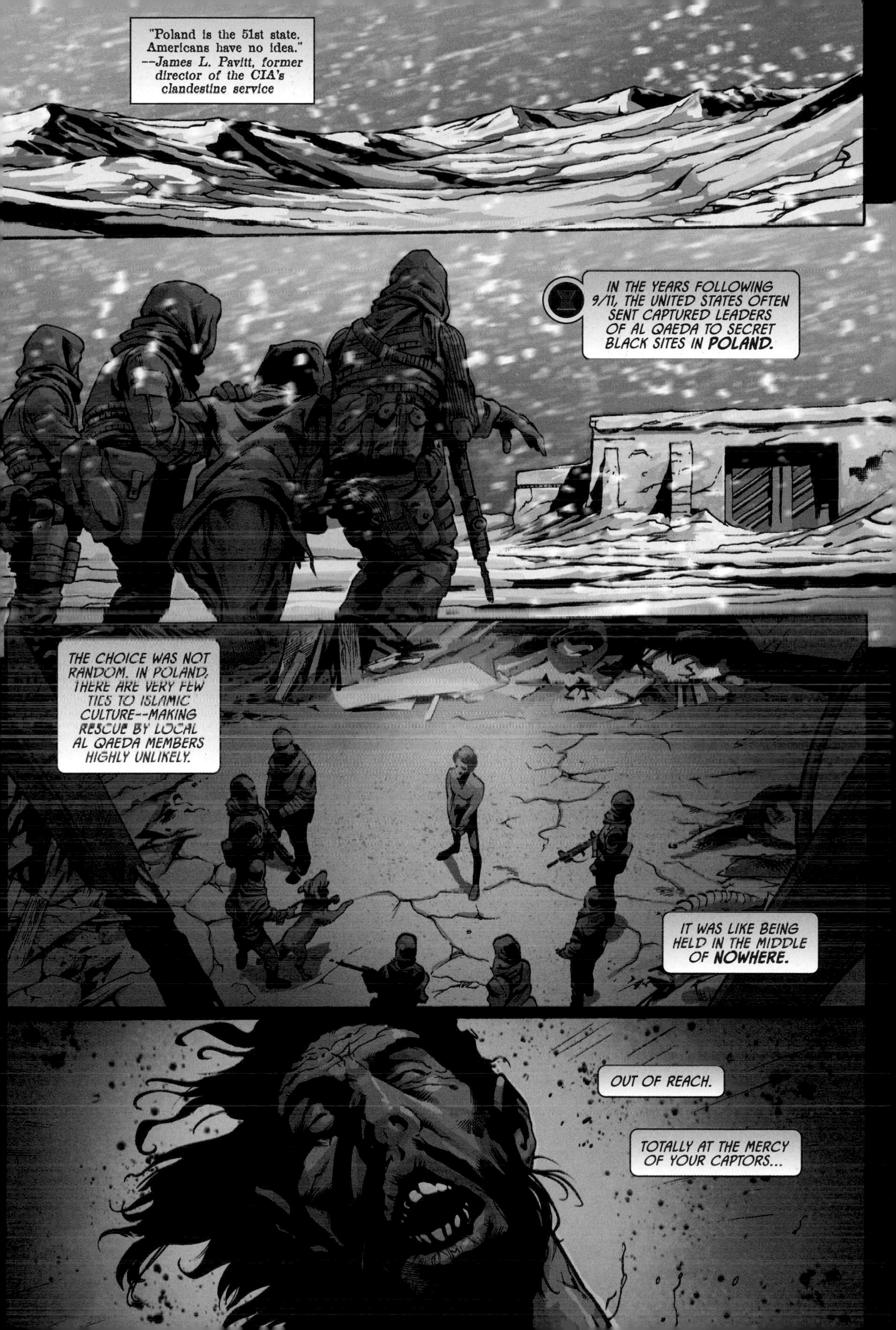
"Poland is the 51st state. Americans have no idea." --James L. Pavitt, former director of the CIA's clandestine service
IN THE YEARS FOLLOWING 9/11, THE UNITED STATES OFTEN SENT CAPTURED LEADERS OF AL QAEDA TO SECRET BLACK SITES IN POLAND.
THE CHOICE WAS NOT RANDOM. IN POLAND, THERE ARE VERY FEW TIES TO ISLAMIC CULTURE--MAKING RESCUE BY LOCAL AL QAEDA MEMBERS HIGHLY UNLIKELY.
IT WAS LIKE BEING HELD IN THE MIDDLE OF NOWHERE.
OUT OF REACH.
TOTALLY AT THE MERCY OF YOUR CAPTORS...

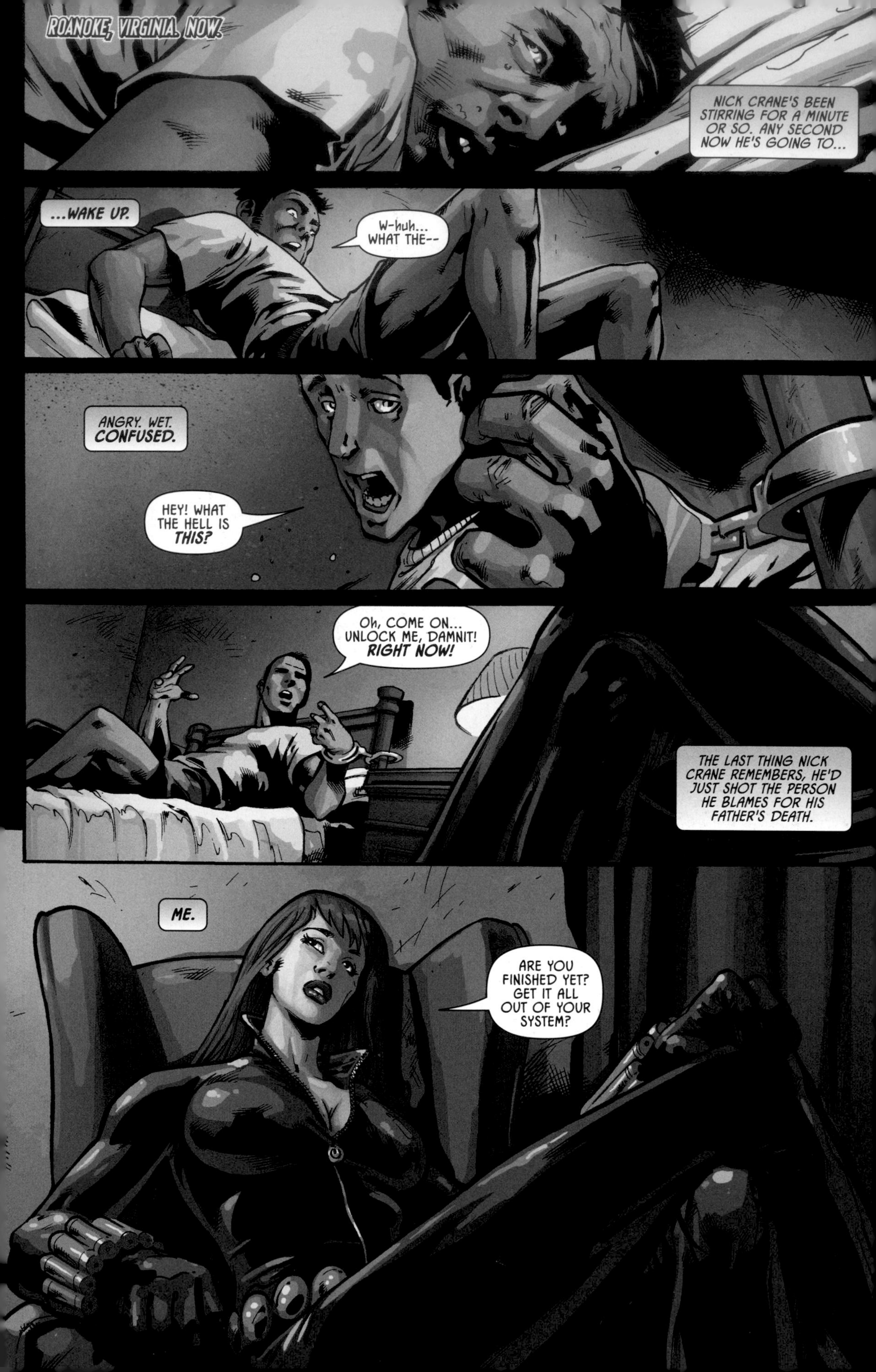
ROANOKE, VIRGINIA. NOW.
NICK CRANE'S BEEN STIRRING FOR A MINUTE OR SO. ANY SECOND NOW HE'S GOING TO...
...WAKE UP.
W-huh... WHAT THE--
ANGRY. WET. CONFUSED.
HEY! WHAT THE HELL IS THIS?
Oh, COME ON... UNLOCK ME, DAMNIT! RIGHT NOW!
THE LAST THING NICK CRANE REMEMBERS, HE'D JUST SHOT THE PERSON HE BLAMES FOR HIS FATHER'S DEATH.
ME.
ARE YOU FINISHED YET? GET IT ALL OUT OF YOUR SYSTEM?

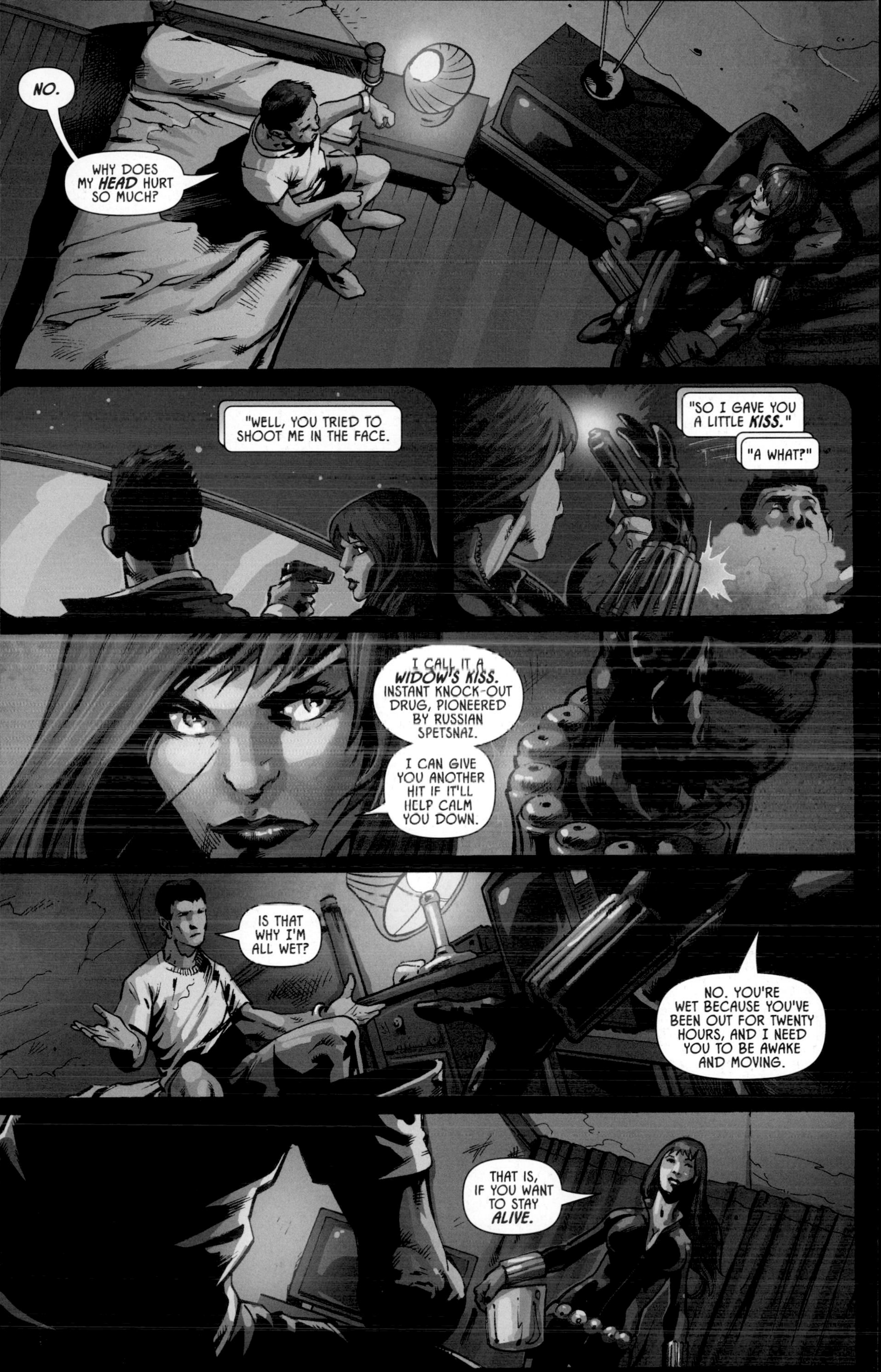

NO.
WHY DOES MY *HEAD* HURT SO MUCH?
"WELL, YOU TRIED TO SHOOT ME IN THE FACE.
"SO I GAVE YOU A LITTLE *KISS.*"
"A WHAT?"
I CALL IT A *WIDOW'S KISS.* INSTANT KNOCK-OUT DRUG, PIONEERED BY RUSSIAN SPETSNAZ.
I CAN GIVE YOU ANOTHER HIT IF IT'LL HELP CALM YOU DOWN.
IS THAT WHY I'M ALL WET?
NO. YOU'RE WET BECAUSE YOU'VE BEEN OUT FOR TWENTY HOURS, AND I NEED YOU TO BE AWAKE AND MOVING.
THAT IS, IF YOU WANT TO STAY *ALIVE.*

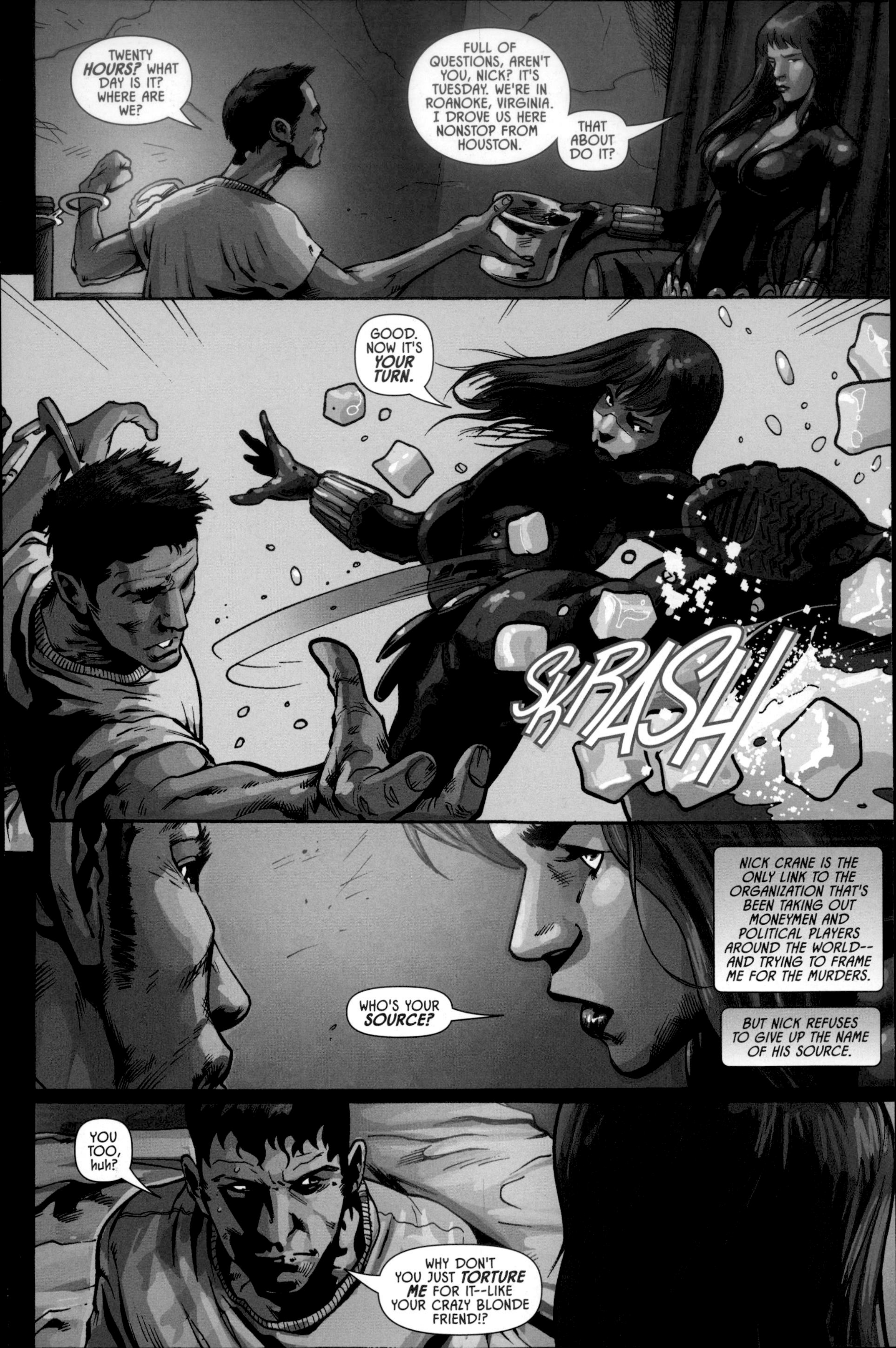

TWENTY HOURS? WHAT DAY IS IT? WHERE ARE WE?
FULL OF QUESTIONS, AREN'T YOU, NICK? IT'S TUESDAY. WE'RE IN ROANOKE, VIRGINIA. I DROVE US HERE NONSTOP FROM HOUSTON.
THAT ABOUT DO IT?
GOOD. NOW IT'S YOUR TURN.
SKRASH
NICK CRANE IS THE ONLY LINK TO THE ORGANIZATION THAT'S BEEN TAKING OUT MONEYMEN AND POLITICAL PLAYERS AROUND THE WORLD--AND TRYING TO FRAME ME FOR THE MURDERS.
BUT NICK REFUSES TO GIVE UP THE NAME OF HIS SOURCE.
WHO'S YOUR SOURCE?
YOU TOO, huh?
WHY DON'T YOU JUST TORTURE ME FOR IT--LIKE YOUR CRAZY BLONDE FRIEND!?

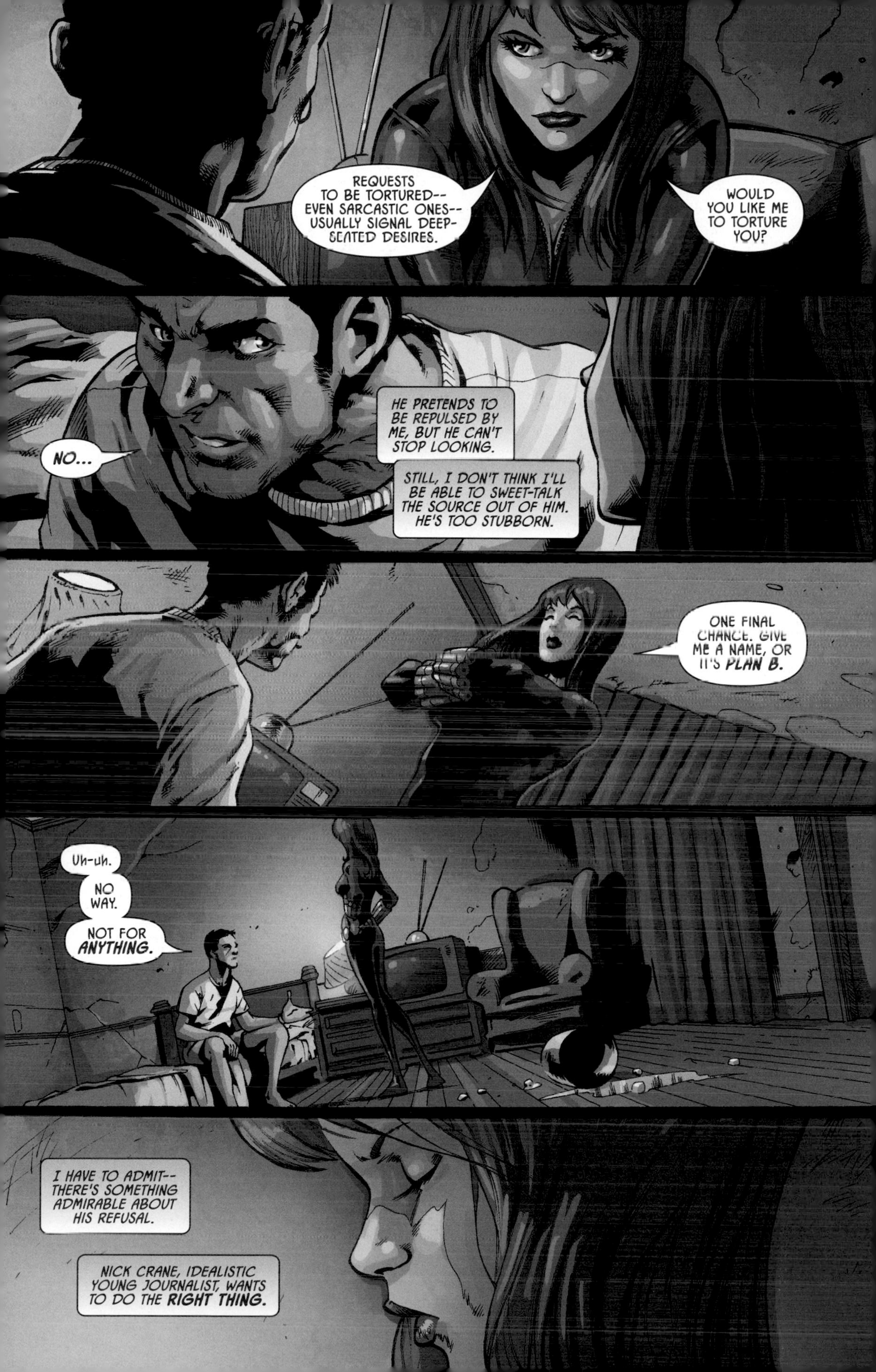
REQUESTS TO BE TORTURED-- EVEN SARCASTIC ONES-- USUALLY SIGNAL DEEP-SEATED DESIRES.
WOULD YOU LIKE ME TO TORTURE YOU?
HE PRETENDS TO BE REPULSED BY ME, BUT HE CAN'T STOP LOOKING.
NO...
STILL, I DON'T THINK I'LL BE ABLE TO SWEET-TALK THE SOURCE OUT OF HIM. HE'S TOO STUBBORN.
ONE FINAL CHANCE. GIVE ME A NAME, OR IT'S PLAN B.
Uh-uh.
NO WAY.
NOT FOR ANYTHING.
I HAVE TO ADMIT-- THERE'S SOMETHING ADMIRABLE ABOUT HIS REFUSAL.
NICK CRANE, IDEALISTIC YOUNG JOURNALIST, WANTS TO DO THE RIGHT THING.

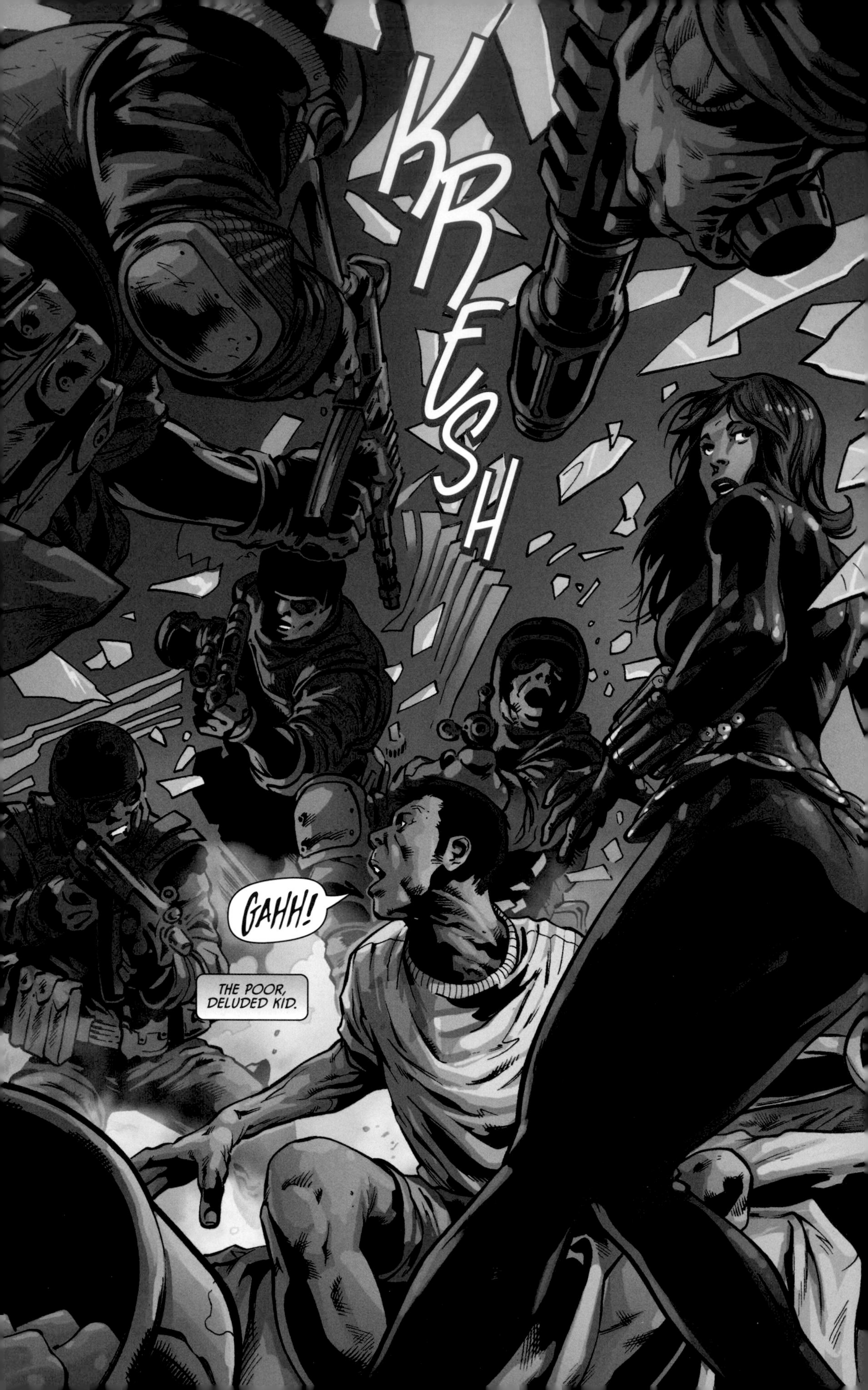
KRESH
GAHH!
THE POOR, DELUDED KID.

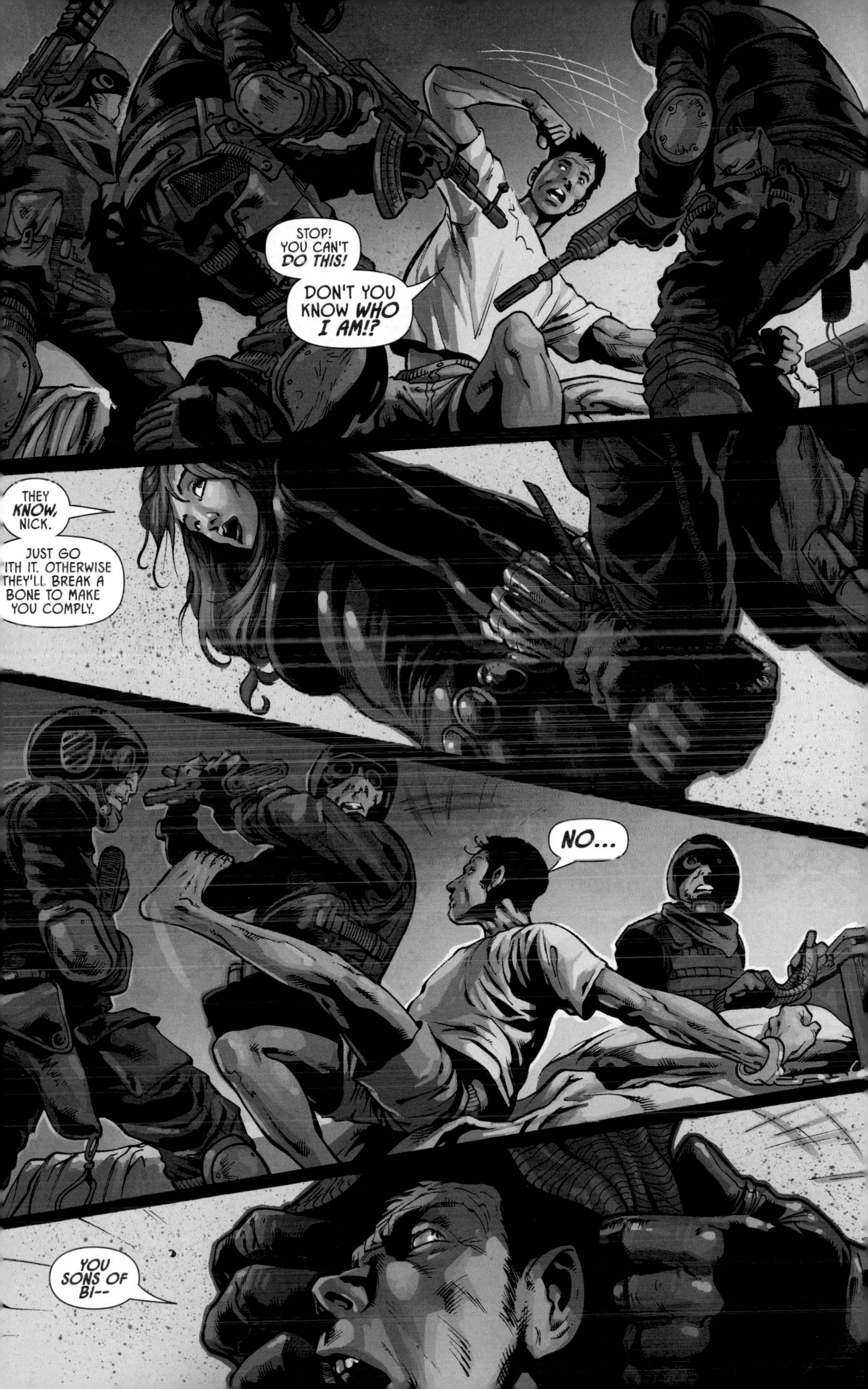
STOP! YOU CAN'T DO THIS!
DON'T YOU KNOW WHO I AM!?
THEY KNOW, NICK.
JUST GO ITH IT. OTHERWISE THEY'LL BREAK A BONE TO MAKE YOU COMPLY.
NO...
YOU SONS OF BI--

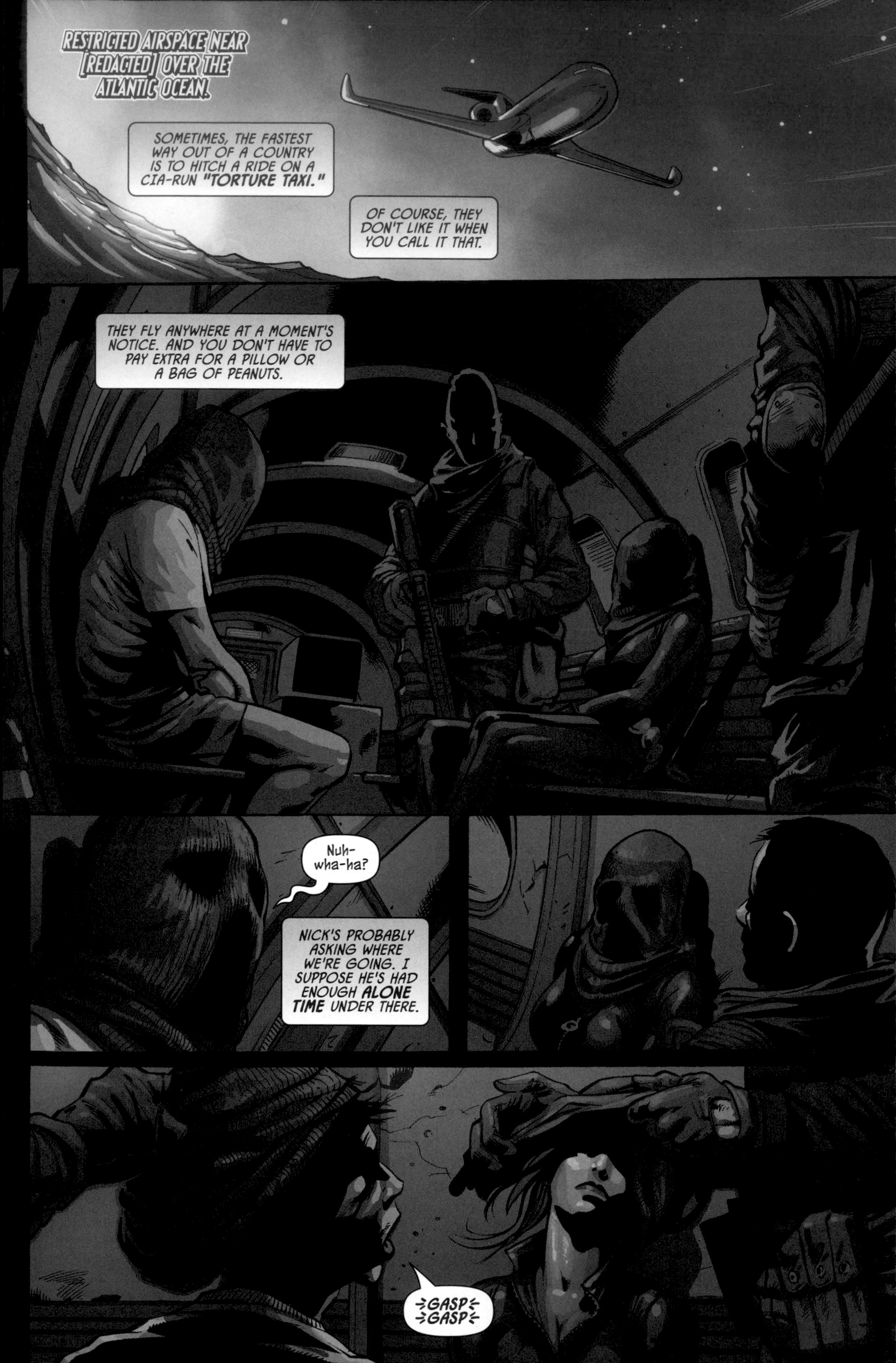
RESTRICTED AIRSPACE NEAR [REDACTED] OVER THE ATLANTIC OCEAN.
SOMETIMES, THE FASTEST WAY OUT OF A COUNTRY IS TO HITCH A RIDE ON A CIA-RUN "TORTURE TAXI."
OF COURSE, THEY DON'T LIKE IT WHEN YOU CALL IT THAT.
THEY FLY ANYWHERE AT A MOMENT'S NOTICE. AND YOU DON'T HAVE TO PAY EXTRA FOR A PILLOW OR A BAG OF PEANUTS.
Nuh-wha-ha?
NICK'S PROBABLY ASKING WHERE WE'RE GOING. I SUPPOSE HE'S HAD ENOUGH ALONE TIME UNDER THERE.
GASP GASP

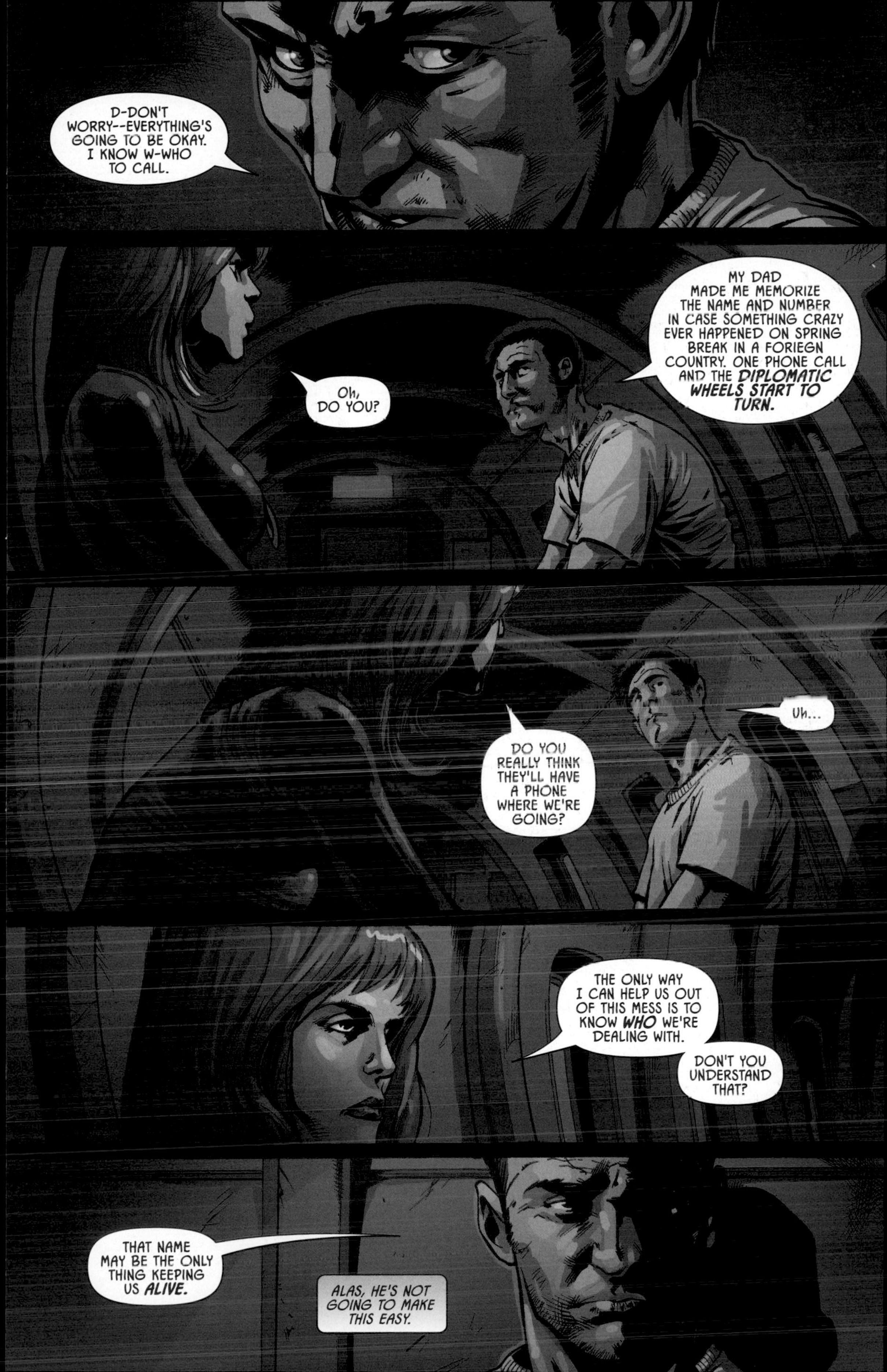
D-DON'T WORRY--EVERYTHING'S GOING TO BE OKAY. I KNOW W-WHO TO CALL.
Oh, DO YOU?
MY DAD MADE ME MEMORIZE THE NAME AND NUMBER IN CASE SOMETHING CRAZY EVER HAPPENED ON SPRING BREAK IN A FORIEGN COUNTRY. ONE PHONE CALL AND THE DIPLOMATIC WHEELS START TO TURN.
DO YOU REALLY THINK THEY'LL HAVE A PHONE WHERE WE'RE GOING?
Uh...
THE ONLY WAY I CAN HELP US OUT OF THIS MESS IS TO KNOW WHO WE'RE DEALING WITH.
DON'T YOU UNDERSTAND THAT?
THAT NAME MAY BE THE ONLY THING KEEPING US ALIVE.
ALAS, HE'S NOT GOING TO MAKE THIS EASY.

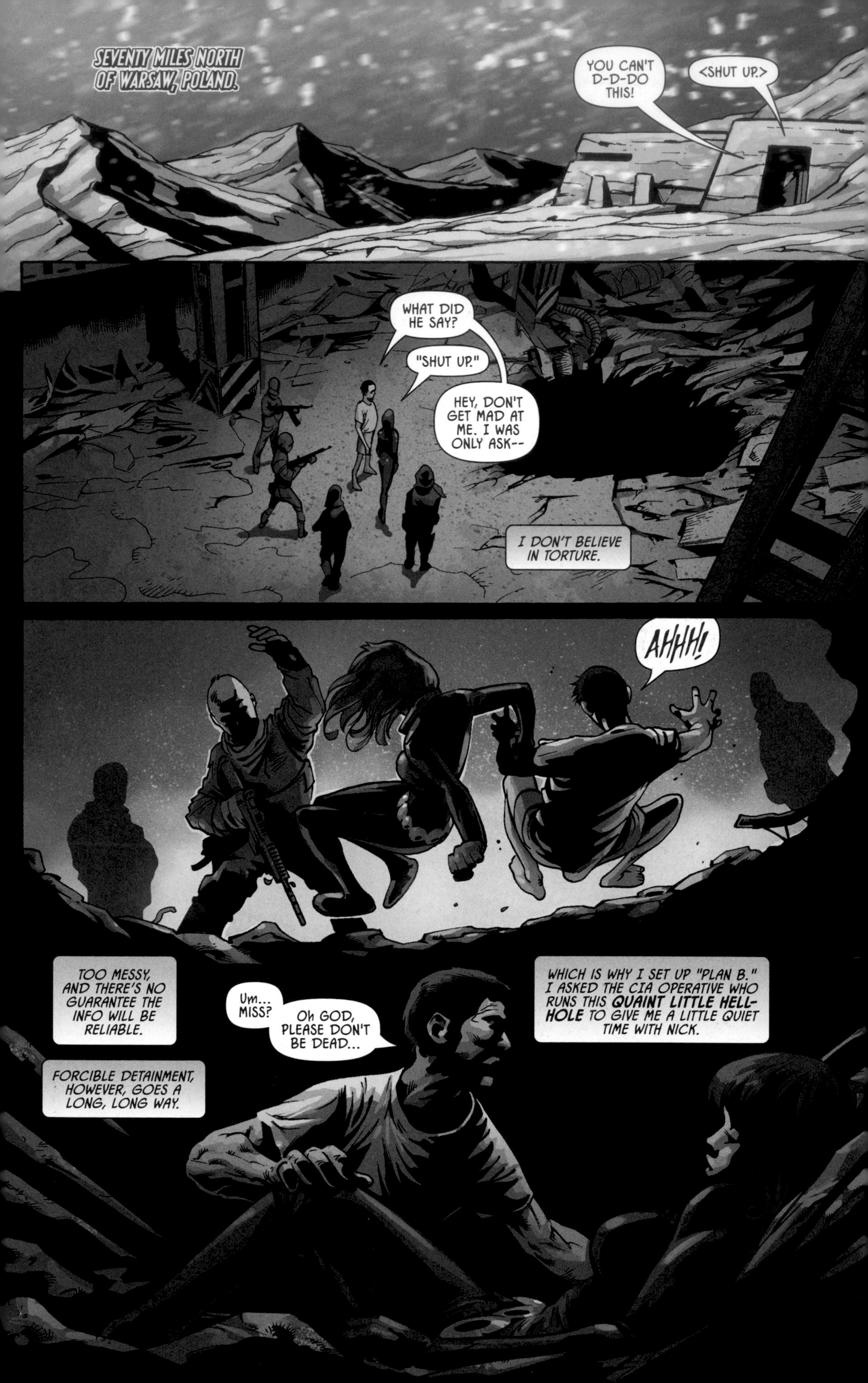
SEVENTY MILES NORTH OF WARSAW, POLAND.
YOU CAN'T D-D-DO THIS!
<SHUT UP.>
WHAT DID HE SAY?
"SHUT UP."
HEY, DON'T GET MAD AT ME. I WAS ONLY ASK--
I DON'T BELIEVE IN TORTURE.
AHHH!
TOO MESSY, AND THERE'S NO GUARANTEE THE INFO WILL BE RELIABLE.
FORCIBLE DETAINMENT, HOWEVER, GOES A LONG, LONG WAY.
Um... MISS?
Oh GOD, PLEASE DON'T BE DEAD...
WHICH IS WHY I SET UP "PLAN B." I ASKED THE CIA OPERATIVE WHO RUNS THIS QUAINT LITTLE HELL-HOLE TO GIVE ME A LITTLE QUIET TIME WITH NICK.

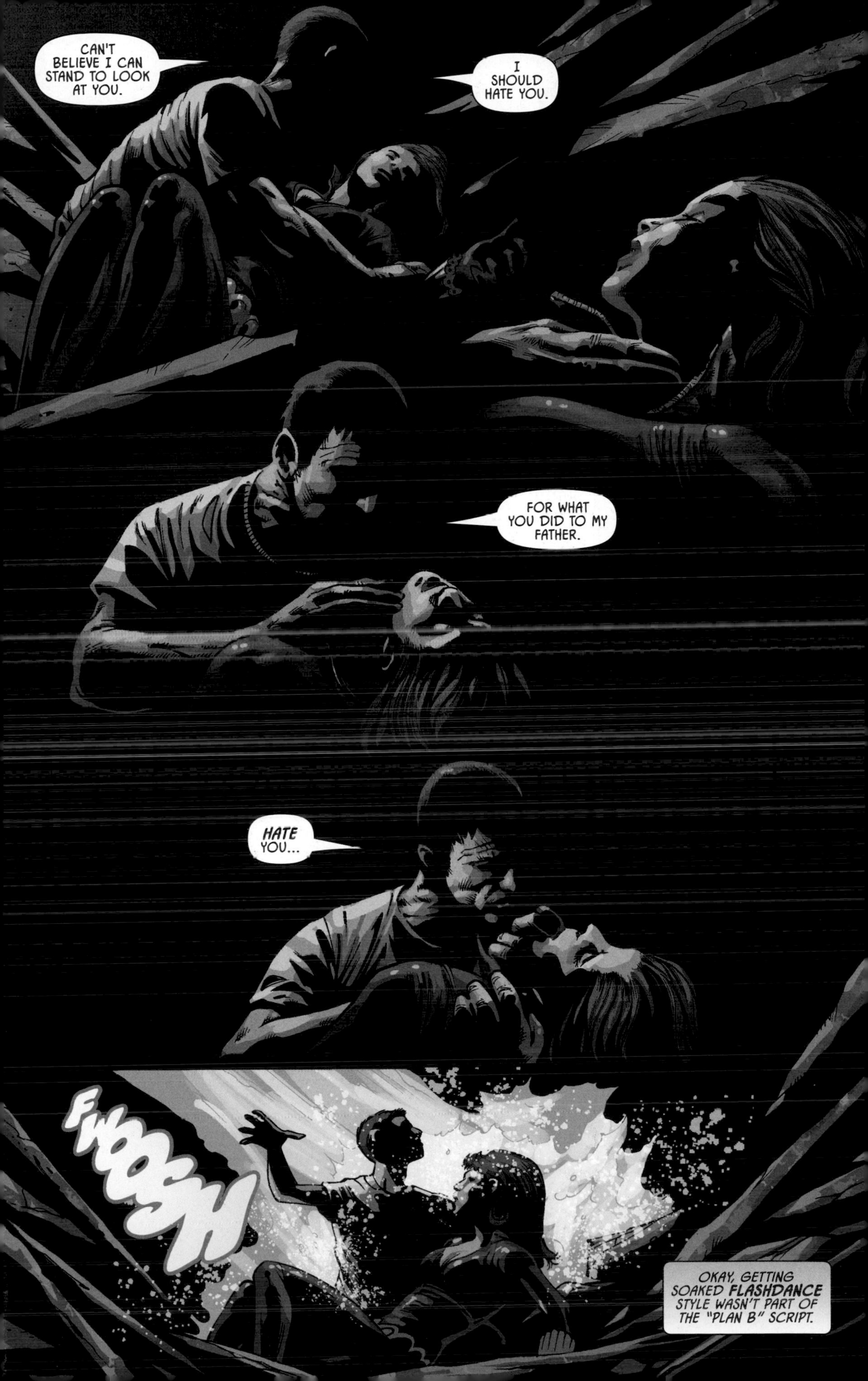
CAN'T BELIEVE I CAN STAND TO LOOK AT YOU.
I SHOULD HATE YOU.
FOR WHAT YOU DID TO MY FATHER.
HATE YOU...
FWOOSH
OKAY, GETTING SOAKED FLASHDANCE STYLE WASN'T PART OF THE "PLAN B" SCRIPT.

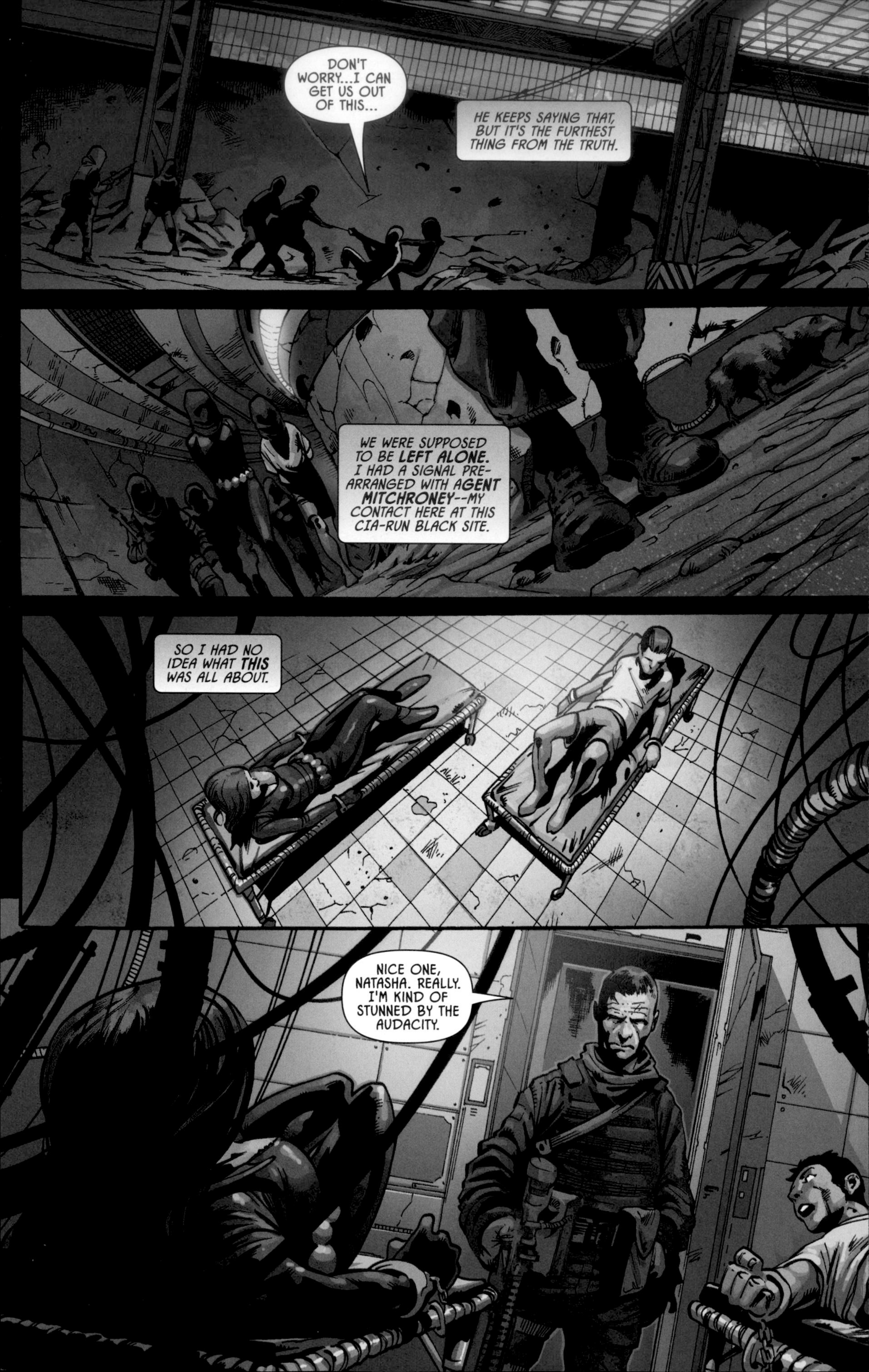
DON'T WORRY...I CAN GET US OUT OF THIS...
HE KEEPS SAYING THAT, BUT IT'S THE FURTHEST THING FROM THE TRUTH.
WE WERE SUPPOSED TO BE LEFT ALONE. I HAD A SIGNAL PRE-ARRANGED WITH AGENT MITCHRONEY--MY CONTACT HERE AT THIS CIA-RUN BLACK SITE.
SO I HAD NO IDEA WHAT THIS WAS ALL ABOUT.
NICE ONE, NATASHA. REALLY. I'M KIND OF STUNNED BY THE AUDACITY.

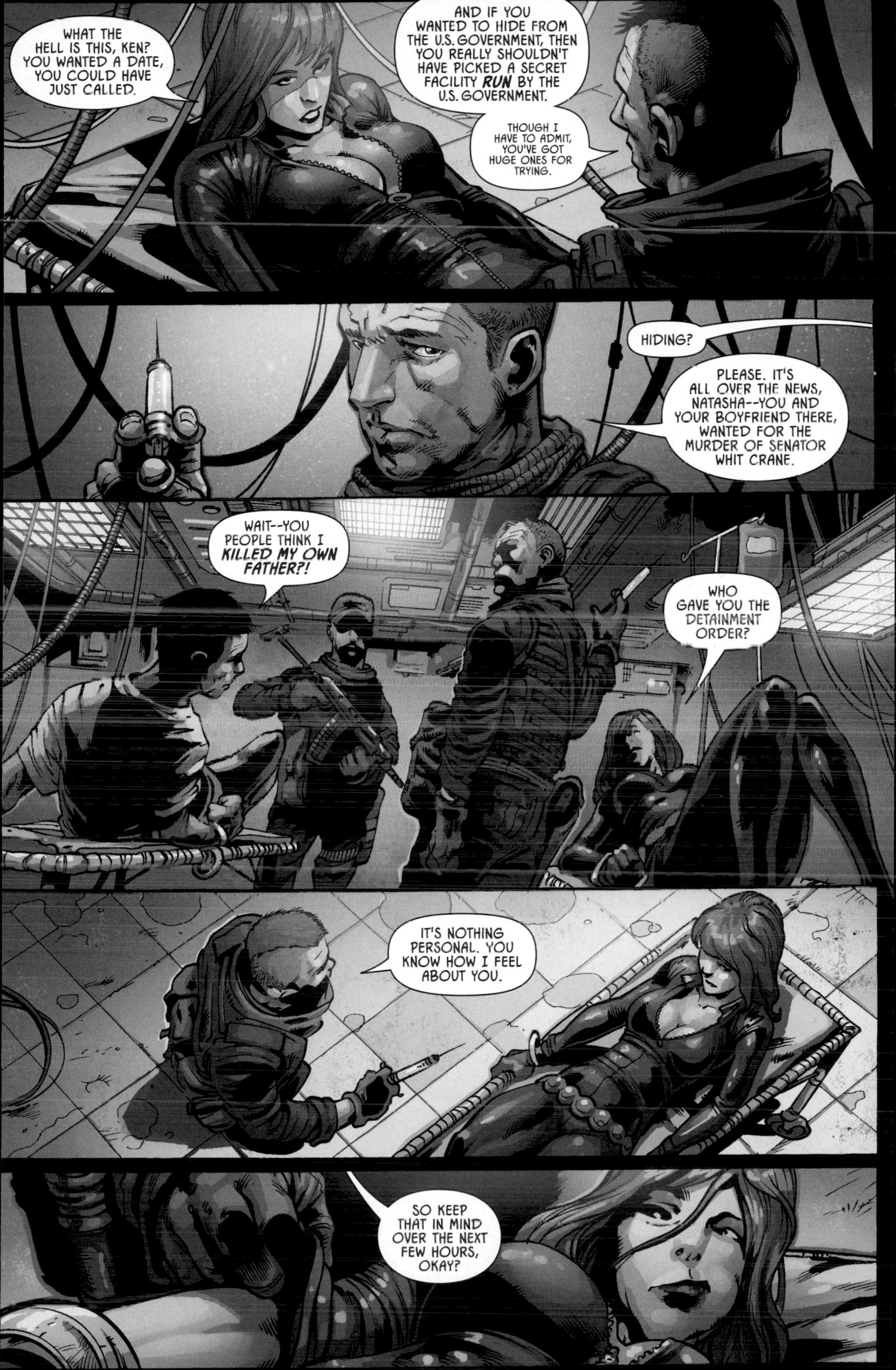
WHAT THE HELL IS THIS, KEN? YOU WANTED A DATE, YOU COULD HAVE JUST CALLED.
AND IF YOU WANTED TO HIDE FROM THE U.S. GOVERNMENT, THEN YOU REALLY SHOULDN'T HAVE PICKED A SECRET FACILITY RUN BY THE U.S. GOVERNMENT.
THOUGH I HAVE TO ADMIT, YOU'VE GOT HUGE ONES FOR TRYING.
HIDING?
PLEASE. IT'S ALL OVER THE NEWS, NATASHA--YOU AND YOUR BOYFRIEND THERE, WANTED FOR THE MURDER OF SENATOR WHIT CRANE.
WAIT--YOU PEOPLE THINK I KILLED MY OWN FATHER?!
WHO GAVE YOU THE DETAINMENT ORDER?
IT'S NOTHING PERSONAL. YOU KNOW HOW I FEEL ABOUT YOU.
SO KEEP THAT IN MIND OVER THE NEXT FEW HOURS, OKAY?

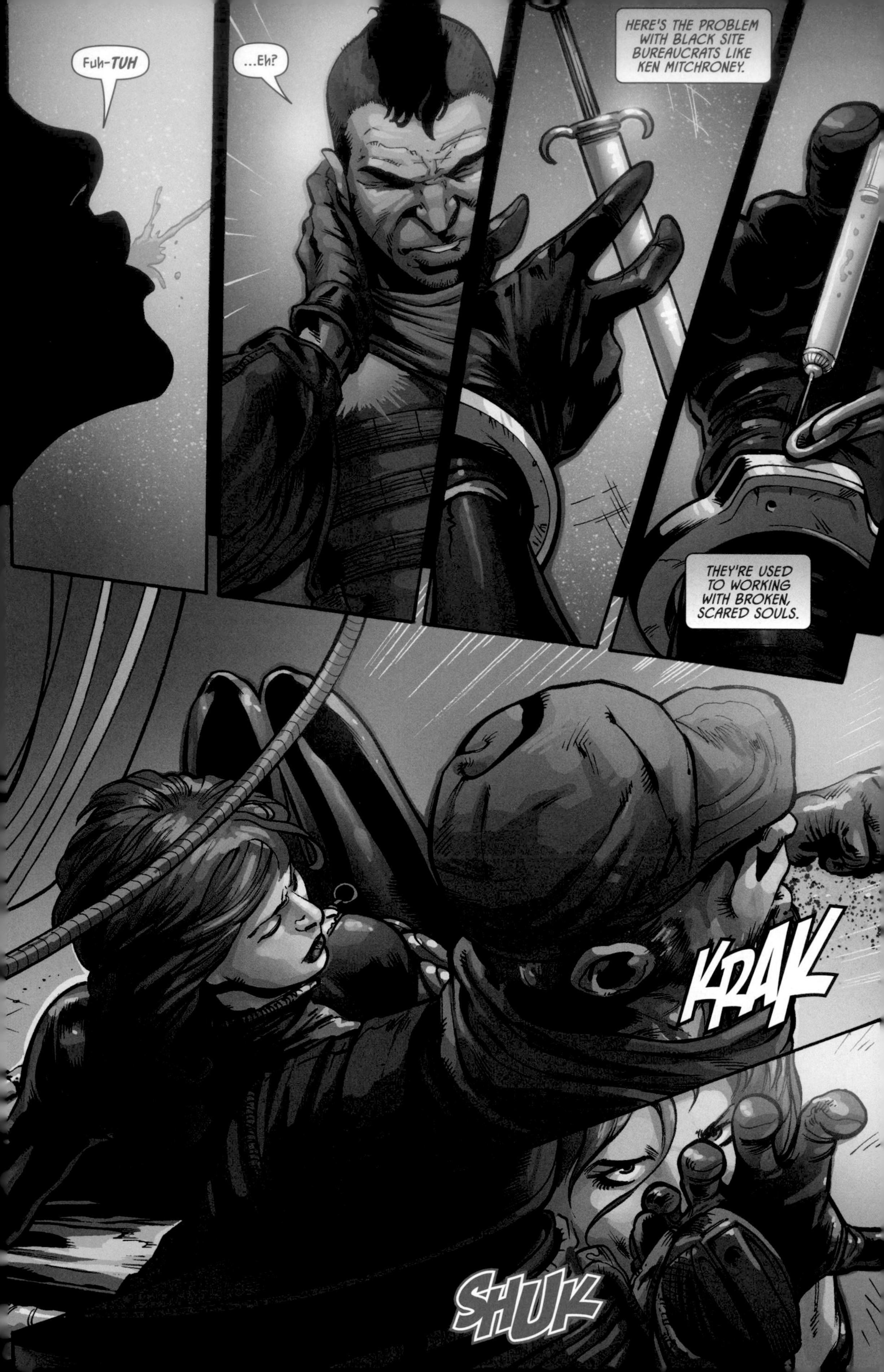
Fuh-TUH
...Eh?
HERE'S THE PROBLEM WITH BLACK SITE BUREAUCRATS LIKE KEN MITCHRONEY.
THEY'RE USED TO WORKING WITH BROKEN, SCARED SOULS.
KRAK
SHUK

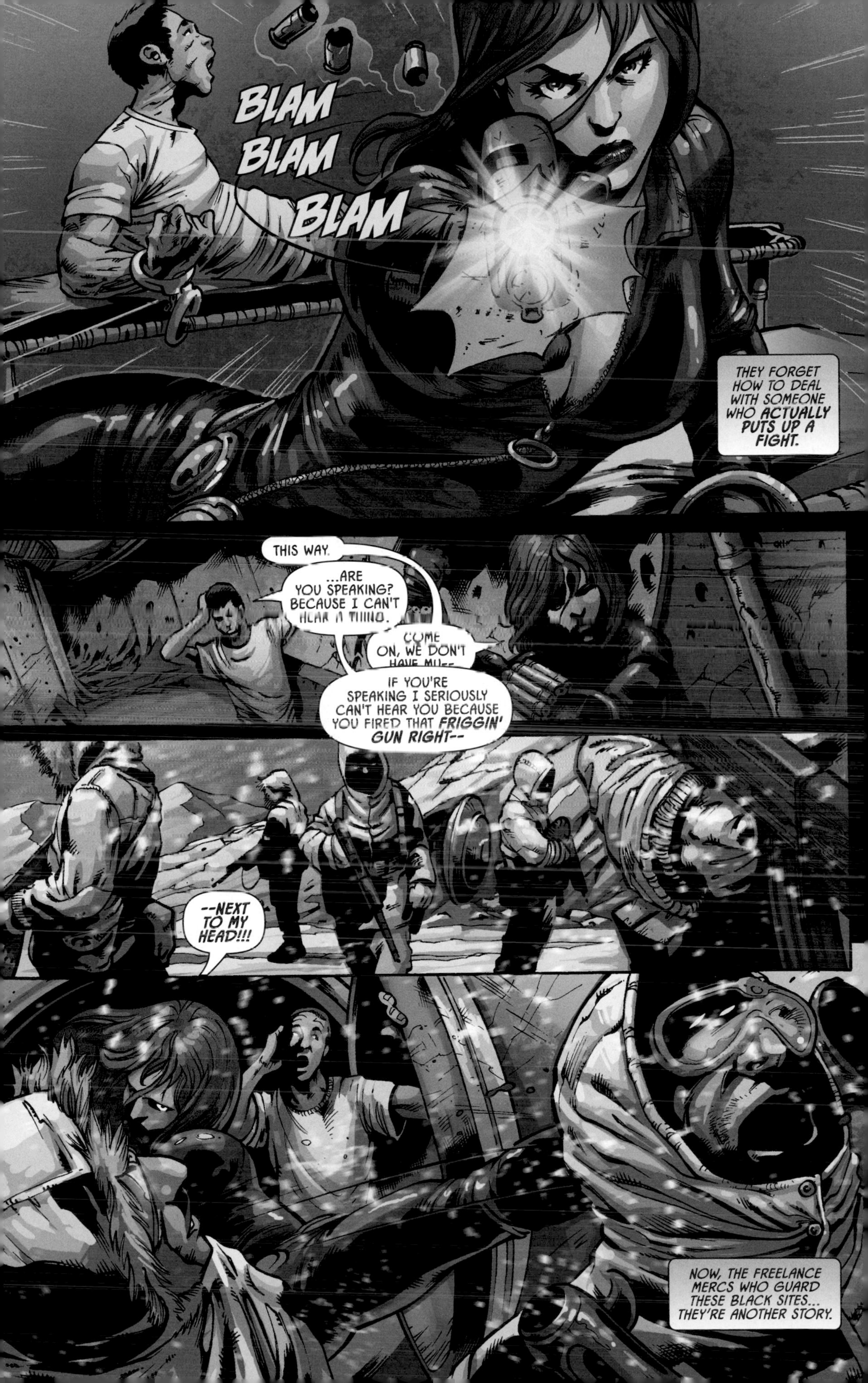
BLAM
BLAM
BLAM
THEY FORGET HOW TO DEAL WITH SOMEONE WHO ACTUALLY PUTS UP A FIGHT.
THIS WAY.
...ARE YOU SPEAKING? BECAUSE I CAN'T HEAR A THING.
COME ON, WE DON'T HAVE MU--
IF YOU'RE SPEAKING I SERIOUSLY CAN'T HEAR YOU BECAUSE YOU FIRED THAT FRIGGIN' GUN RIGHT--
--NEXT TO MY HEAD!!!
NOW, THE FREELANCE MERCS WHO GUARD THESE BLACK SITES... THEY'RE ANOTHER STORY.

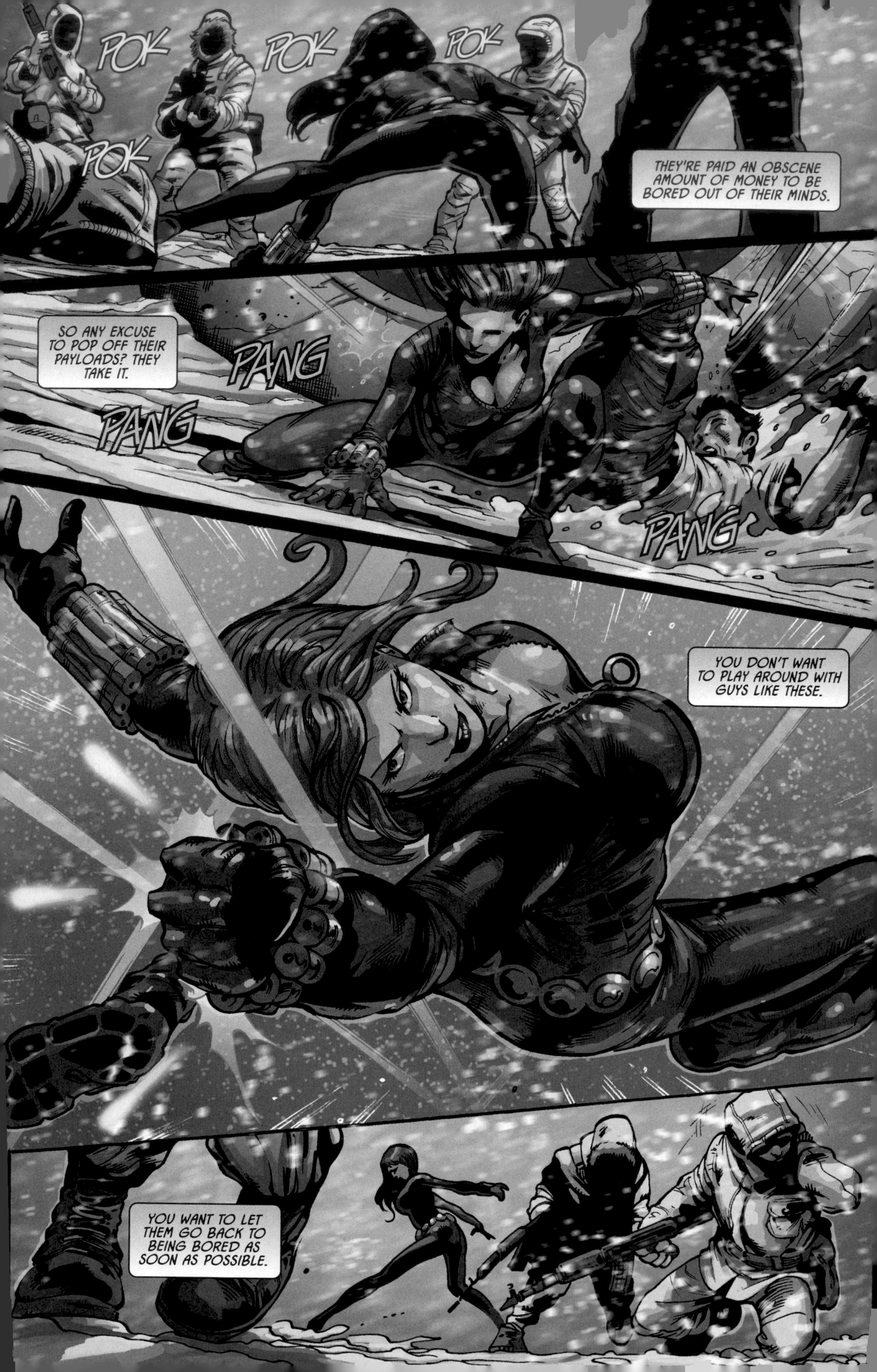
POK
POK
POK
POK
THEY'RE PAID AN OBSCENE AMOUNT OF MONEY TO BE BORED OUT OF THEIR MINDS.
SO ANY EXCUSE TO POP OFF THEIR PAYLOADS? THEY TAKE IT.
PANG
PANG
PANG
YOU DON'T WANT TO PLAY AROUND WITH GUYS LIKE THESE.
YOU WANT TO LET THEM GO BACK TO BEING BORED AS SOON AS POSSIBLE.

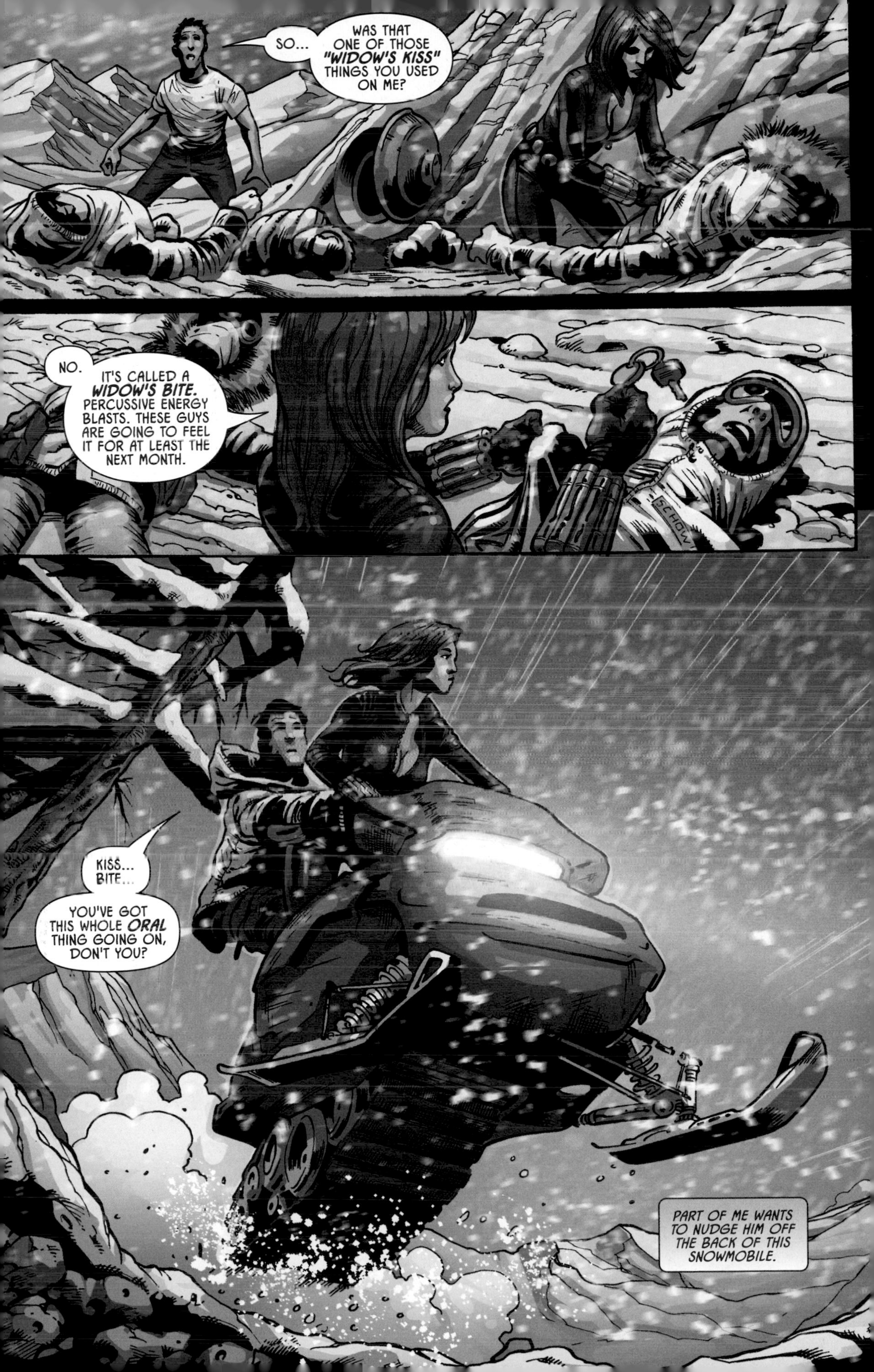
SO...
WAS THAT ONE OF THOSE "WIDOW'S KISS" THINGS YOU USED ON ME?
NO.
IT'S CALLED A WIDOW'S BITE. PERCUSSIVE ENERGY BLASTS. THESE GUYS ARE GOING TO FEEL IT FOR AT LEAST THE NEXT MONTH.
SCHOW
KISS... BITE...
YOU'VE GOT THIS WHOLE ORAL THING GOING ON, DON'T YOU?
PART OF ME WANTS TO NUDGE HIM OFF THE BACK OF THIS SNOWMOBILE.

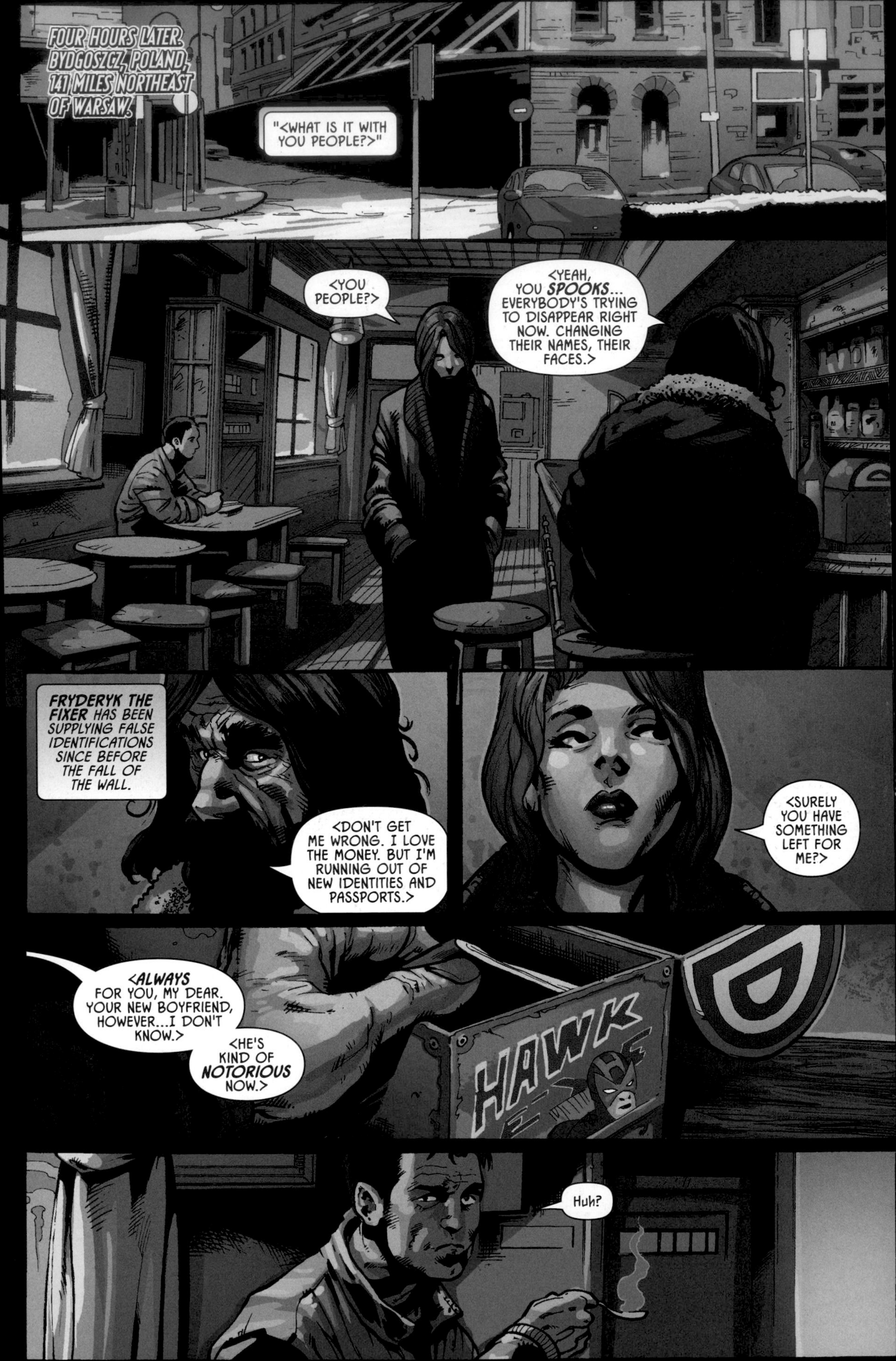
FOUR HOURS LATER. BYDGOSZCZ, POLAND, 141 MILES NORTHEAST OF WARSAW.
"<WHAT IS IT WITH YOU PEOPLE?>"
<YOU PEOPLE?>
<YEAH, YOU SPOOKS... EVERYBODY'S TRYING TO DISAPPEAR RIGHT NOW. CHANGING THEIR NAMES, THEIR FACES.>
FRYDERYK THE FIXER HAS BEEN SUPPLYING FALSE IDENTIFICATIONS SINCE BEFORE THE FALL OF THE WALL.
<DON'T GET ME WRONG. I LOVE THE MONEY. BUT I'M RUNNING OUT OF NEW IDENTITIES AND PASSPORTS.>
<SURELY YOU HAVE SOMETHING LEFT FOR ME?>
<ALWAYS FOR YOU, MY DEAR. YOUR NEW BOYFRIEND, HOWEVER...I DON'T KNOW.>
<HE'S KIND OF NOTORIOUS NOW.>
HAWK
Huh?

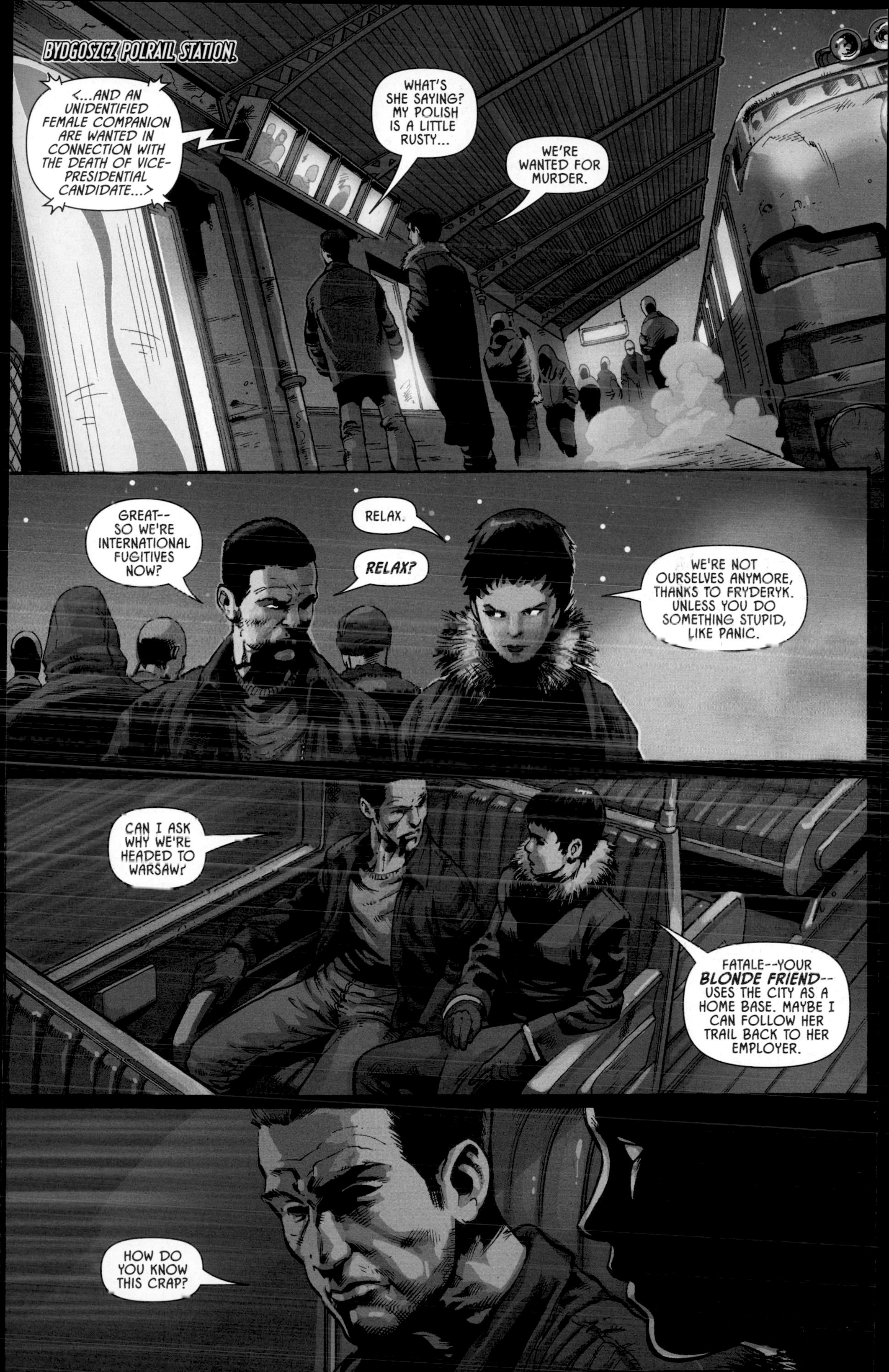

BYDGOSZCZ POLRAIL STATION.
<...AND AN UNIDENTIFIED FEMALE COMPANION ARE WANTED IN CONNECTION WITH THE DEATH OF VICE-PRESIDENTIAL CANDIDATE...>
WHAT'S SHE SAYING? MY POLISH IS A LITTLE RUSTY...
WE'RE WANTED FOR MURDER.
GREAT-- SO WE'RE INTERNATIONAL FUGITIVES NOW?
RELAX.
RELAX?
WE'RE NOT OURSELVES ANYMORE, THANKS TO FRYDERYK. UNLESS YOU DO SOMETHING STUPID, LIKE PANIC.
CAN I ASK WHY WE'RE HEADED TO WARSAW?
FATALE--YOUR BLONDE FRIEND-- USES THE CITY AS A HOME BASE. MAYBE I CAN FOLLOW HER TRAIL BACK TO HER EMPLOYER.
HOW DO YOU KNOW THIS CRAP?

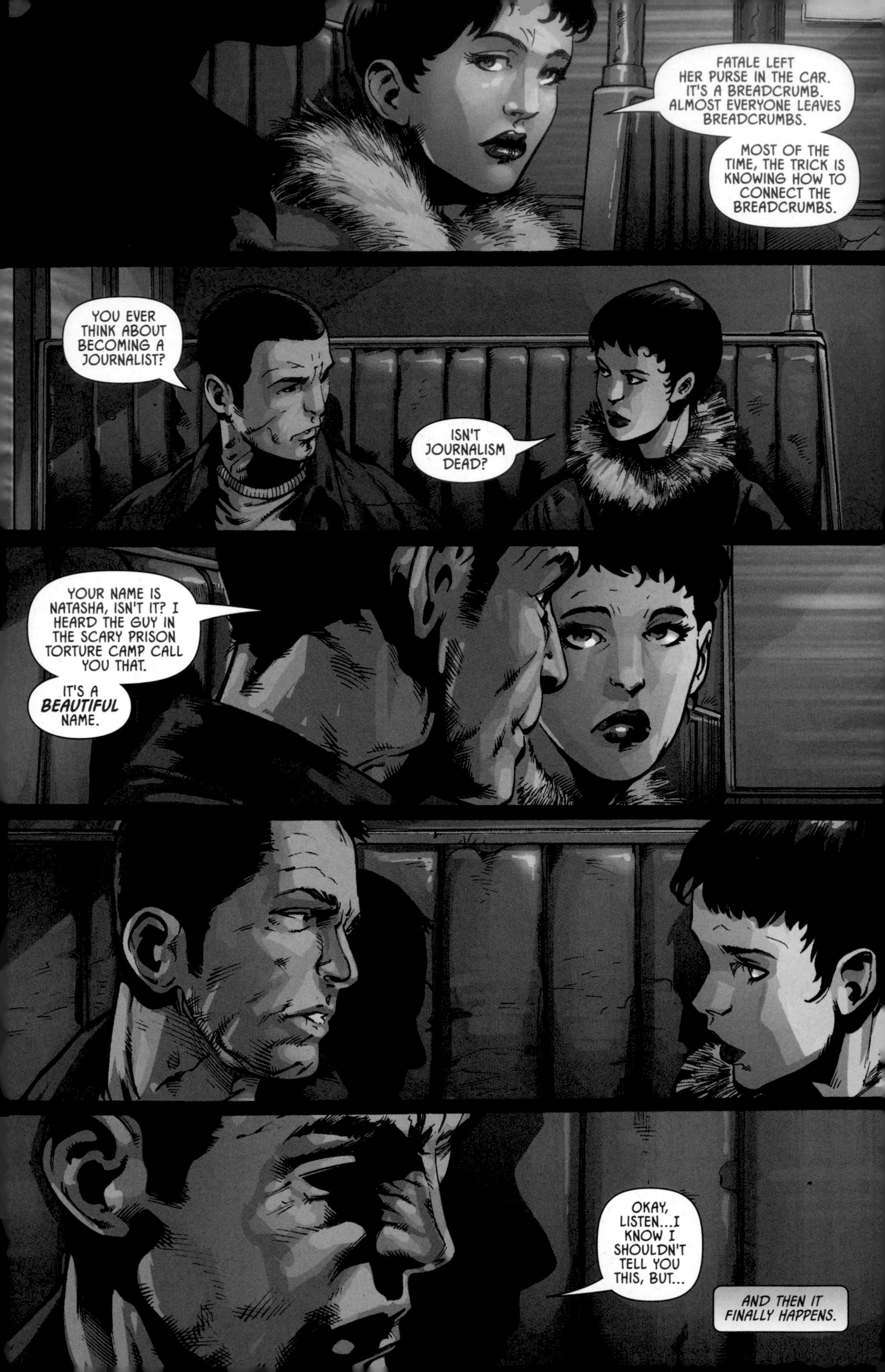
FATALE LEFT HER PURSE IN THE CAR. IT'S A BREADCRUMB. ALMOST EVERYONE LEAVES BREADCRUMBS.
MOST OF THE TIME, THE TRICK IS KNOWING HOW TO CONNECT THE BREADCRUMBS.
YOU EVER THINK ABOUT BECOMING A JOURNALIST?
ISN'T JOURNALISM DEAD?
YOUR NAME IS NATASHA, ISN'T IT? I HEARD THE GUY IN THE SCARY PRISON TORTURE CAMP CALL YOU THAT.
IT'S A *BEAUTIFUL* NAME.
OKAY, LISTEN...I KNOW I SHOULDN'T TELL YOU THIS, BUT...
AND THEN IT FINALLY HAPPENS.

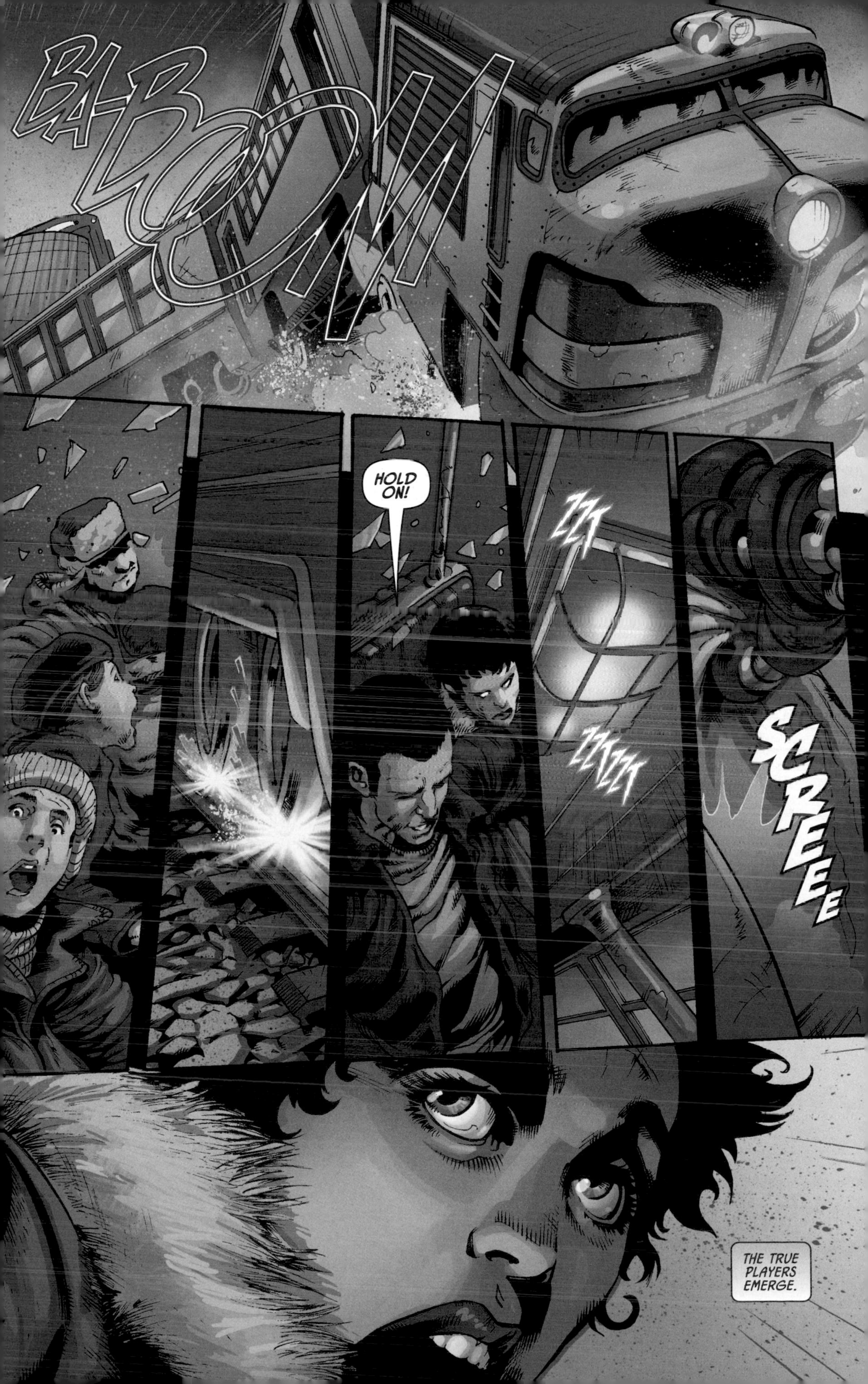
BA-BOOM
HOLD ON!
ZZZT
ZZZZZZT
SCREEEE
THE TRUE PLAYERS EMERGE.

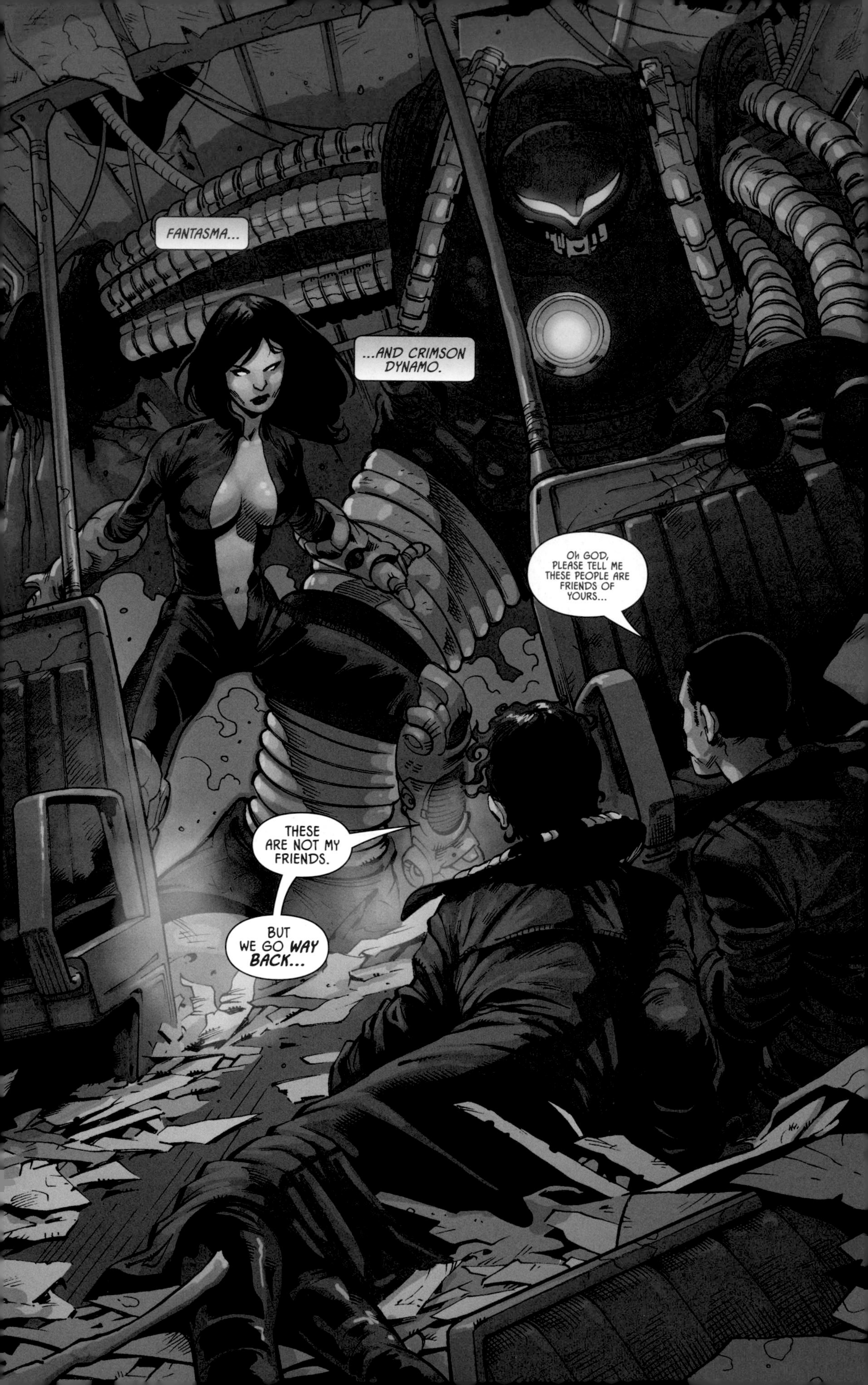
FANTASMA...
...AND CRIMSON DYNAMO.
Oh GOD, PLEASE TELL ME THESE PEOPLE ARE FRIENDS OF YOURS...
THESE ARE NOT MY FRIENDS.
BUT WE GO WAY BACK...

8

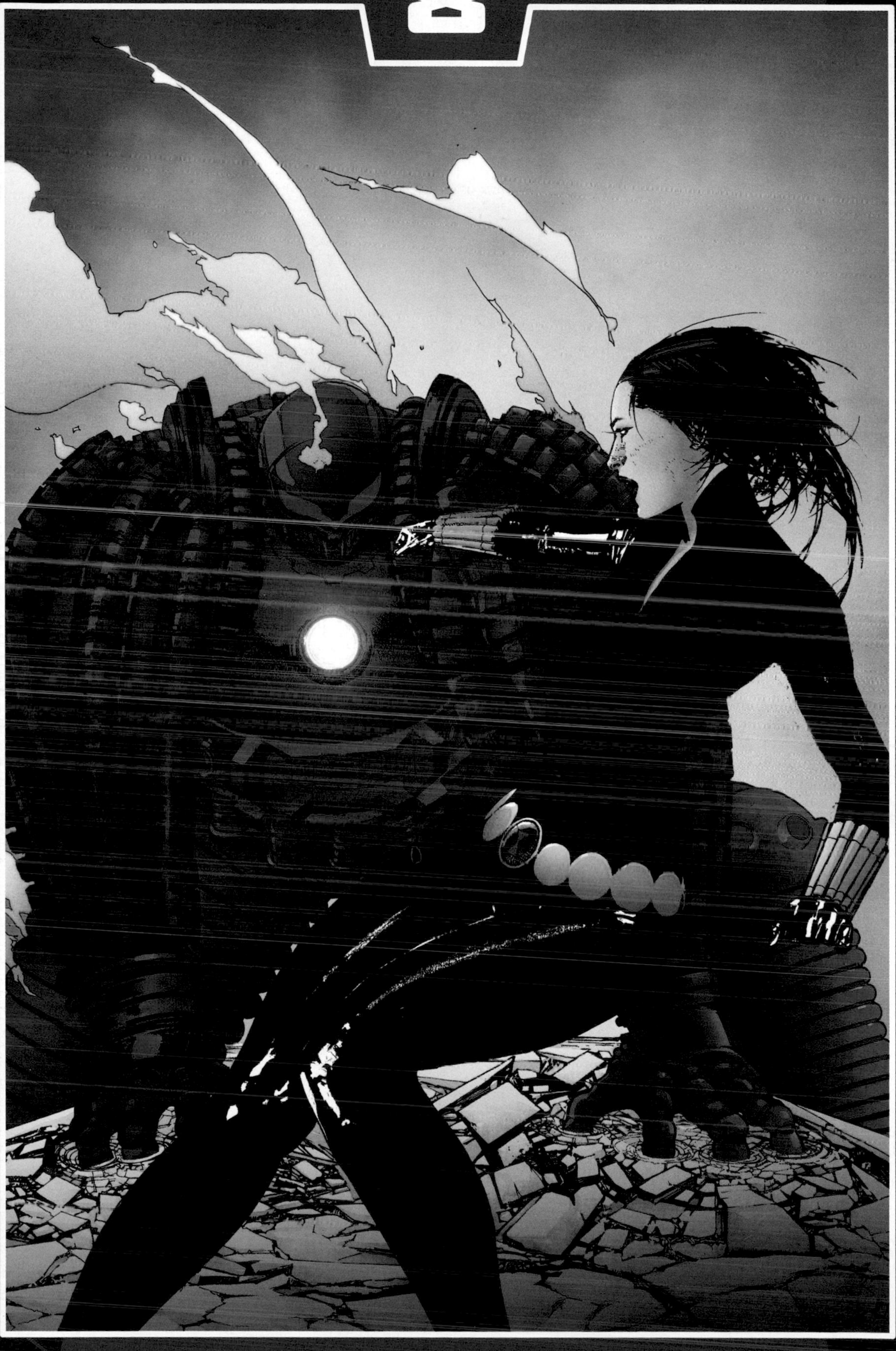

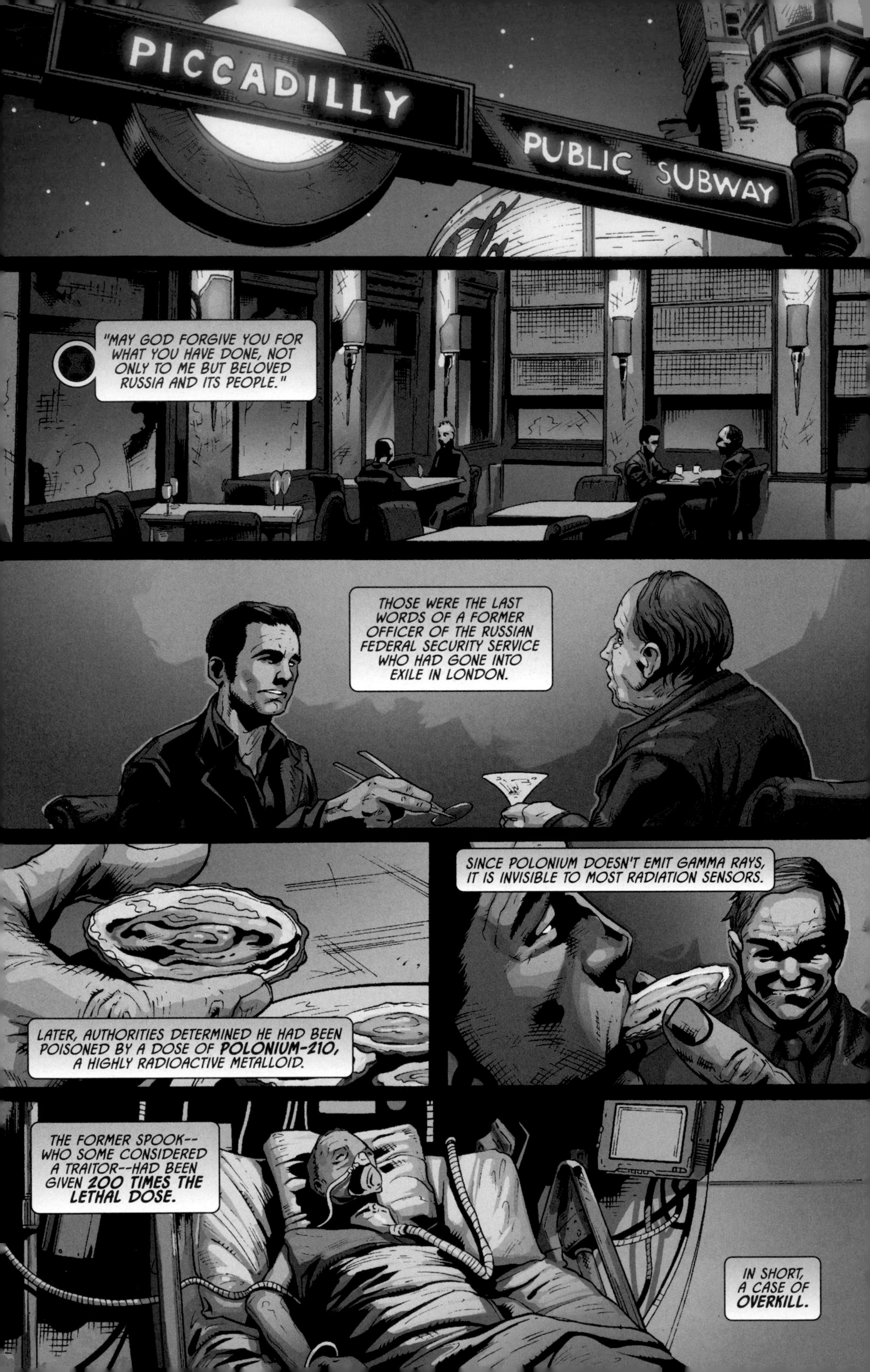
PICCADILLY
PUBLIC SUBWAY
"MAY GOD FORGIVE YOU FOR WHAT YOU HAVE DONE, NOT ONLY TO ME BUT BELOVED RUSSIA AND ITS PEOPLE."
THOSE WERE THE LAST WORDS OF A FORMER OFFICER OF THE RUSSIAN FEDERAL SECURITY SERVICE WHO HAD GONE INTO EXILE IN LONDON.
LATER, AUTHORITIES DETERMINED HE HAD BEEN POISONED BY A DOSE OF **POLONIUM-210,** A HIGHLY RADIOACTIVE METALLOID.
SINCE POLONIUM DOESN'T EMIT GAMMA RAYS, IT IS INVISIBLE TO MOST RADIATION SENSORS.
THE FORMER SPOOK--WHO SOME CONSIDERED A TRAITOR--HAD BEEN GIVEN **200 TIMES THE LETHAL DOSE.**
IN SHORT, A CASE OF **OVERKILL.**

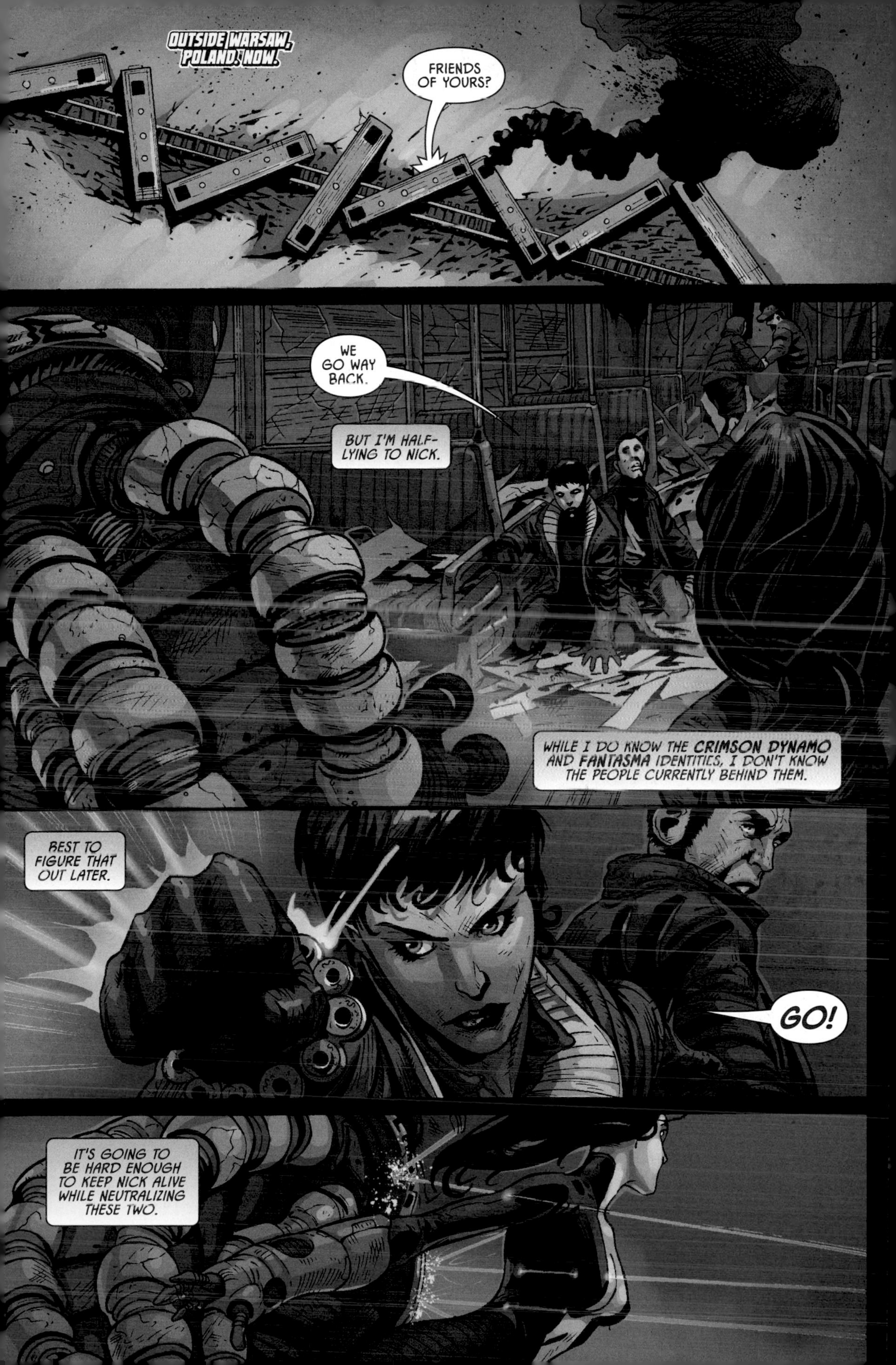
OUTSIDE WARSAW, POLAND. NOW.
FRIENDS OF YOURS?
WE GO WAY BACK.
BUT I'M HALF-LYING TO NICK.
WHILE I DO KNOW THE CRIMSON DYNAMO AND FANTASMA IDENTITIES, I DON'T KNOW THE PEOPLE CURRENTLY BEHIND THEM.
BEST TO FIGURE THAT OUT LATER.
GO!
IT'S GOING TO BE HARD ENOUGH TO KEEP NICK ALIVE WHILE NEUTRALIZING THESE TWO.

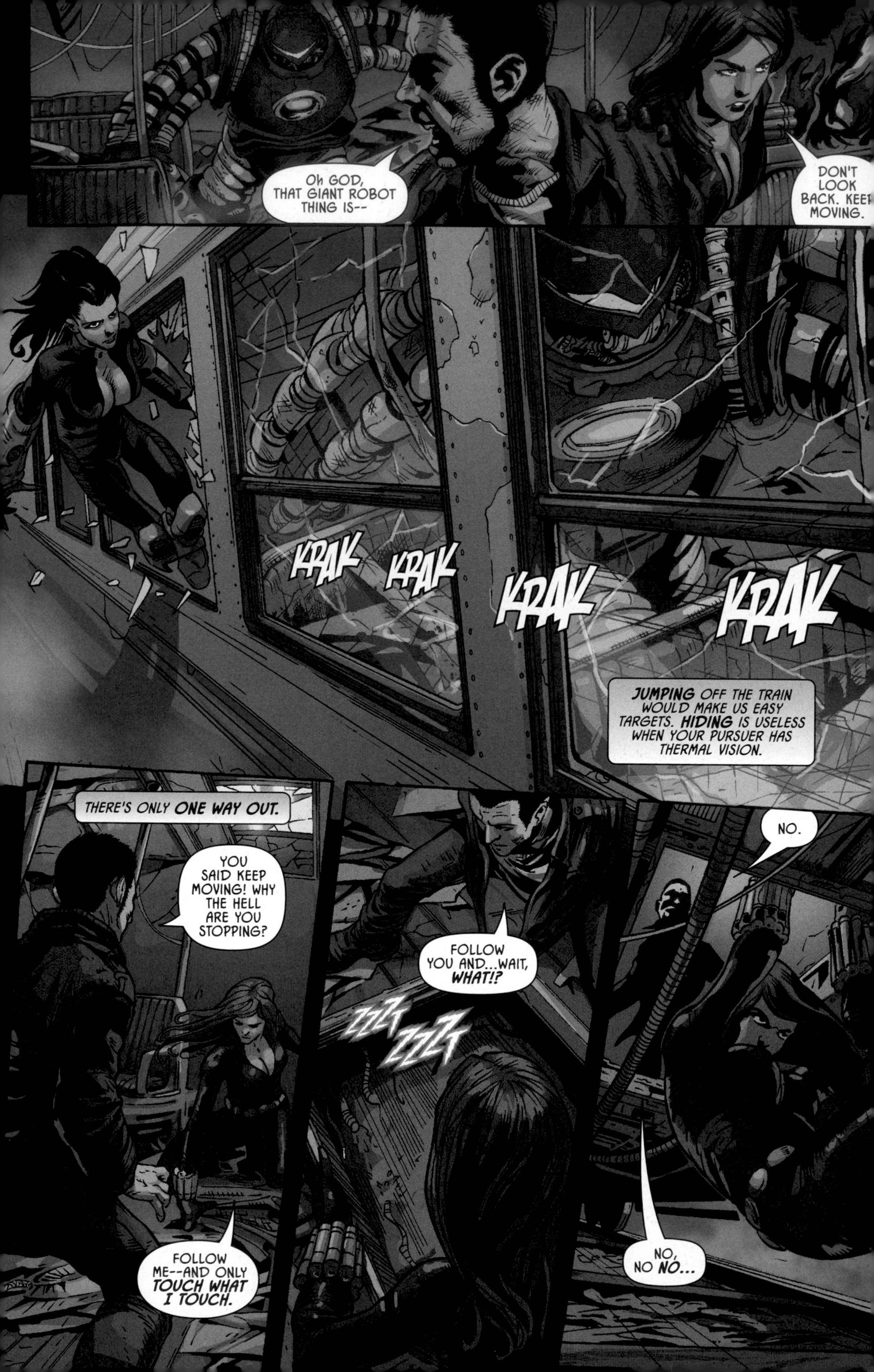
Oh GOD, THAT GIANT ROBOT THING IS--
DON'T LOOK BACK. KEEP MOVING.
KRAK
KRAK
KRAK
KRAK
JUMPING OFF THE TRAIN WOULD MAKE US EASY TARGETS. HIDING IS USELESS WHEN YOUR PURSUER HAS THERMAL VISION.
THERE'S ONLY ONE WAY OUT.
YOU SAID KEEP MOVING! WHY THE HELL ARE YOU STOPPING?
FOLLOW ME--AND ONLY TOUCH WHAT I TOUCH.
FOLLOW YOU AND...WAIT, WHAT!?
ZZZT
ZZZT
NO.
NO, NO NO...

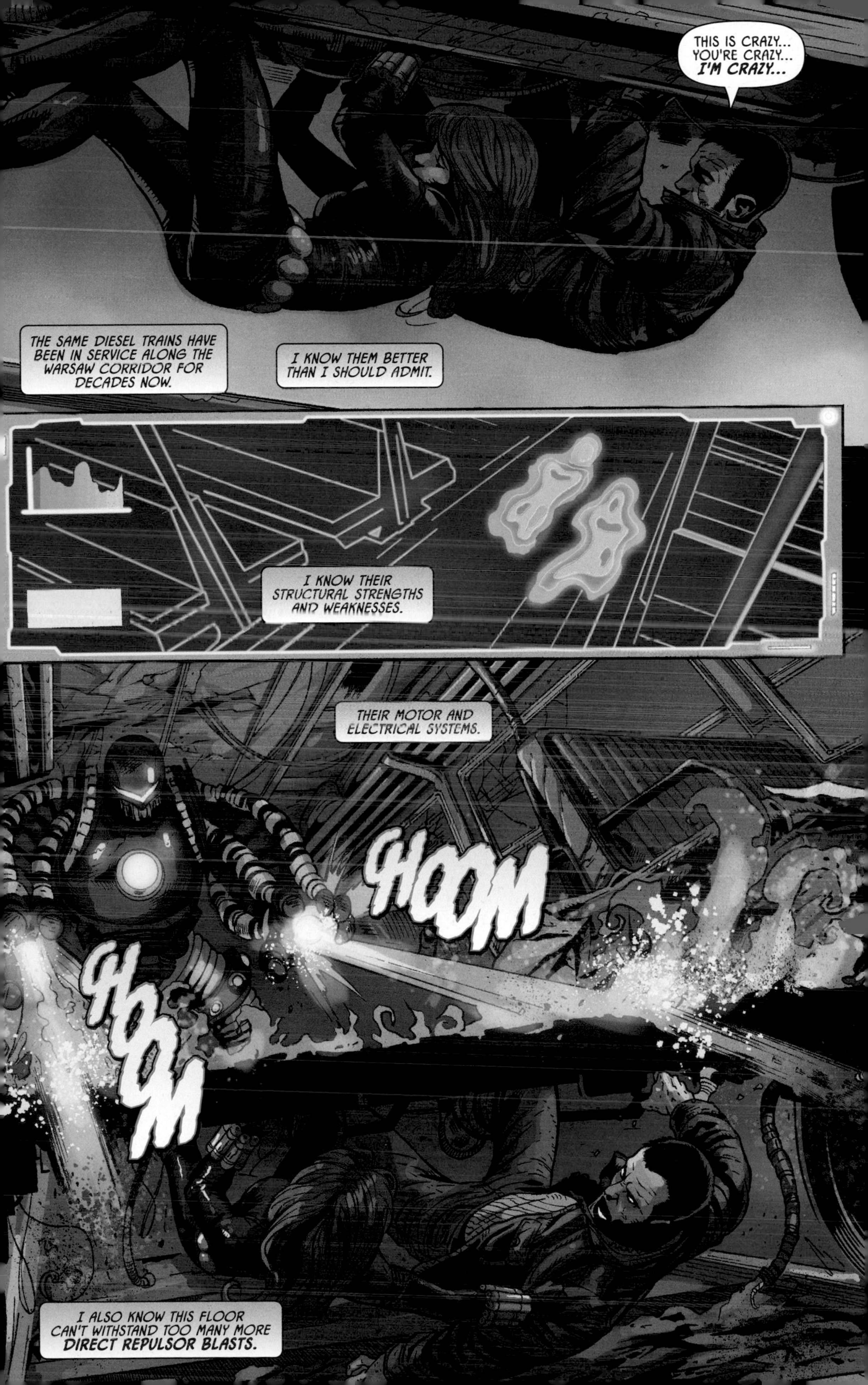
THIS IS CRAZY... YOU'RE CRAZY... I'M CRAZY...
THE SAME DIESEL TRAINS HAVE BEEN IN SERVICE ALONG THE WARSAW CORRIDOR FOR DECADES NOW.
I KNOW THEM BETTER THAN I SHOULD ADMIT.
I KNOW THEIR STRUCTURAL STRENGTHS AND WEAKNESSES.
THEIR MOTOR AND ELECTRICAL SYSTEMS.
HOOM
HOOM
I ALSO KNOW THIS FLOOR CAN'T WITHSTAND TOO MANY MORE DIRECT REPULSOR BLASTS.

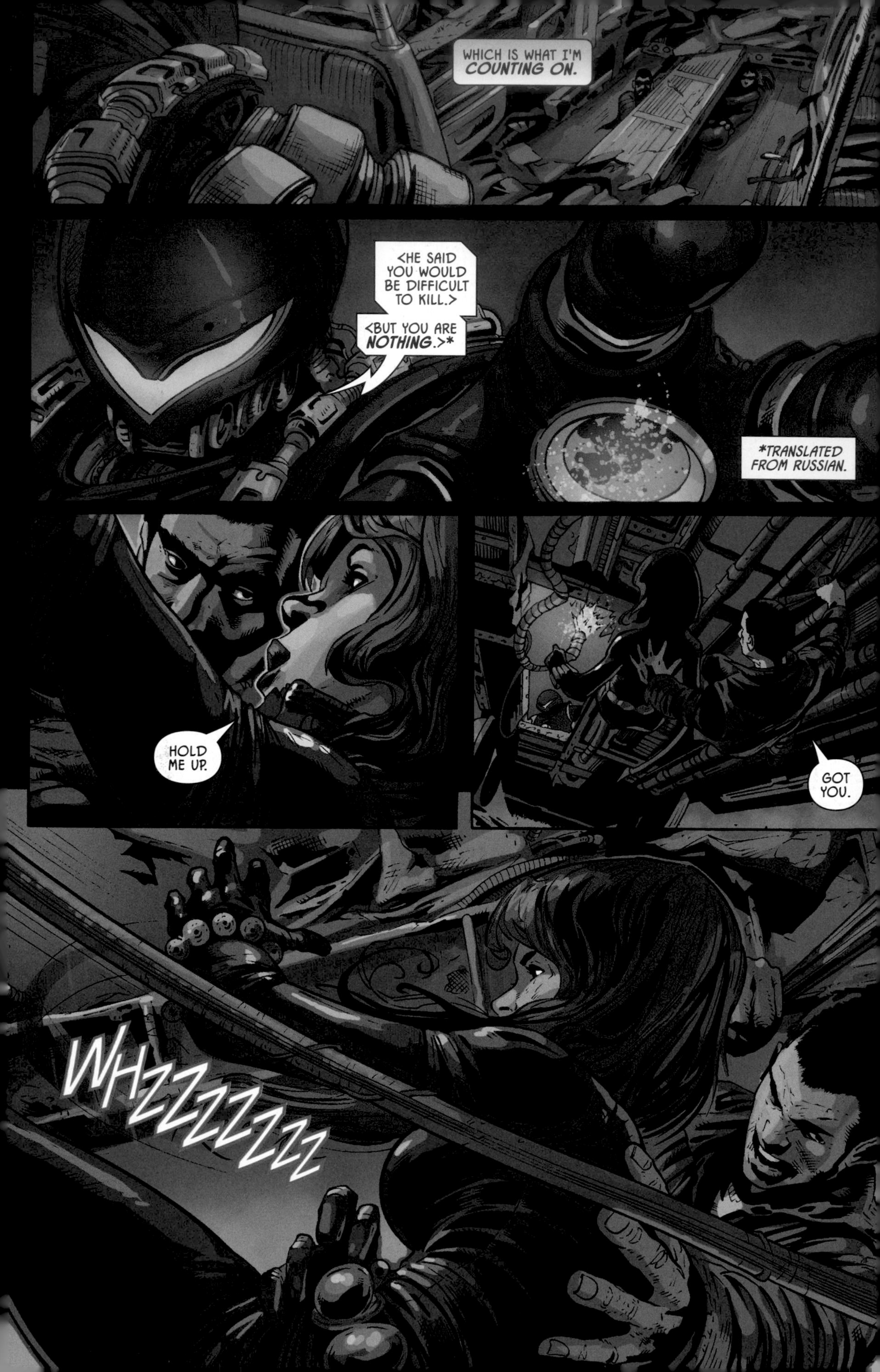
WHICH IS WHAT I'M COUNTING ON.
<HE SAID YOU WOULD BE DIFFICULT TO KILL.>
<BUT YOU ARE NOTHING.>*
*TRANSLATED FROM RUSSIAN.
HOLD ME UP.
GOT YOU.
WHZZZZZZZ

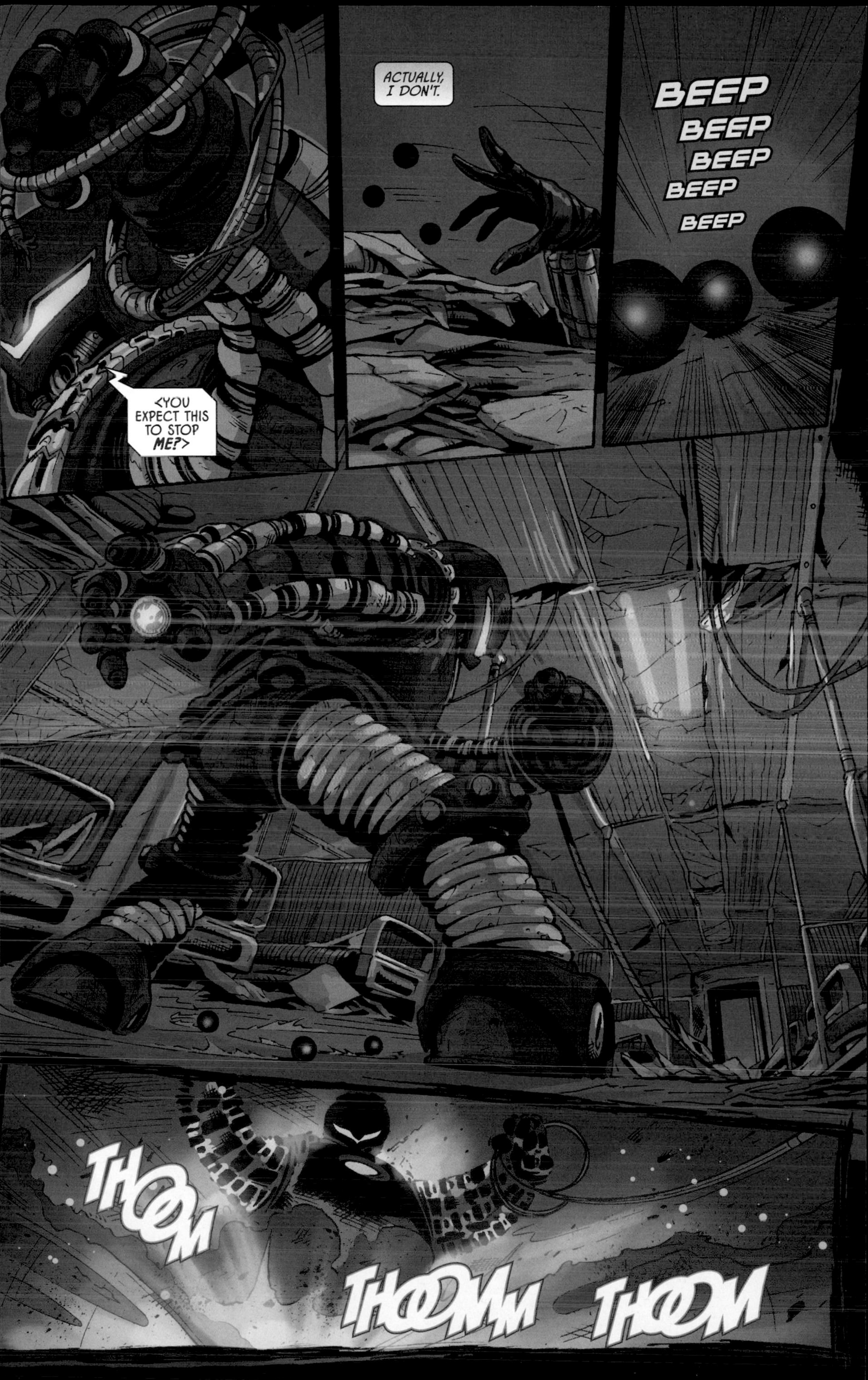

<YOU EXPECT THIS TO STOP ME?>
ACTUALLY, I DON'T.
BEEP BEEP BEEP BEEP BEEP
THOOM
THOOMM
THOOM

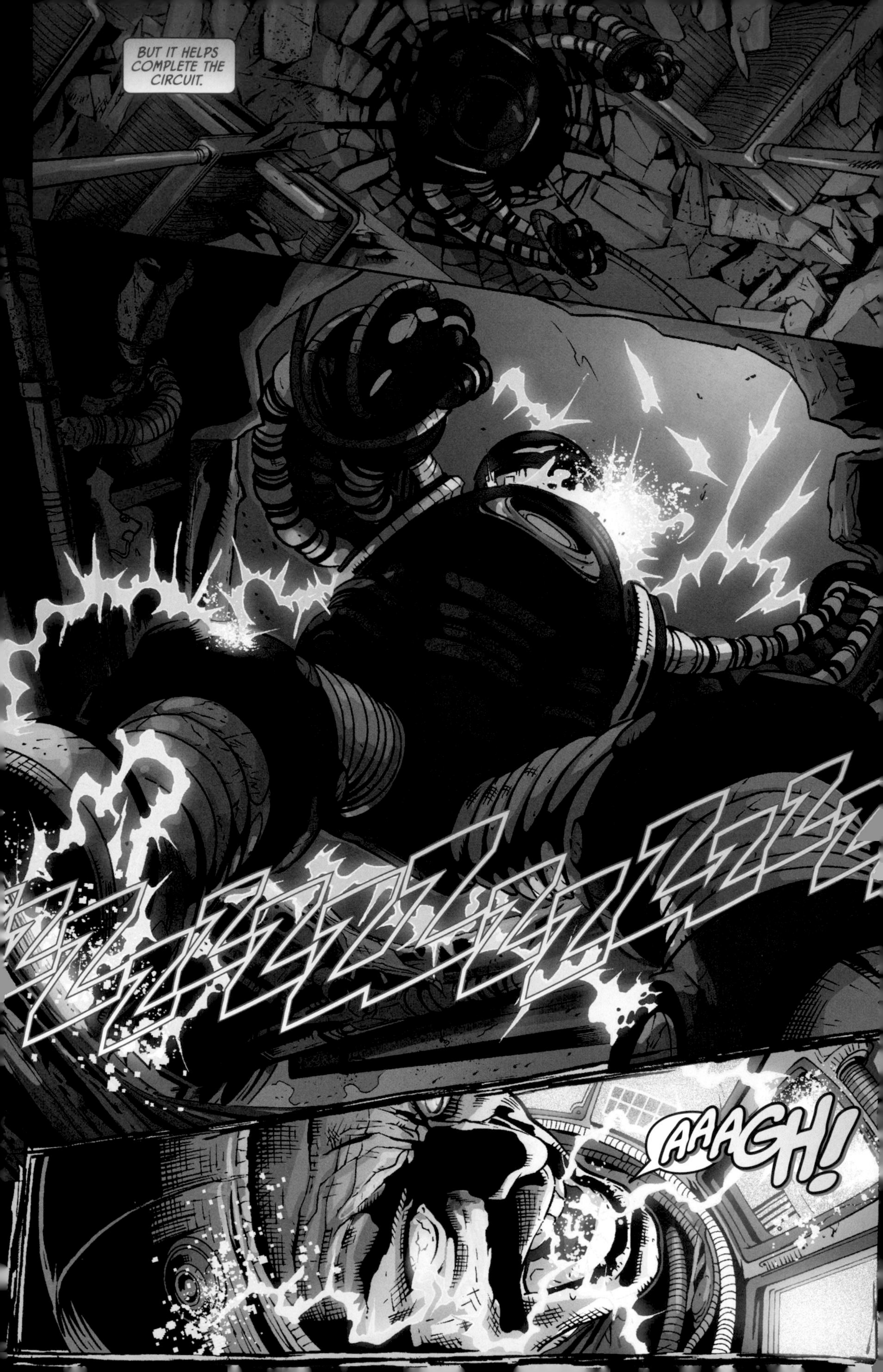
BUT IT HELPS COMPLETE THE CIRCUIT.
AAAGH!

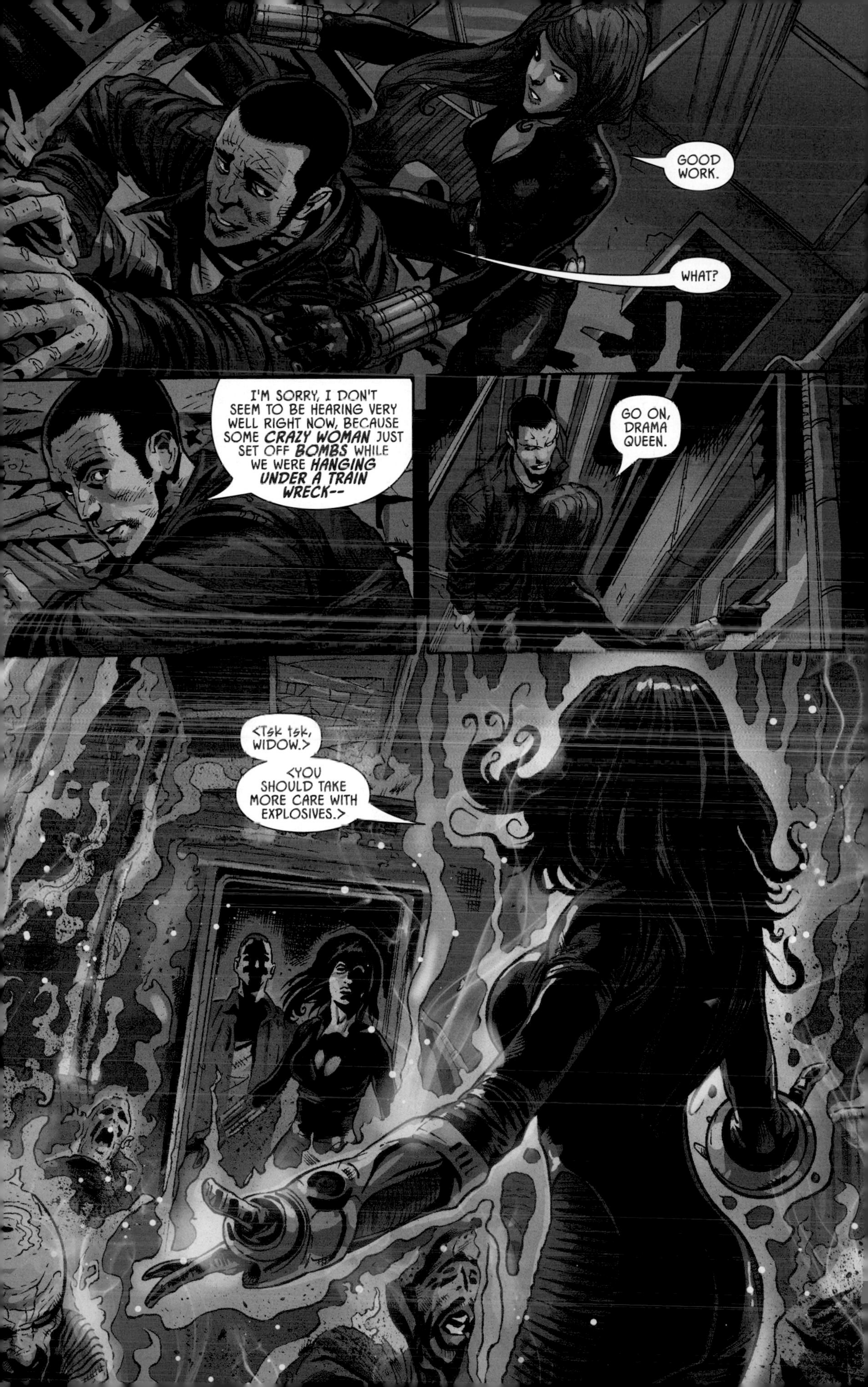
GOOD WORK.
WHAT?
I'M SORRY, I DON'T SEEM TO BE HEARING VERY WELL RIGHT NOW, BECAUSE SOME CRAZY WOMAN JUST SET OFF BOMBS WHILE WE WERE HANGING UNDER A TRAIN WRECK--
GO ON, DRAMA QUEEN.
<Tsk tsk, WIDOW.>
<YOU SHOULD TAKE MORE CARE WITH EXPLOSIVES.>

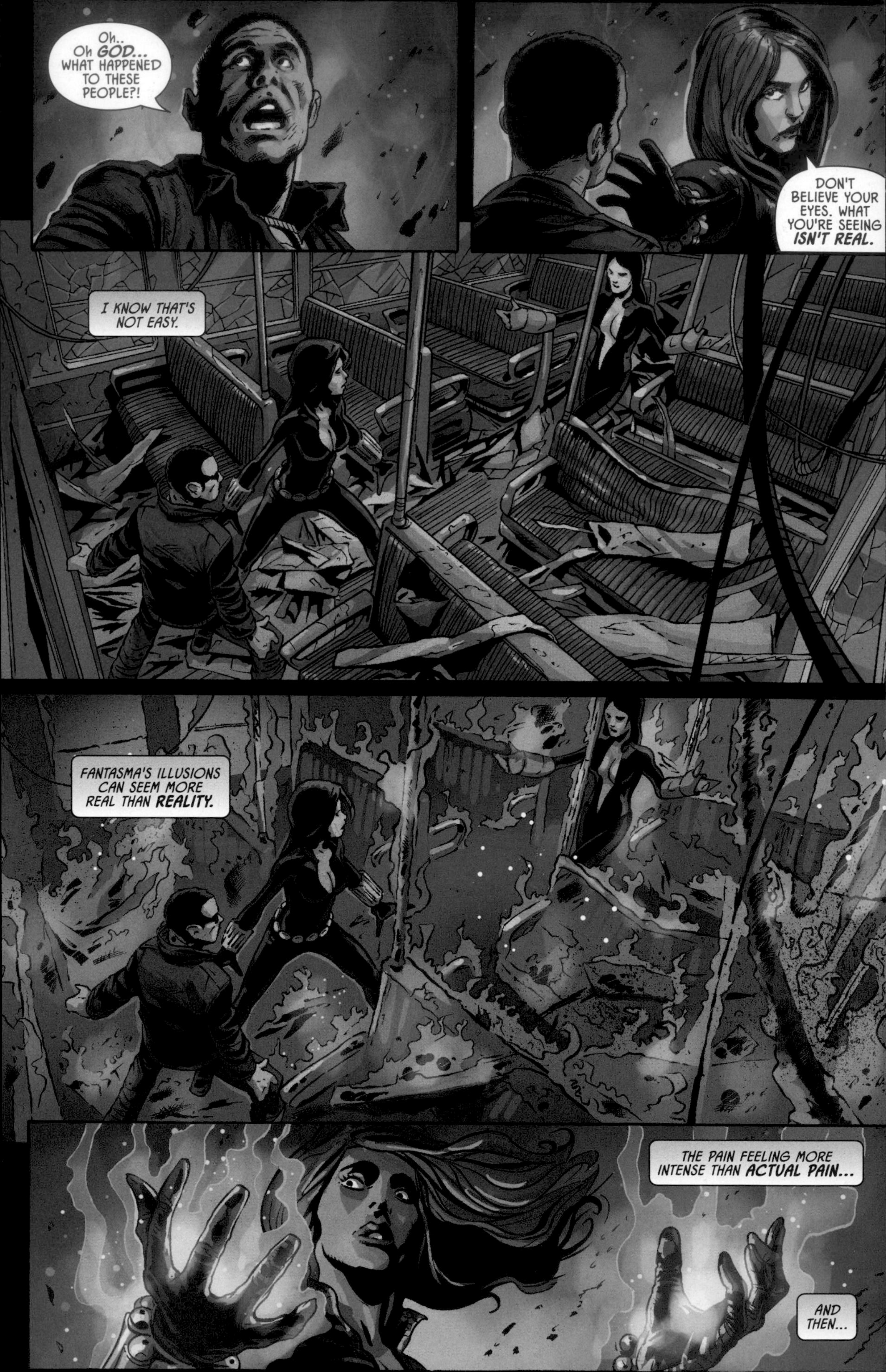
Oh.. Oh GOD... WHAT HAPPENED TO THESE PEOPLE?!
DON'T BELIEVE YOUR EYES. WHAT YOU'RE SEEING ISN'T REAL.
I KNOW THAT'S NOT EASY.
FANTASMA'S ILLUSIONS CAN SEEM MORE REAL THAN REALITY.
THE PAIN FEELING MORE INTENSE THAN ACTUAL PAIN...
AND THEN...

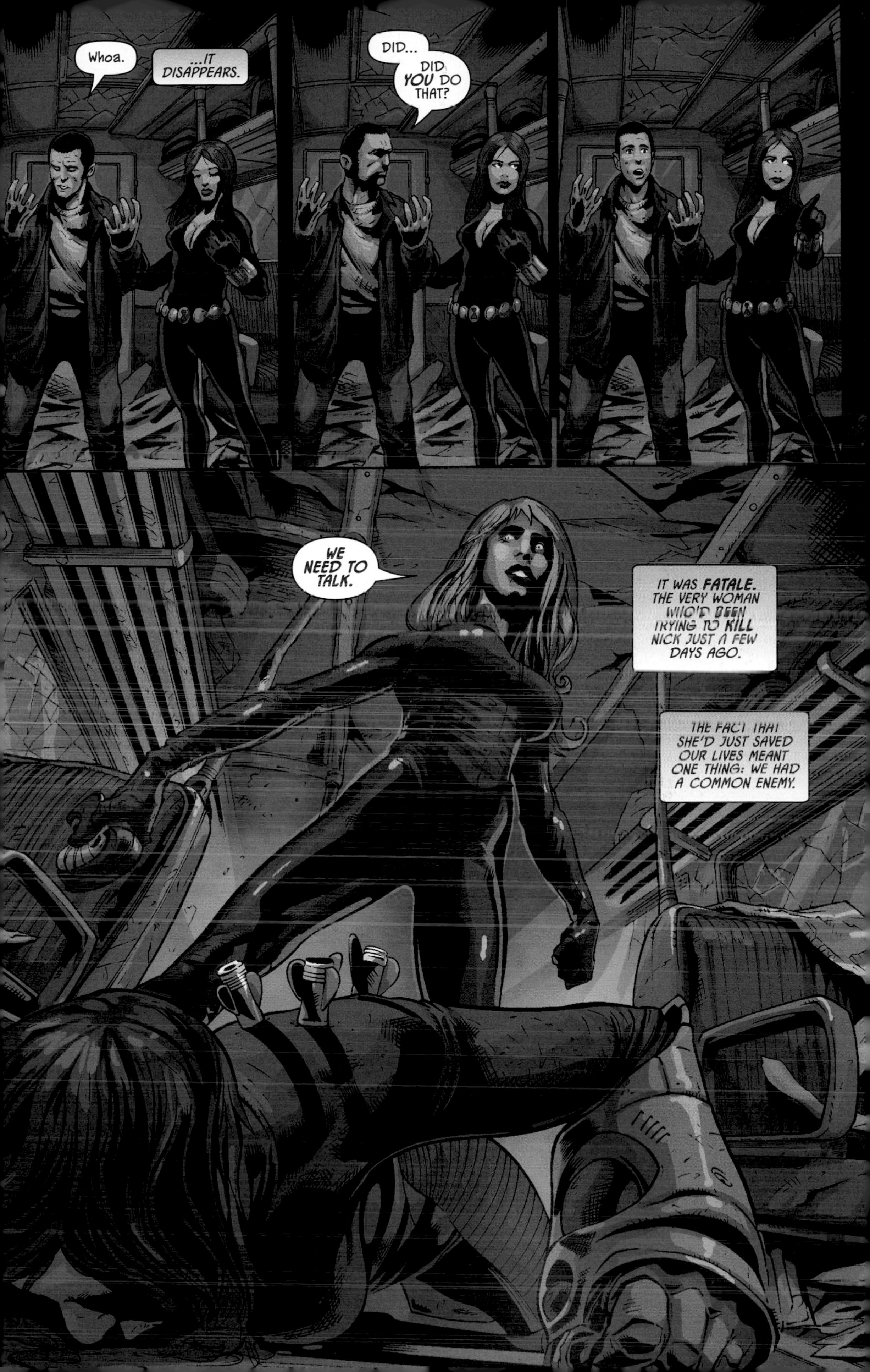

Whoa.
...IT DISAPPEARS.
DID... DID YOU DO THAT?
WE NEED TO TALK.
IT WAS FATALE. THE VERY WOMAN WHO'D BEEN TRYING TO KILL NICK JUST A FEW DAYS AGO.
THE FACT THAT SHE'D JUST SAVED OUR LIVES MEANT ONE THING: WE HAD A COMMON ENEMY.

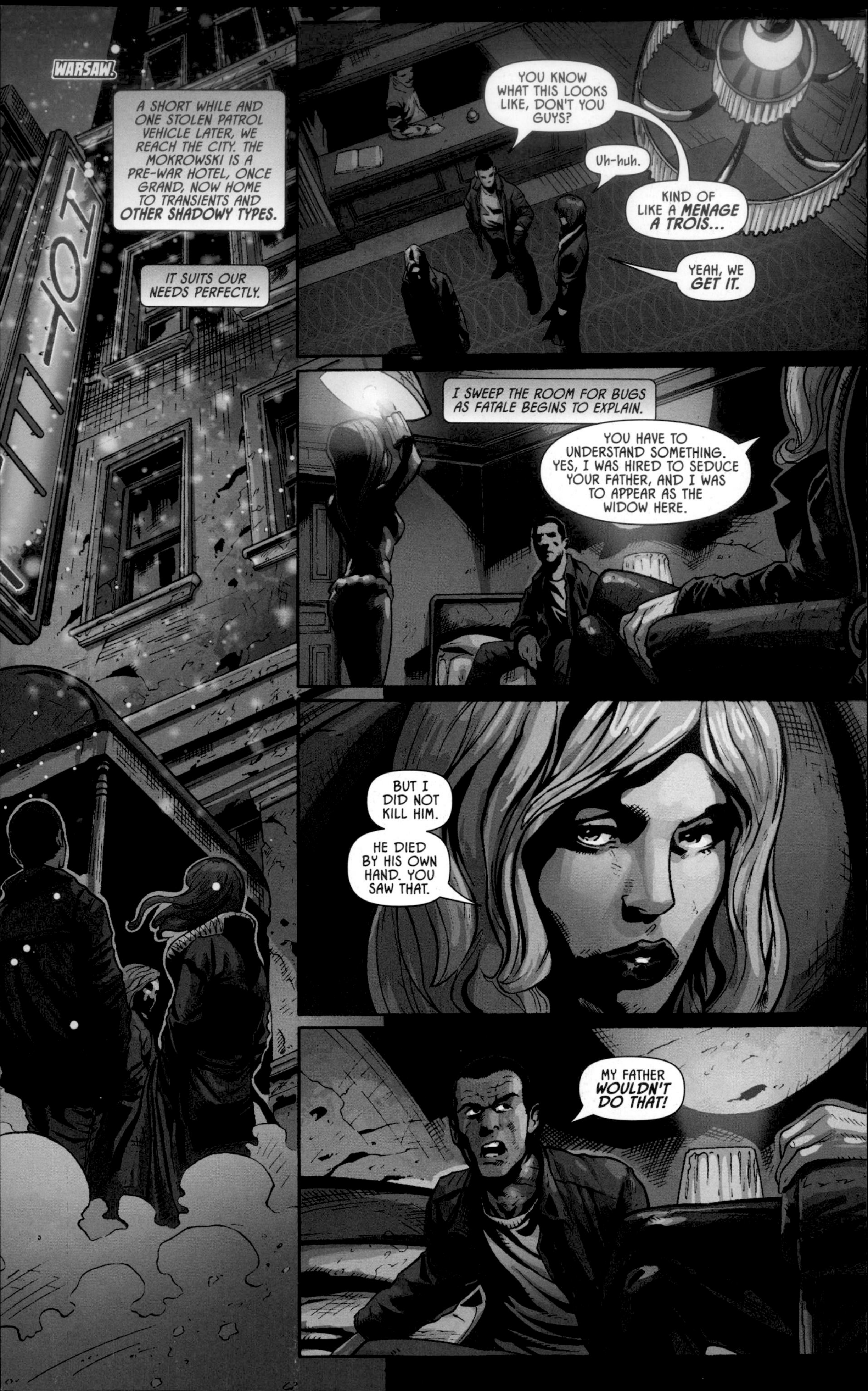
WARSAW.
A SHORT WHILE AND ONE STOLEN PATROL VEHICLE LATER, WE REACH THE CITY. THE MOKROWSKI IS A PRE-WAR HOTEL, ONCE GRAND, NOW HOME TO TRANSIENTS AND OTHER SHADOWY TYPES.
IT SUITS OUR NEEDS PERFECTLY.
YOU KNOW WHAT THIS LOOKS LIKE, DON'T YOU GUYS?
Uh-huh.
KIND OF LIKE A MENAGE A TROIS...
YEAH, WE GET IT.
I SWEEP THE ROOM FOR BUGS AS FATALE BEGINS TO EXPLAIN.
YOU HAVE TO UNDERSTAND SOMETHING. YES, I WAS HIRED TO SEDUCE YOUR FATHER, AND I WAS TO APPEAR AS THE WIDOW HERE.
BUT I DID NOT KILL HIM.
HE DIED BY HIS OWN HAND. YOU SAW THAT.
MY FATHER WOULDN'T DO THAT!

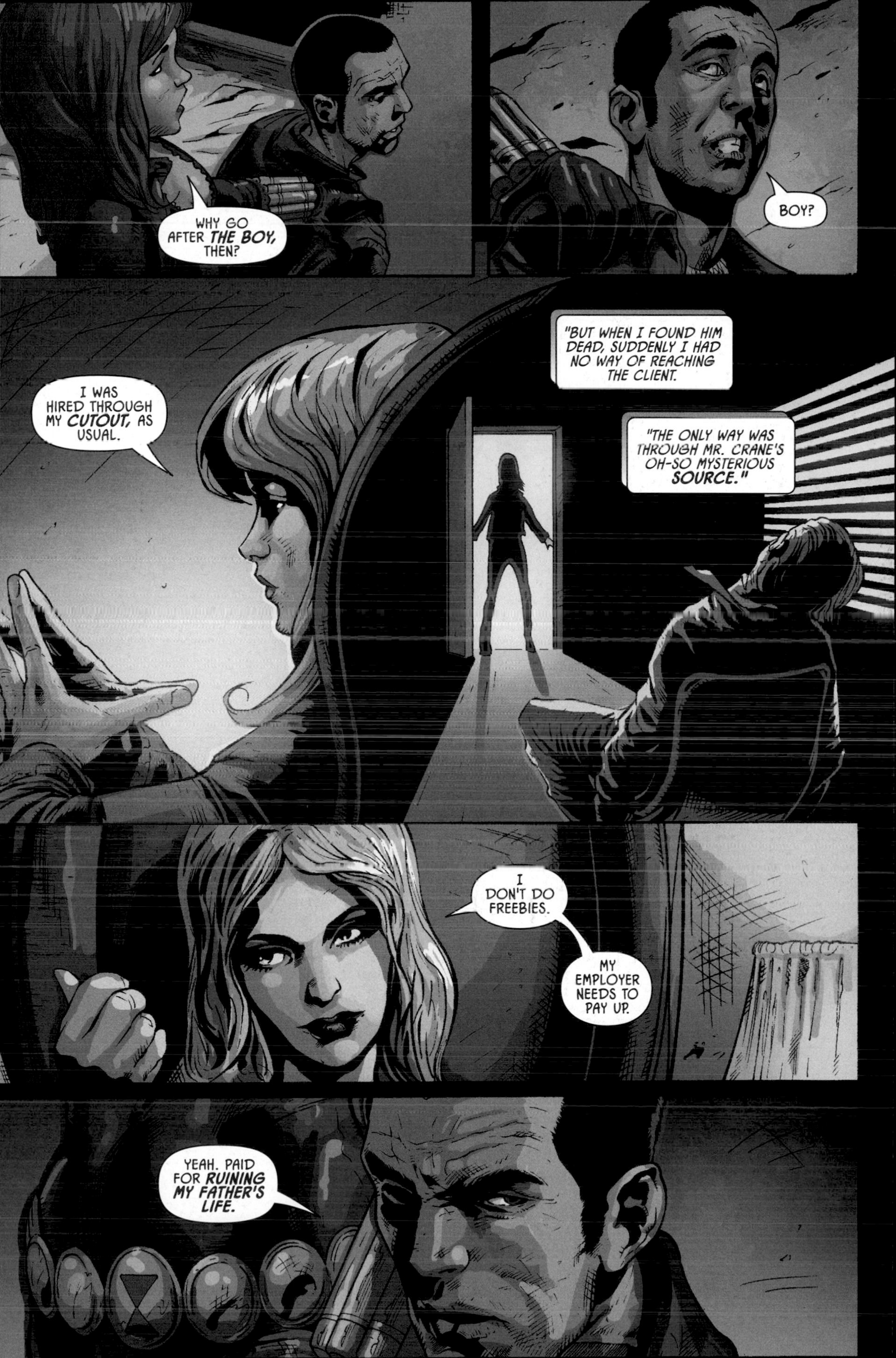
WHY GO AFTER THE BOY, THEN?
BOY?
I WAS HIRED THROUGH MY CUTOUT, AS USUAL.
"BUT WHEN I FOUND HIM DEAD, SUDDENLY I HAD NO WAY OF REACHING THE CLIENT.
"THE ONLY WAY WAS THROUGH MR. CRANE'S OH-SO MYSTERIOUS SOURCE."
I DON'T DO FREEBIES.
MY EMPLOYER NEEDS TO PAY UP.
YEAH. PAID FOR RUINING MY FATHER'S LIFE.

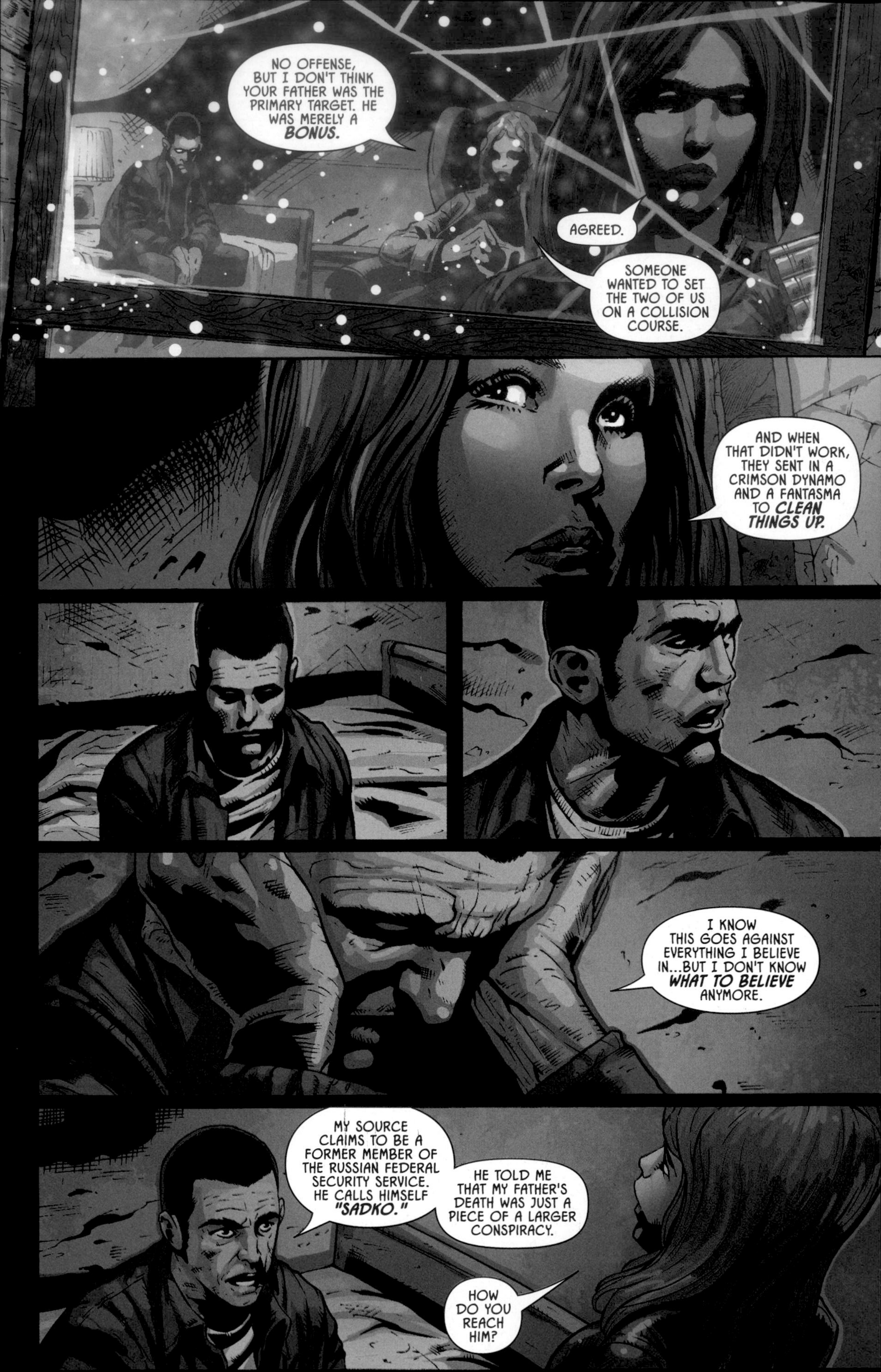
NO OFFENSE, BUT I DON'T THINK YOUR FATHER WAS THE PRIMARY TARGET. HE WAS MERELY A BONUS.
AGREED.
SOMEONE WANTED TO SET THE TWO OF US ON A COLLISION COURSE.
AND WHEN THAT DIDN'T WORK, THEY SENT IN A CRIMSON DYNAMO AND A FANTASMA TO CLEAN THINGS UP.
I KNOW THIS GOES AGAINST EVERYTHING I BELIEVE IN...BUT I DON'T KNOW WHAT TO BELIEVE ANYMORE.
MY SOURCE CLAIMS TO BE A FORMER MEMBER OF THE RUSSIAN FEDERAL SECURITY SERVICE. HE CALLS HIMSELF "SADKO."
HE TOLD ME THAT MY FATHER'S DEATH WAS JUST A PIECE OF A LARGER CONSPIRACY.
HOW DO YOU REACH HIM?

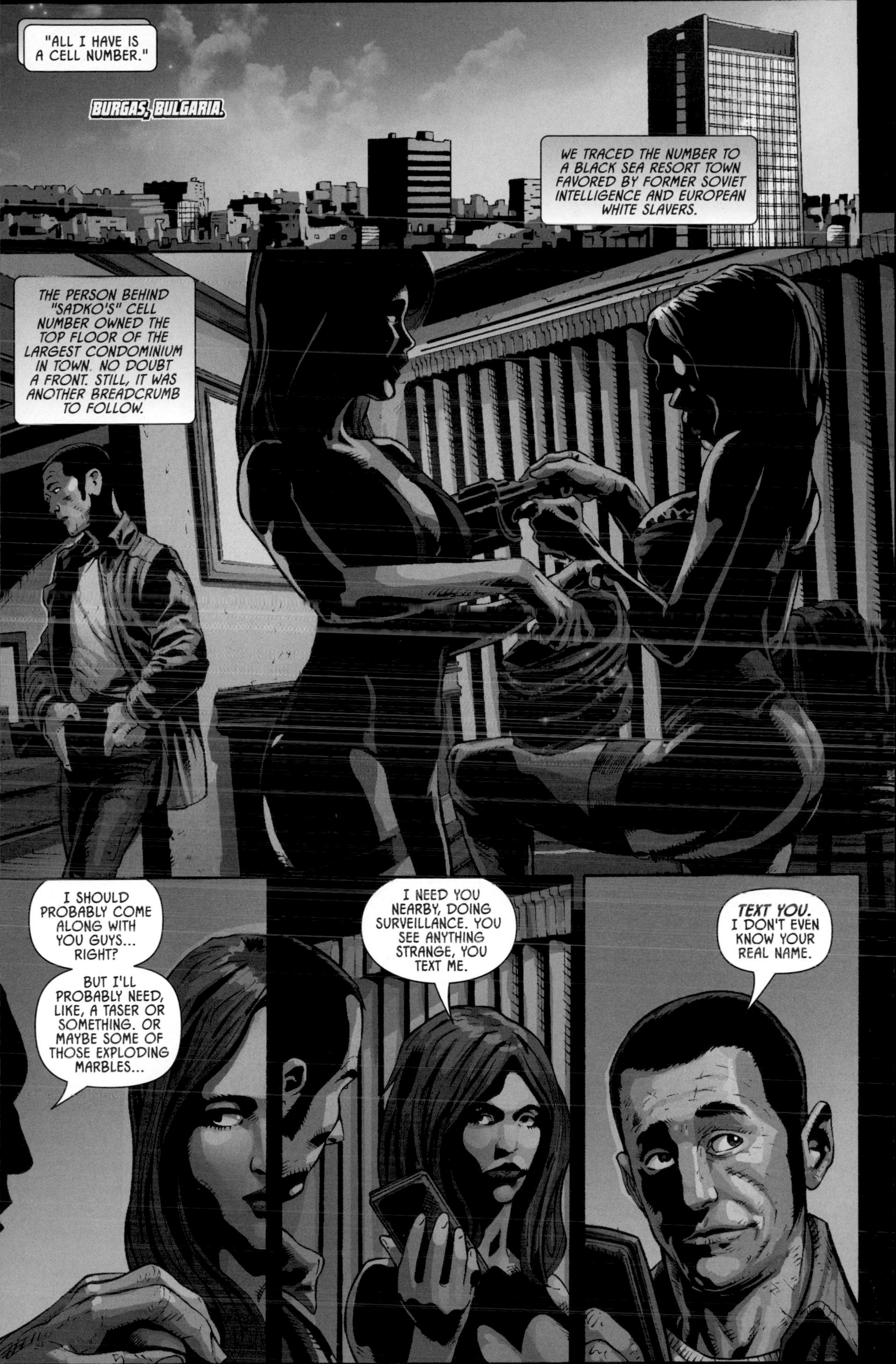
"ALL I HAVE IS A CELL NUMBER."
BURGAS, BULGARIA.
WE TRACED THE NUMBER TO A BLACK SEA RESORT TOWN FAVORED BY FORMER SOVIET INTELLIGENCE AND EUROPEAN WHITE SLAVERS.
THE PERSON BEHIND "SADKO'S" CELL NUMBER OWNED THE TOP FLOOR OF THE LARGEST CONDOMINIUM IN TOWN. NO DOUBT A FRONT. STILL, IT WAS ANOTHER BREADCRUMB TO FOLLOW.
I SHOULD PROBABLY COME ALONG WITH YOU GUYS... RIGHT?
BUT I'LL PROBABLY NEED, LIKE, A TASER OR SOMETHING. OR MAYBE SOME OF THOSE EXPLODING MARBLES...
I NEED YOU NEARBY, DOING SURVEILLANCE. YOU SEE ANYTHING STRANGE, YOU TEXT ME.
TEXT YOU. I DON'T EVEN KNOW YOUR REAL NAME.

"IT'S NATALIA."

CAMERA E-3

CAMERA F-5

PING

Natalia
Romanoff (A.K.A.
Black Widow)

PING

Kate Horsley
(a.k.a. Fatale)

CAMERA E-7

1:28

CAMERA L-3

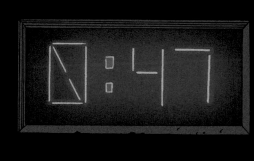

0:47

CAMERA P-2

0:04

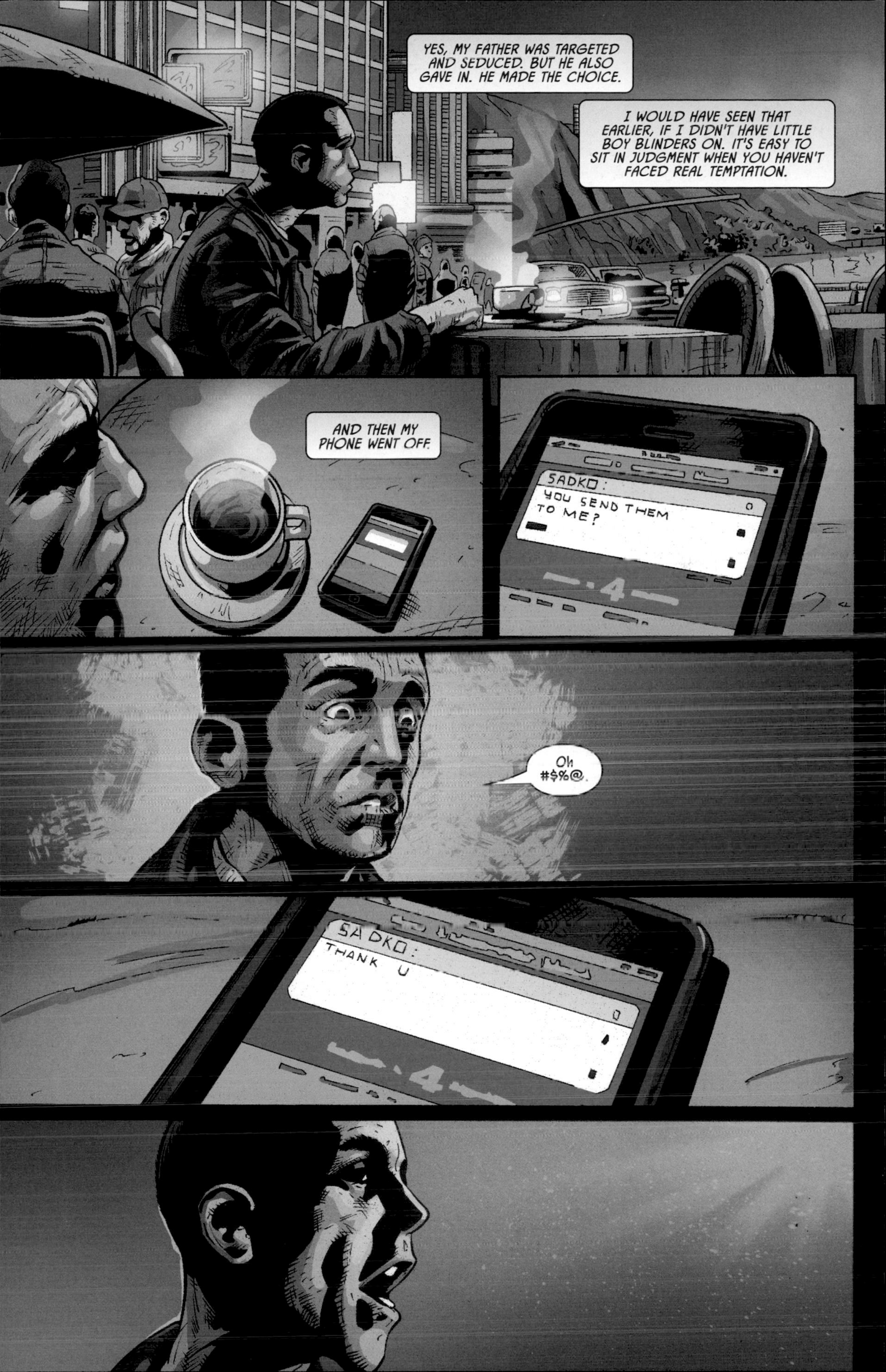
YES, MY FATHER WAS TARGETED AND SEDUCED. BUT HE ALSO GAVE IN. HE MADE THE CHOICE.
I WOULD HAVE SEEN THAT EARLIER, IF I DIDN'T HAVE LITTLE BOY BLINDERS ON. IT'S EASY TO SIT IN JUDGMENT WHEN YOU HAVEN'T FACED REAL TEMPTATION.
AND THEN MY PHONE WENT OFF.
SADKO:
YOU SEND THEM TO ME?
Oh #$%@.
SADKO:
THANK U

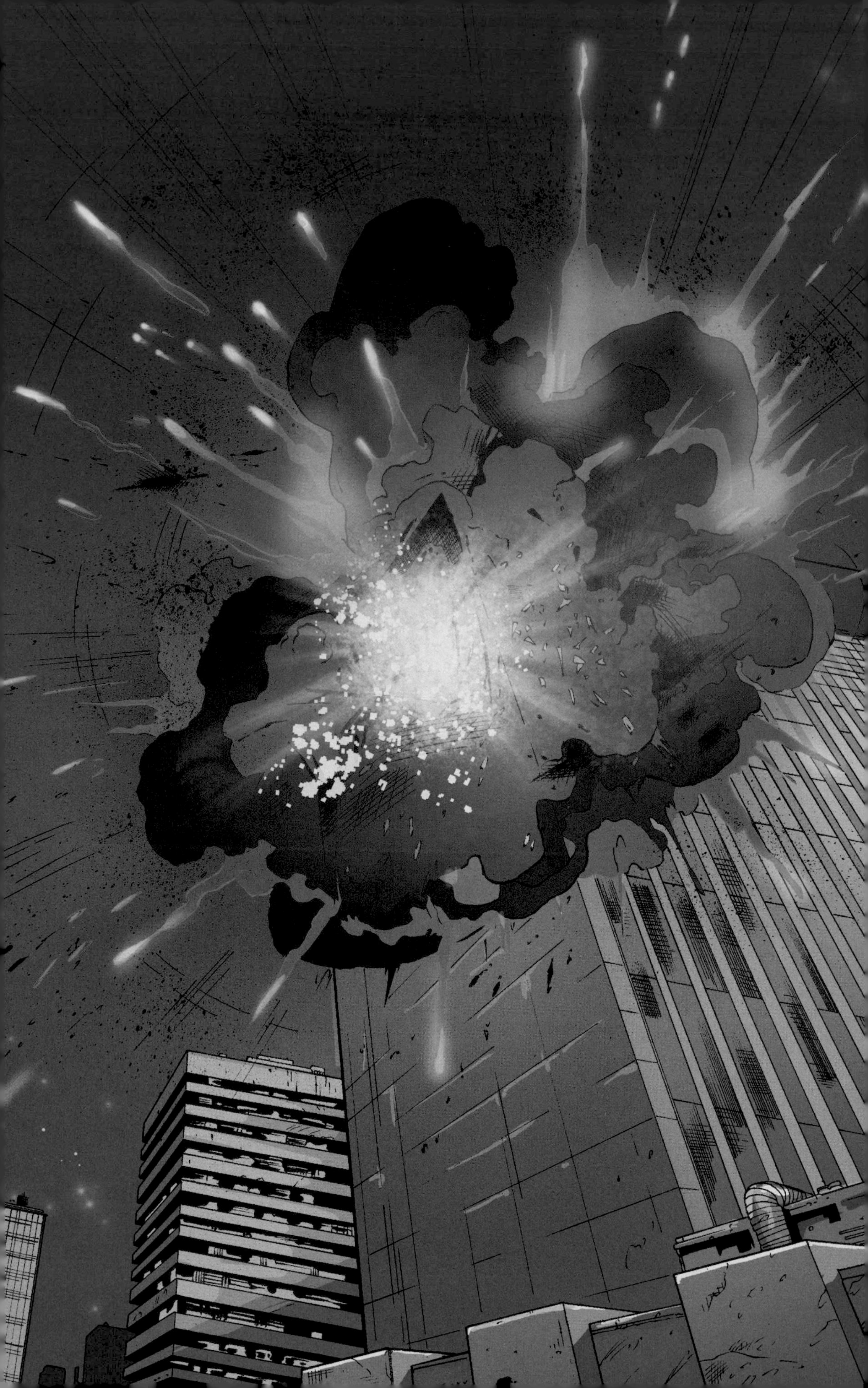

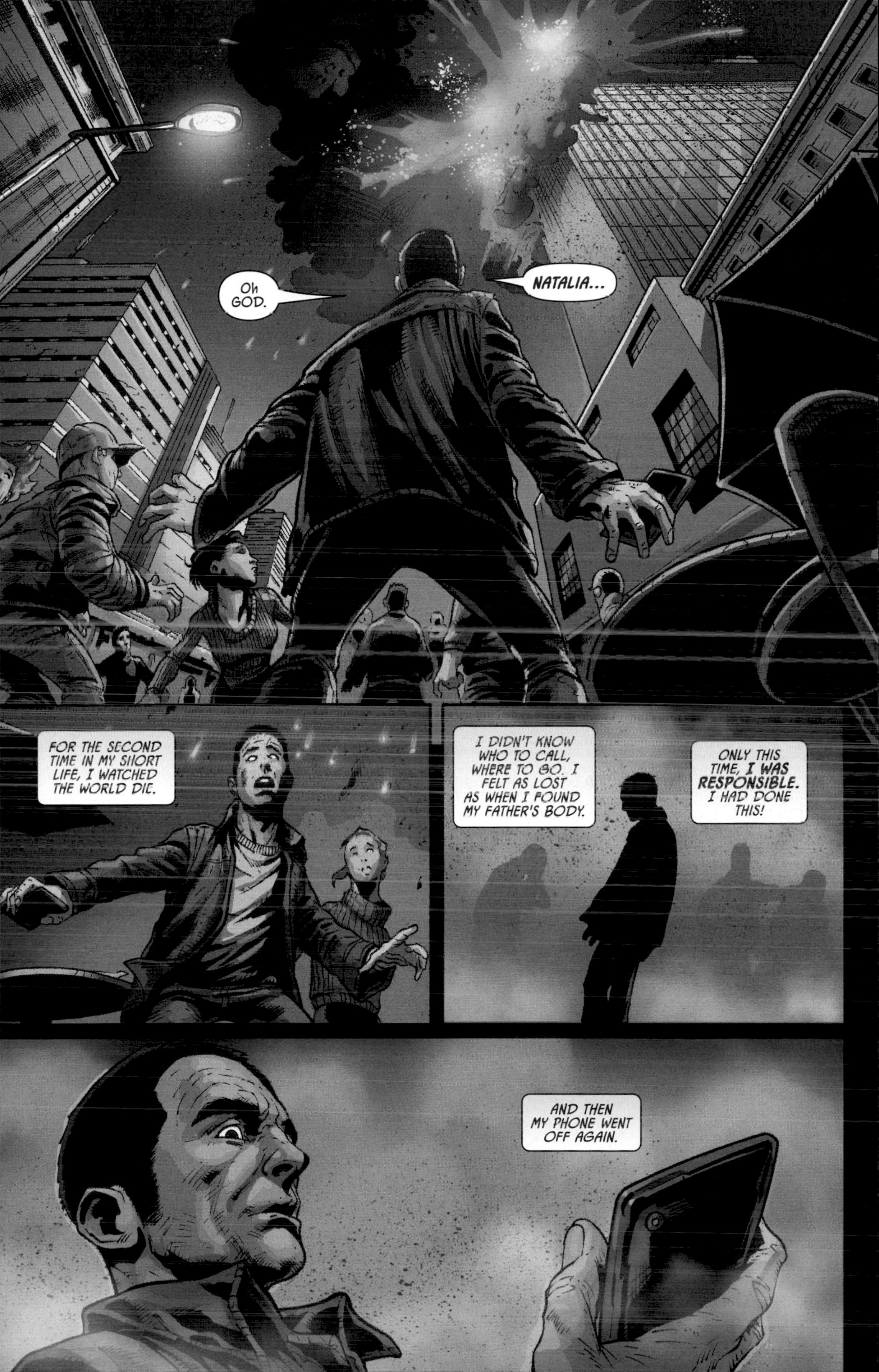

Oh GOD.
NATALIA...
FOR THE SECOND TIME IN MY SHORT LIFE, I WATCHED THE WORLD DIE.
I DIDN'T KNOW WHO TO CALL, WHERE TO GO. I FELT AS LOST AS WHEN I FOUND MY FATHER'S BODY.
ONLY THIS TIME, I WAS RESPONSIBLE. I HAD DONE THIS!
AND THEN MY PHONE WENT OFF AGAIN.

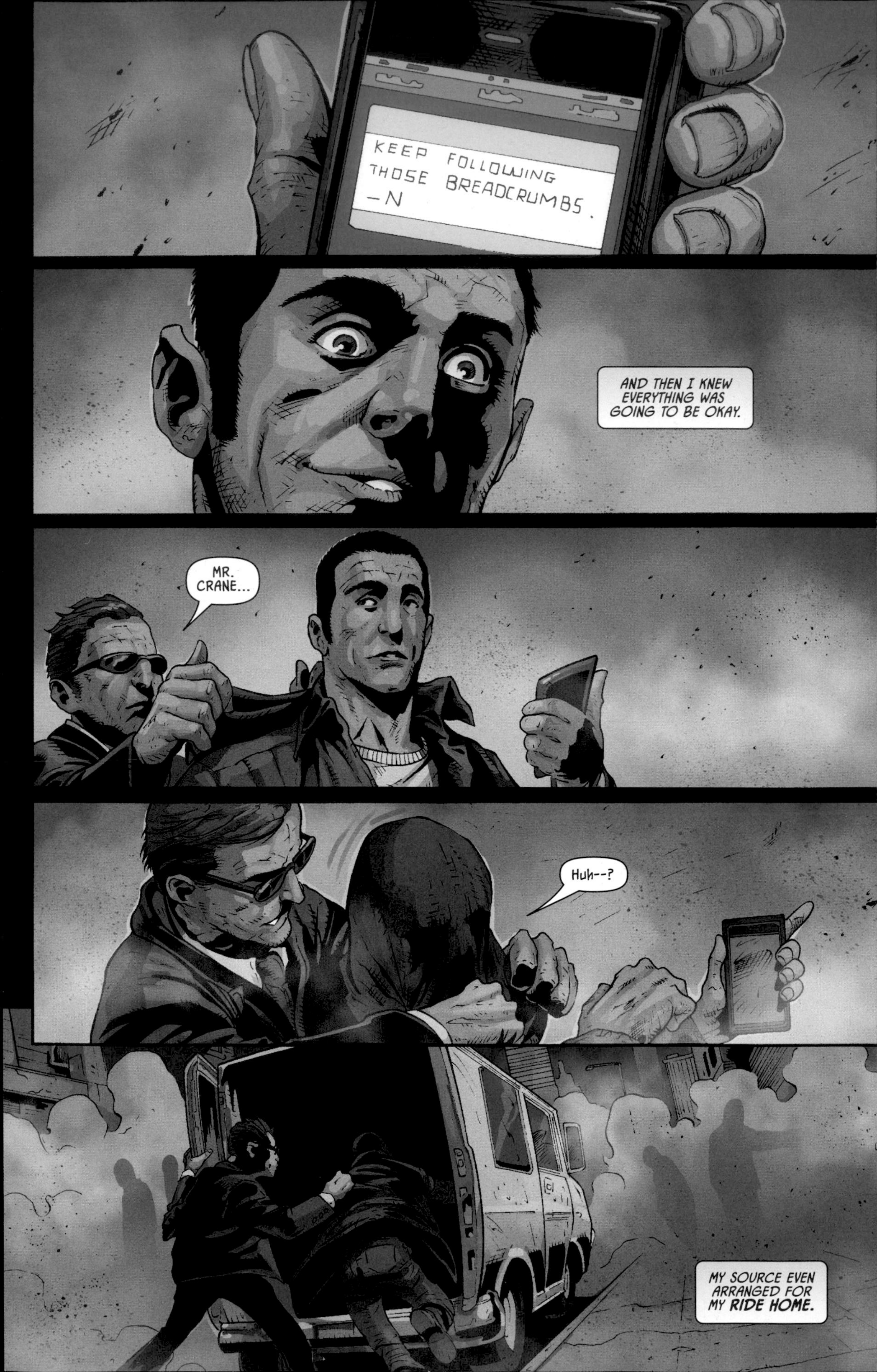
KEEP FOLLOWING THOSE BREADCRUMBS. -N
AND THEN I KNEW EVERYTHING WAS GOING TO BE OKAY.
MR. CRANE...
Huh--?
MY SOURCE EVEN ARRANGED FOR MY RIDE HOME.

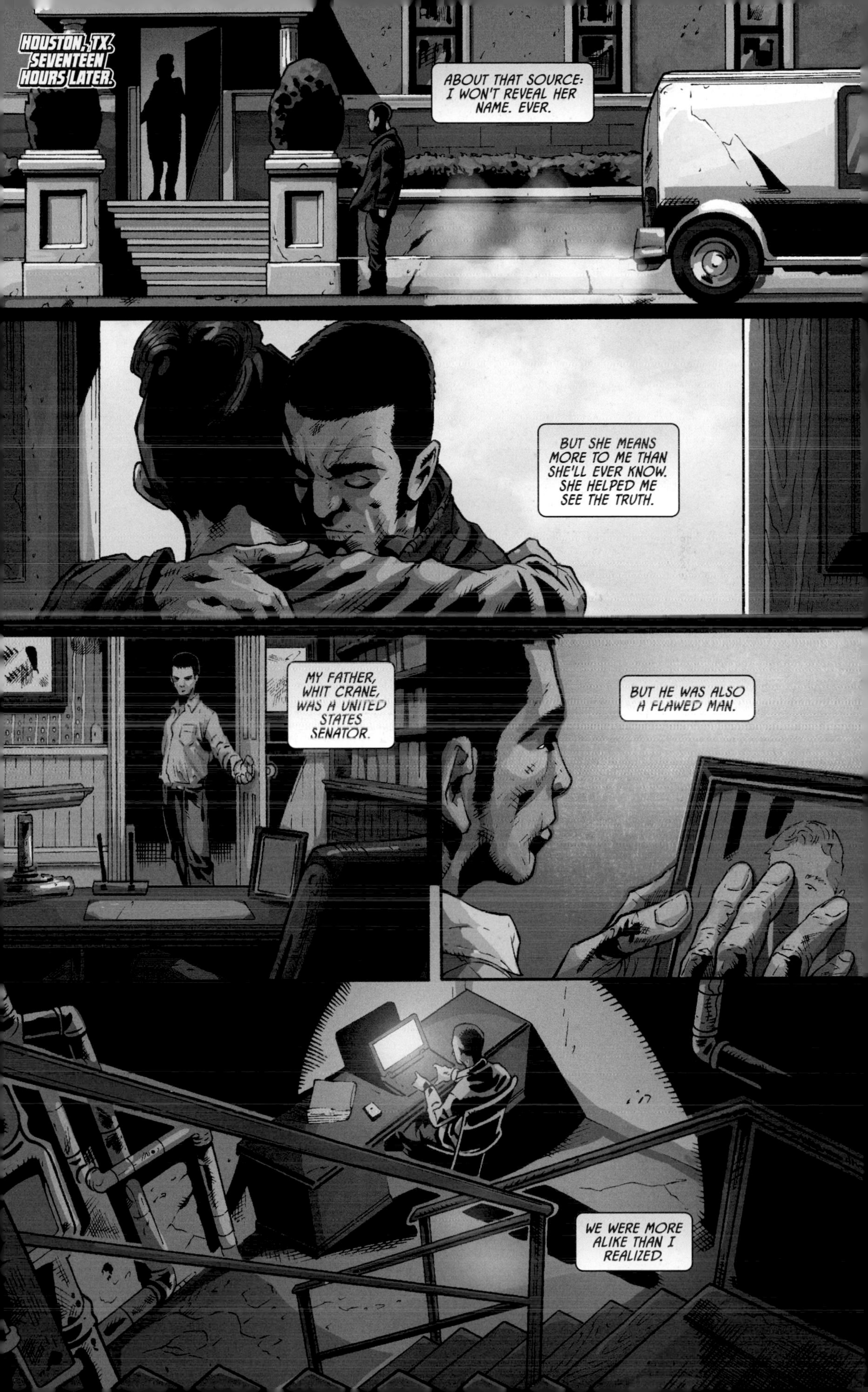
HOUSTON, TX. SEVENTEEN HOURS LATER.
ABOUT THAT SOURCE: I WON'T REVEAL HER NAME. EVER.
BUT SHE MEANS MORE TO ME THAN SHE'LL EVER KNOW. SHE HELPED ME SEE THE TRUTH.
MY FATHER, WHIT CRANE, WAS A UNITED STATES SENATOR.
BUT HE WAS ALSO A FLAWED MAN.
WE WERE MORE ALIKE THAN I REALIZED.

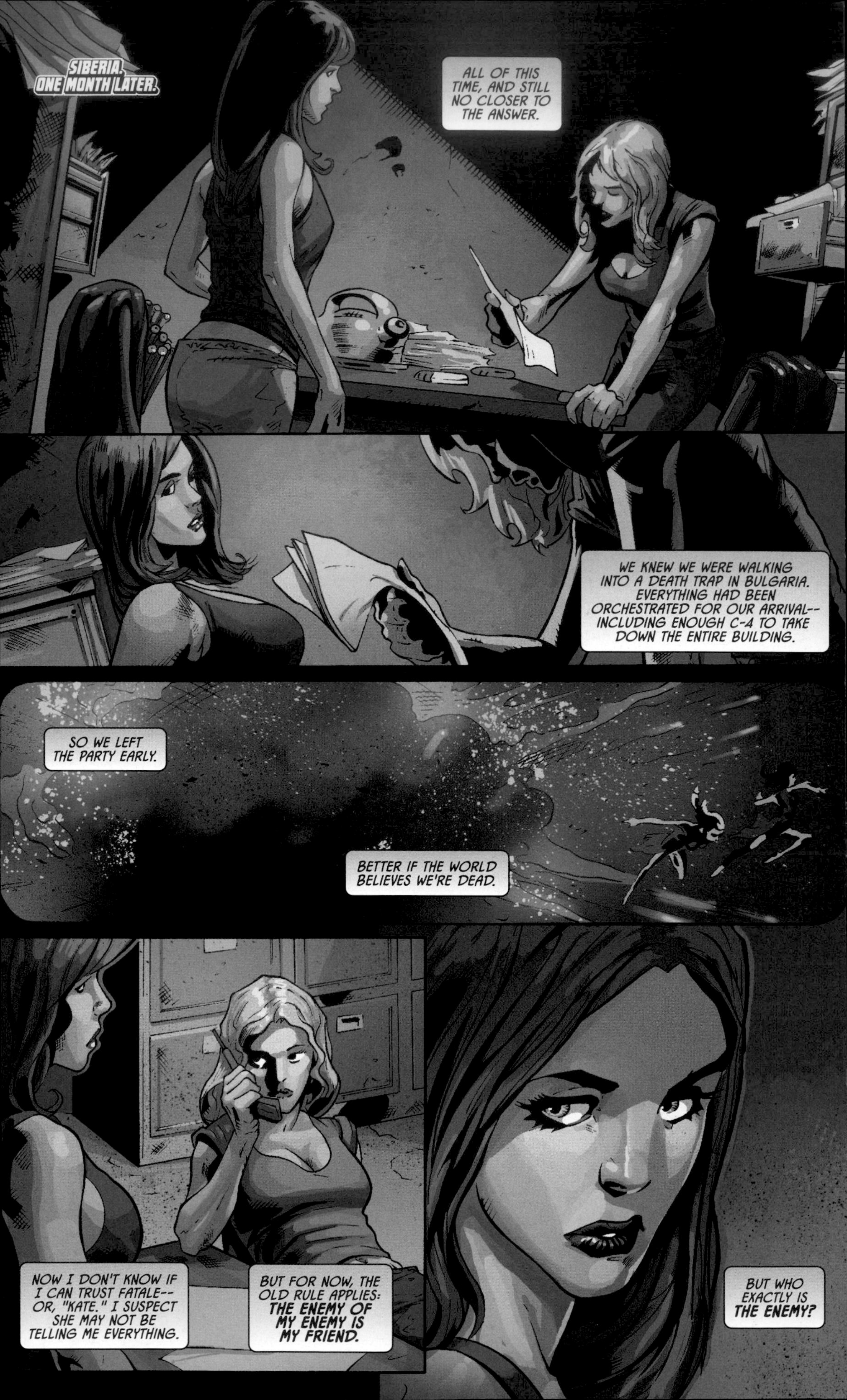
SIBERIA. ONE MONTH LATER.
ALL OF THIS TIME, AND STILL NO CLOSER TO THE ANSWER.
WE KNEW WE WERE WALKING INTO A DEATH TRAP IN BULGARIA. EVERYTHING HAD BEEN ORCHESTRATED FOR OUR ARRIVAL--INCLUDING ENOUGH C-4 TO TAKE DOWN THE ENTIRE BUILDING.
SO WE LEFT THE PARTY EARLY.
BETTER IF THE WORLD BELIEVES WE'RE DEAD.
NOW I DON'T KNOW IF I CAN TRUST FATALE--OR, "KATE." I SUSPECT SHE MAY NOT BE TELLING ME EVERYTHING.
BUT FOR NOW, THE OLD RULE APPLIES: THE ENEMY OF MY ENEMY IS MY FRIEND.
BUT WHO EXACTLY IS THE ENEMY?

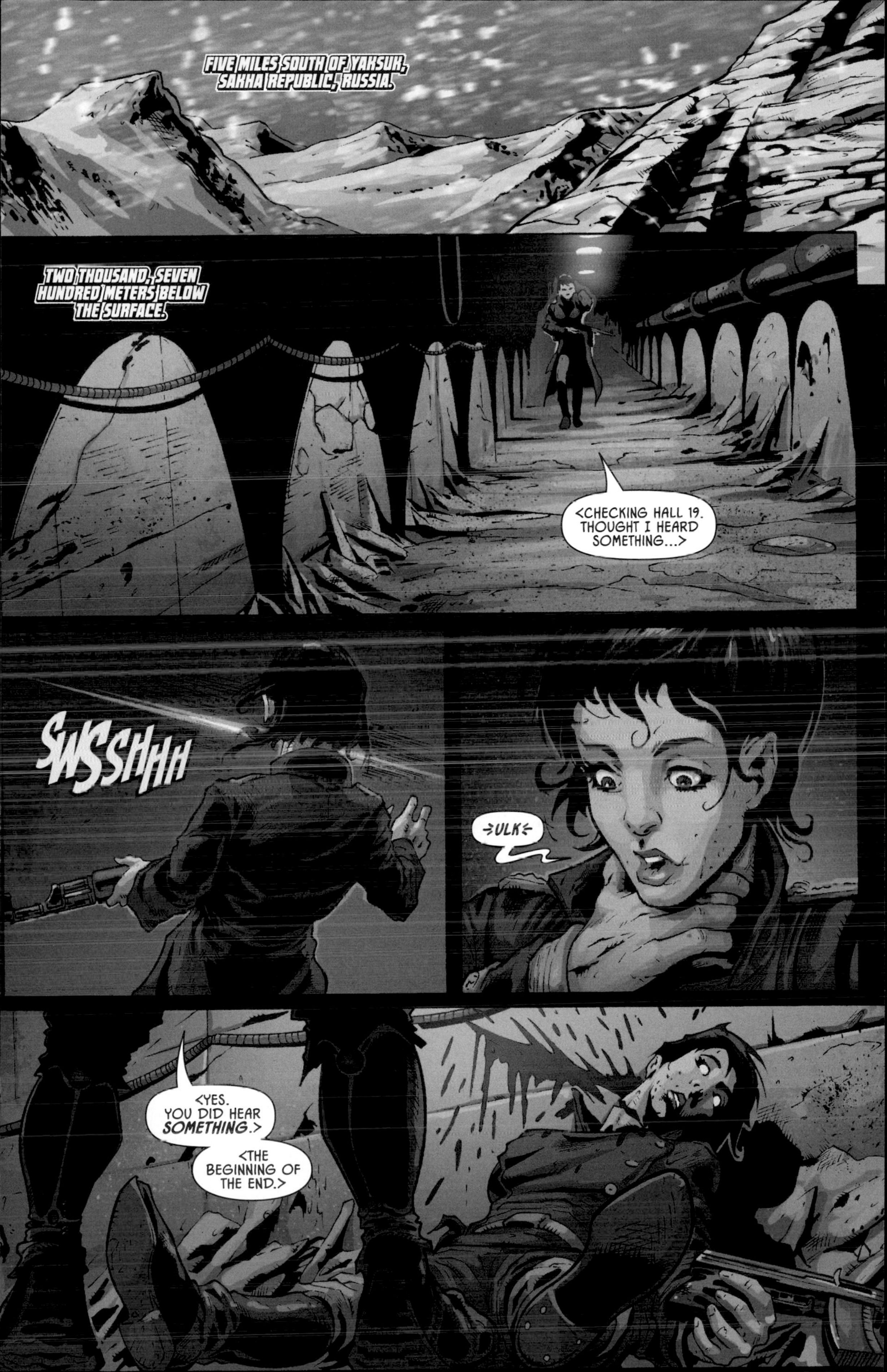
FIVE MILES SOUTH OF YAKSUK, SAKHA REPUBLIC, RUSSIA.
TWO THOUSAND, SEVEN HUNDRED METERS BELOW THE SURFACE.
<CHECKING HALL 19. THOUGHT I HEARD SOMETHING...>
SWSSHHH
ULK
<YES. YOU DID HEAR SOMETHING.>
<THE BEGINNING OF THE END.>

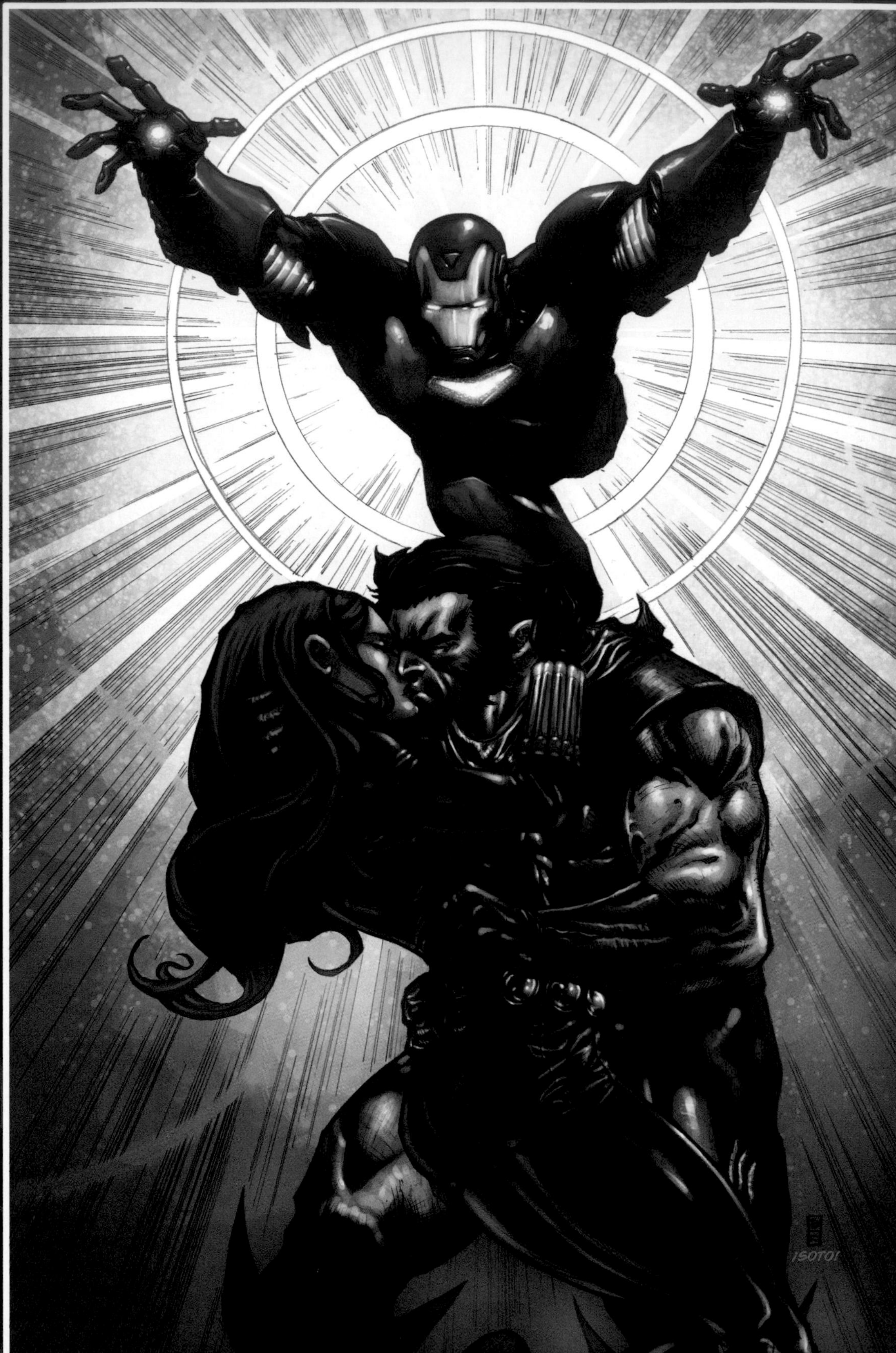

IRON MAN: KISS AND KILL

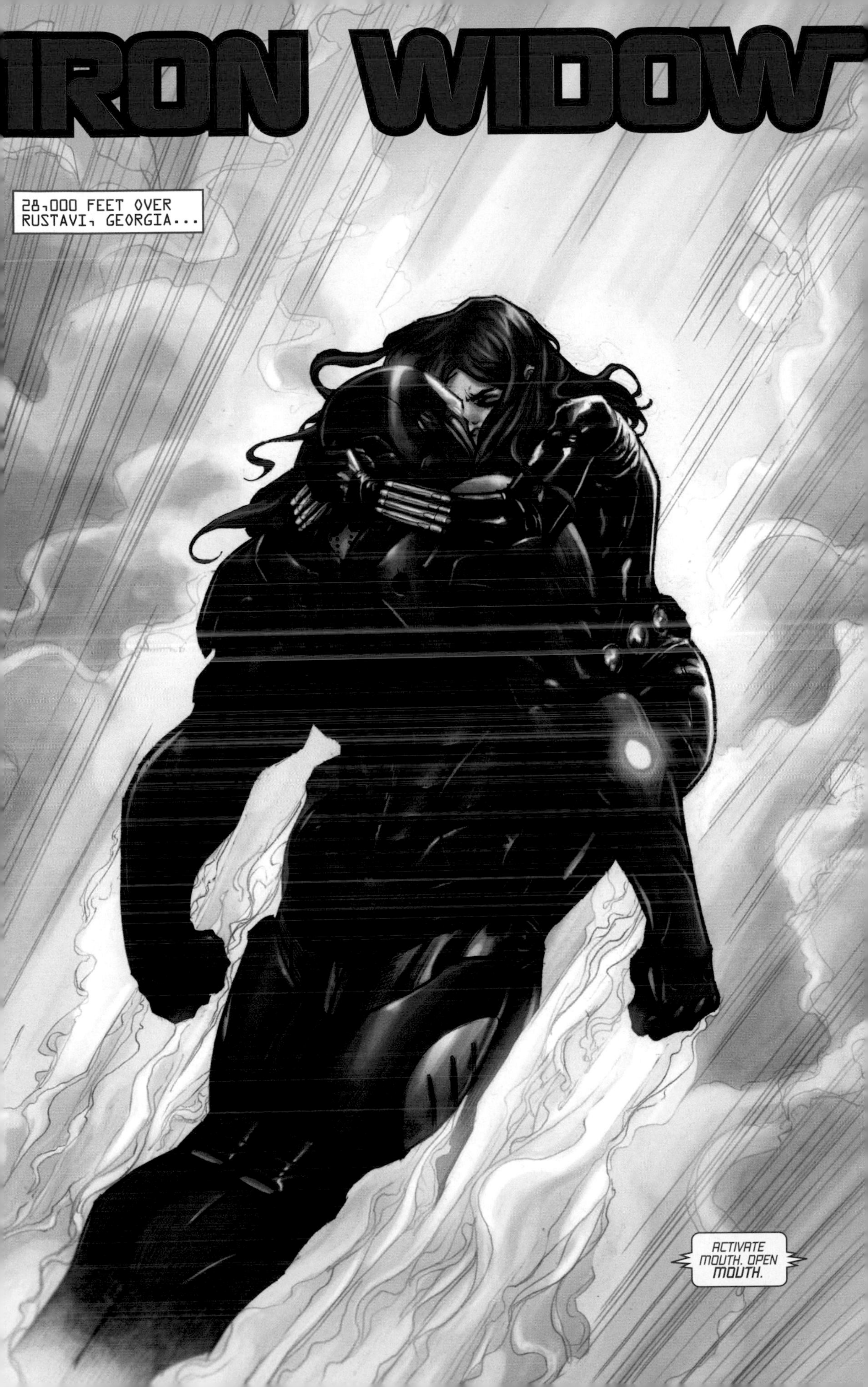
IRON WIDOW
28,000 FEET OVER RUSTAVI, GEORGIA...
ACTIVATE MOUTH. OPEN MOUTH.

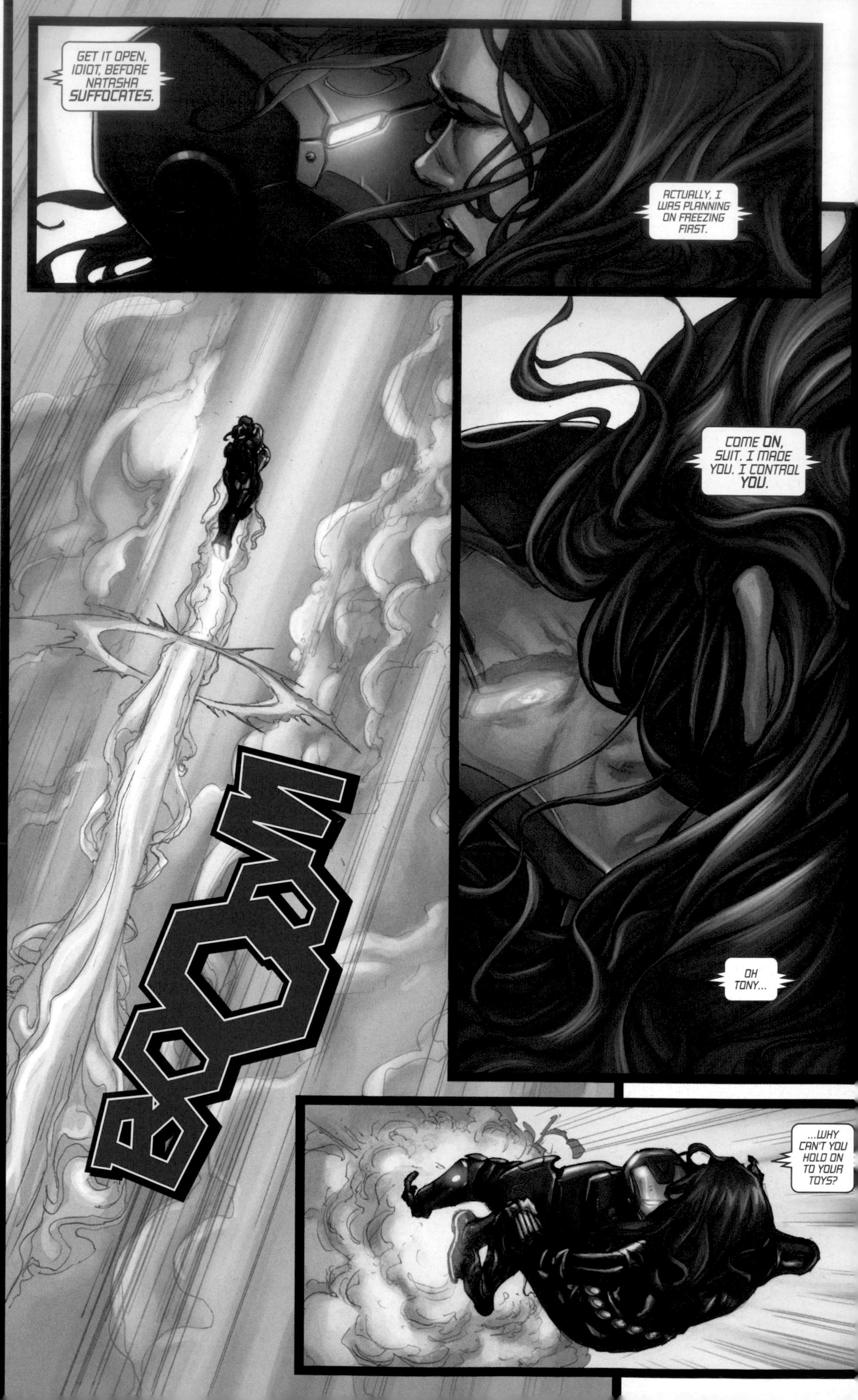
GET IT OPEN, IDIOT, BEFORE NATASHA SUFFOCATES.
ACTUALLY, I WAS PLANNING ON FREEZING FIRST.
COME ON, SUIT. I MADE YOU. I CONTROL YOU.
BOOM
OH TONY...
...WHY CAN'T YOU HOLD ON TO YOUR TOYS?

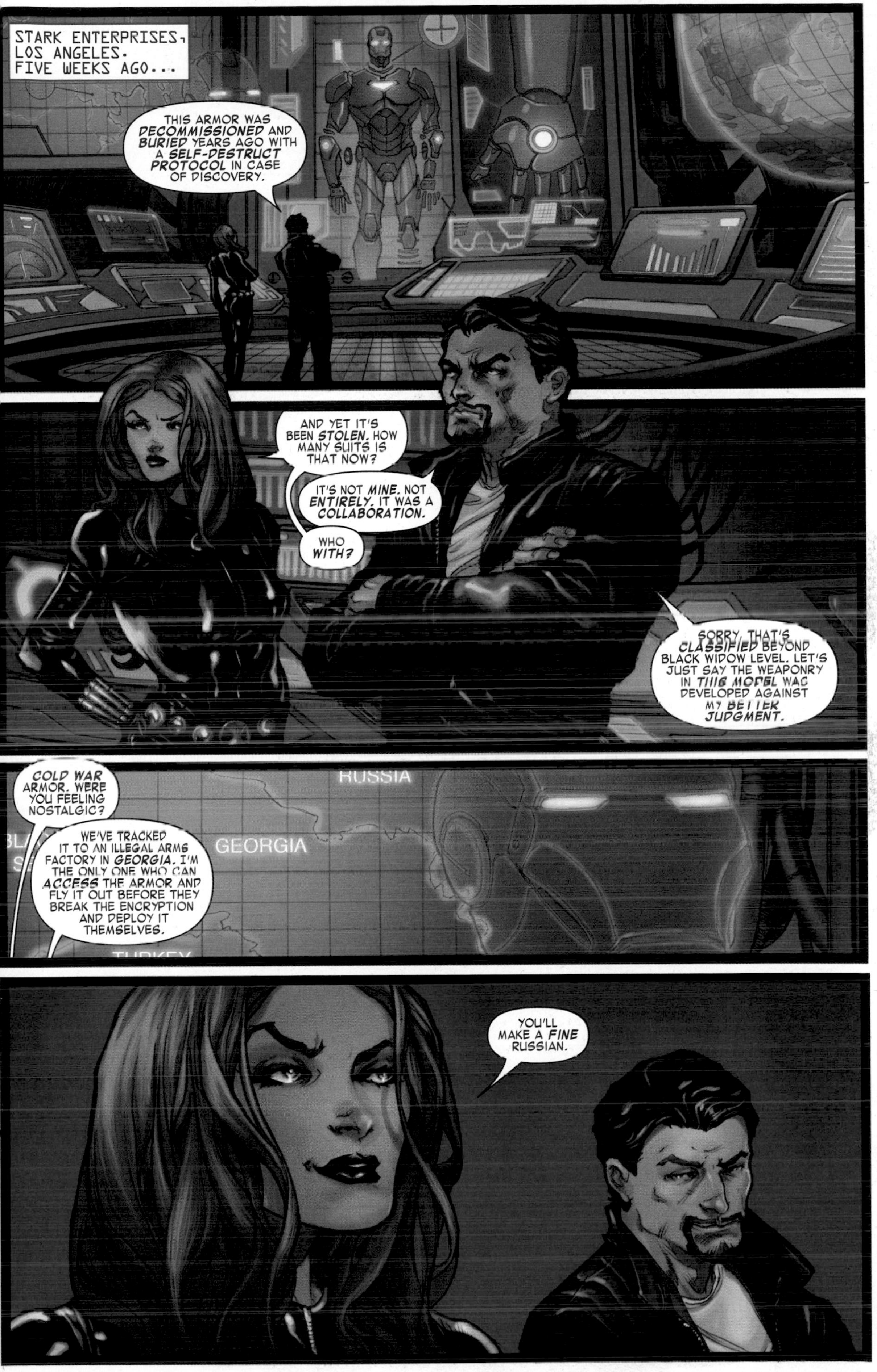
STARK ENTERPRISES, LOS ANGELES. FIVE WEEKS AGO...
THIS ARMOR WAS DECOMMISSIONED AND BURIED YEARS AGO WITH A SELF-DESTRUCT PROTOCOL IN CASE OF DISCOVERY.
AND YET IT'S BEEN STOLEN. HOW MANY SUITS IS THAT NOW?
IT'S NOT MINE. NOT ENTIRELY. IT WAS A COLLABORATION.
WHO WITH?
SORRY, THAT'S CLASSIFIED BEYOND BLACK WIDOW LEVEL. LET'S JUST SAY THE WEAPONRY IN THIS MODEL WAS DEVELOPED AGAINST MY BETTER JUDGMENT.
RUSSIA
GEORGIA
COLD WAR ARMOR. WERE YOU FEELING NOSTALGIC?
WE'VE TRACKED IT TO AN ILLEGAL ARMS FACTORY IN GEORGIA. I'M THE ONLY ONE WHO CAN ACCESS THE ARMOR AND FLY IT OUT BEFORE THEY BREAK THE ENCRYPTION AND DEPLOY IT THEMSELVES.
YOU'LL MAKE A FINE RUSSIAN.

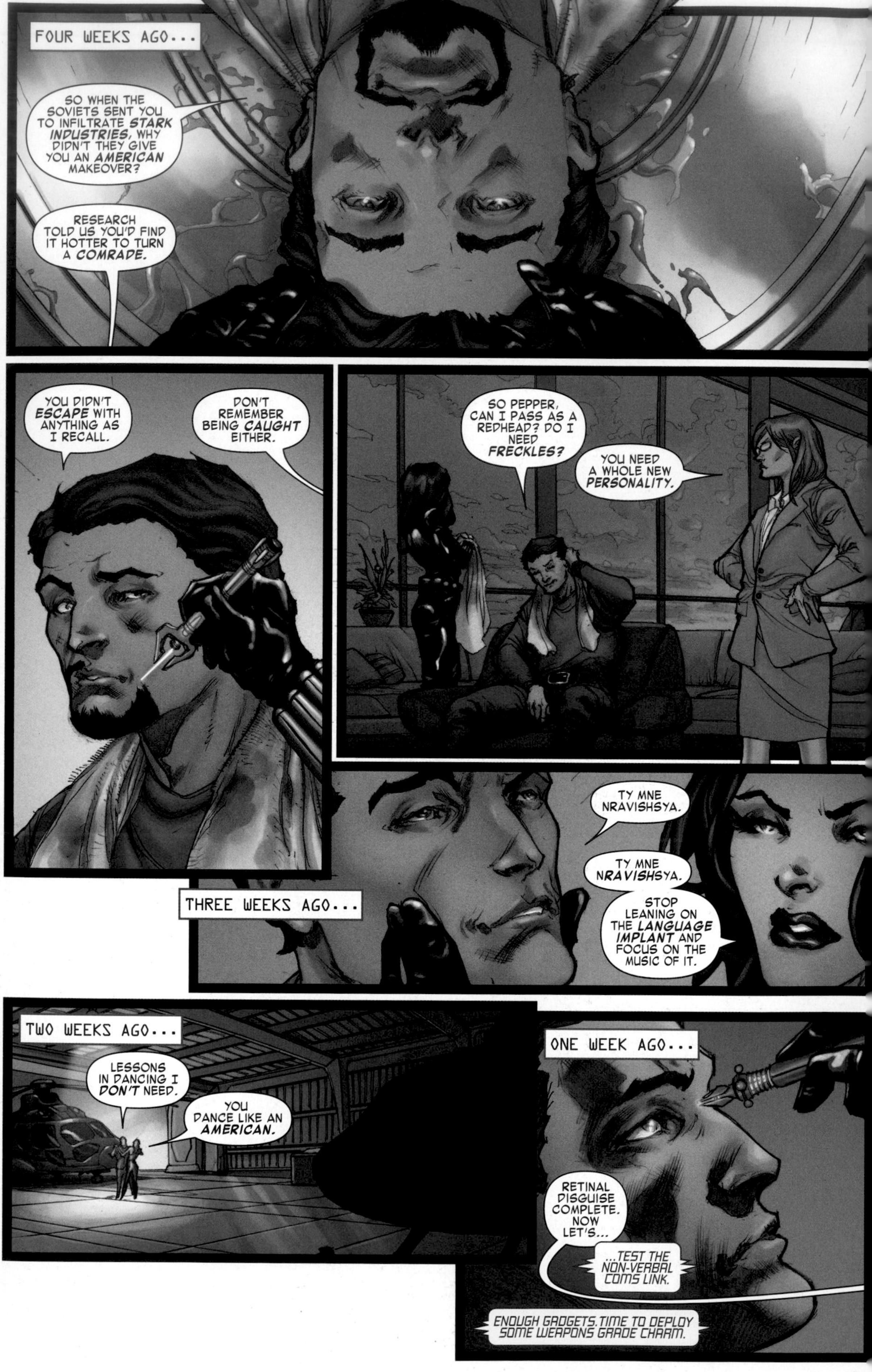
FOUR WEEKS AGO...
SO WHEN THE SOVIETS SENT YOU TO INFILTRATE STARK INDUSTRIES, WHY DIDN'T THEY GIVE YOU AN AMERICAN MAKEOVER?
RESEARCH TOLD US YOU'D FIND IT HOTTER TO TURN A COMRADE.
YOU DIDN'T ESCAPE WITH ANYTHING AS I RECALL.
DON'T REMEMBER BEING CAUGHT EITHER.
SO PEPPER, CAN I PASS AS A REDHEAD? DO I NEED FRECKLES?
YOU NEED A WHOLE NEW PERSONALITY.
THREE WEEKS AGO...
TY MNE NRAVISHSYA.
TY MNE NRAVISHSYA.
STOP LEANING ON THE LANGUAGE IMPLANT AND FOCUS ON THE MUSIC OF IT.
TWO WEEKS AGO...
LESSONS IN DANCING I DON'T NEED.
YOU DANCE LIKE AN AMERICAN.
ONE WEEK AGO...
RETINAL DISGUISE COMPLETE. NOW LET'S...
...TEST THE NON-VERBAL COMS LINK.
ENOUGH GADGETS. TIME TO DEPLOY SOME WEAPONS GRADE CHARM.

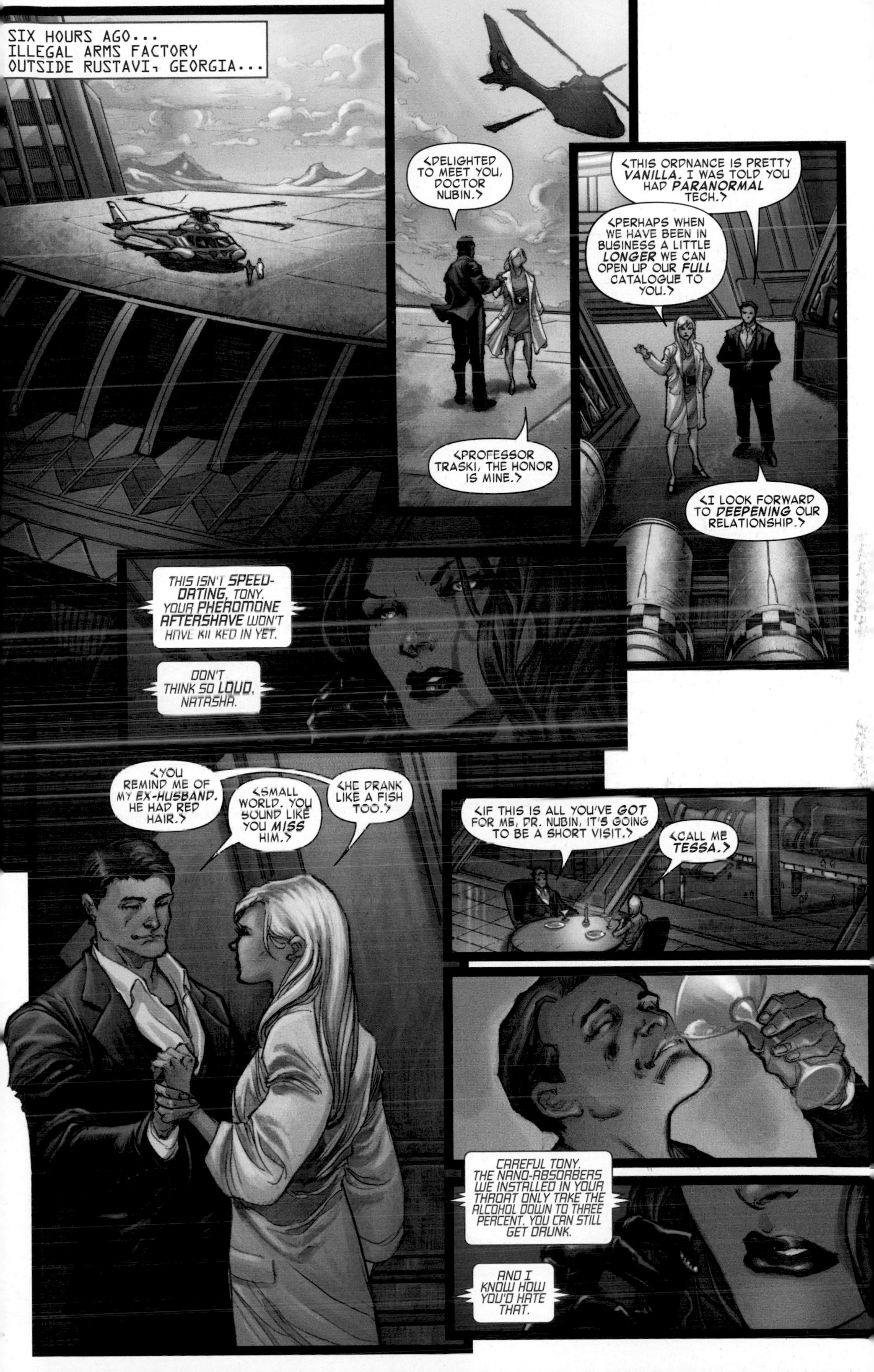
SIX HOURS AGO...
ILLEGAL ARMS FACTORY
OUTSIDE RUSTAVI, GEORGIA...
<DELIGHTED TO MEET YOU, DOCTOR NUBIN.>
<PROFESSOR TRASKI, THE HONOR IS MINE.>
<THIS ORDNANCE IS PRETTY VANILLA. I WAS TOLD YOU HAD PARANORMAL TECH.>
<PERHAPS WHEN WE HAVE BEEN IN BUSINESS A LITTLE LONGER WE CAN OPEN UP OUR FULL CATALOGUE TO YOU.>
<I LOOK FORWARD TO DEEPENING OUR RELATIONSHIP.>
THIS ISN'T SPEED-DATING, TONY. YOUR PHEROMONE AFTERSHAVE WON'T HAVE KICKED IN YET.
DON'T THINK SO LOUD, NATASHA.
<YOU REMIND ME OF MY EX-HUSBAND. HE HAD RED HAIR.>
<SMALL WORLD. YOU SOUND LIKE YOU MISS HIM.>
<HE DRANK LIKE A FISH TOO.>
<IF THIS IS ALL YOU'VE GOT FOR ME, DR. NUBIN, IT'S GOING TO BE A SHORT VISIT.>
<CALL ME TESSA.>
CAREFUL TONY. THE NANO-ABSORBERS WE INSTALLED IN YOUR THROAT ONLY TAKE THE ALCOHOL DOWN TO THREE PERCENT. YOU CAN STILL GET DRUNK.
AND I KNOW HOW YOU'D HATE THAT.

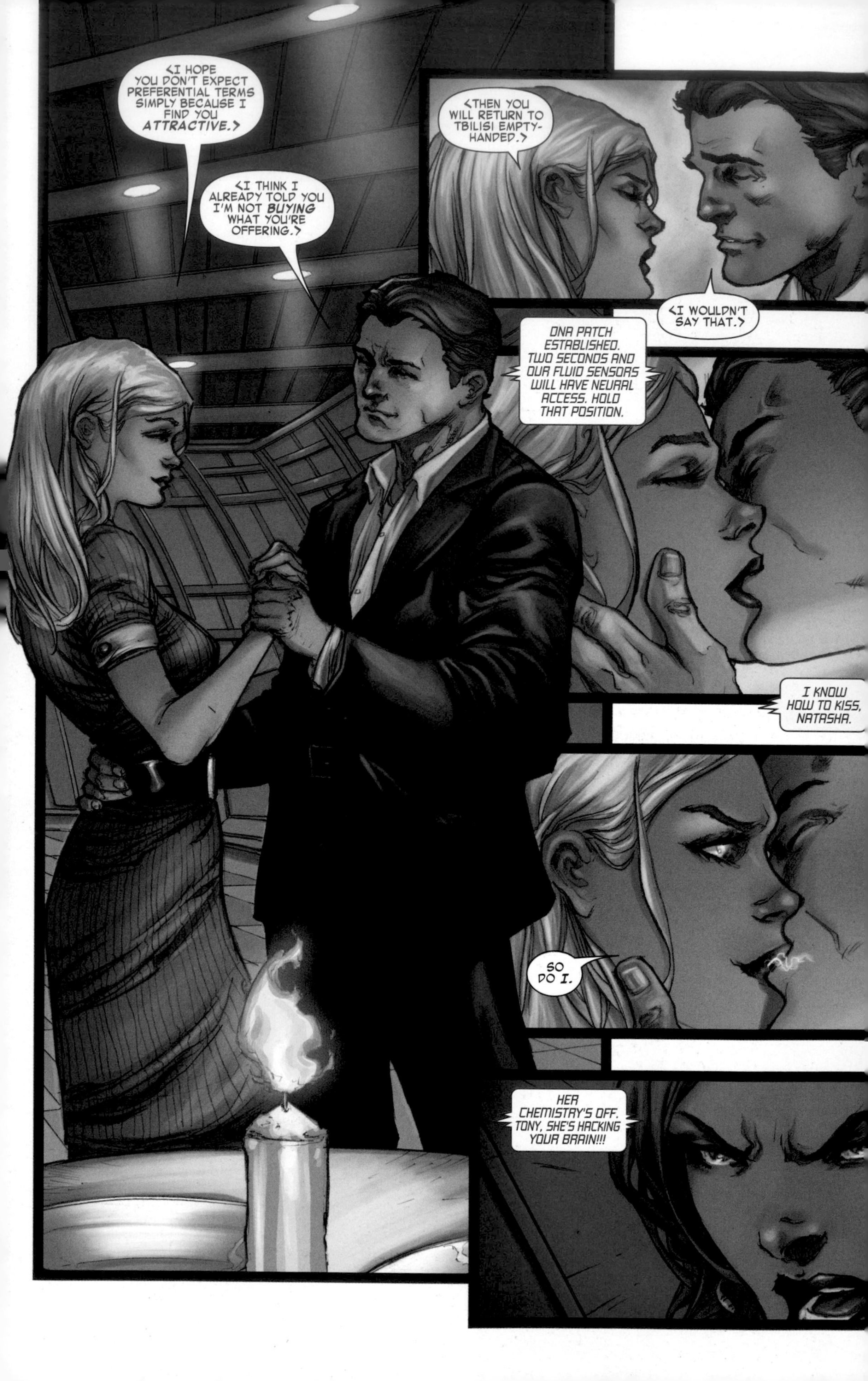

<I HOPE YOU DON'T EXPECT PREFERENTIAL TERMS SIMPLY BECAUSE I FIND YOU ATTRACTIVE.>
<I THINK I ALREADY TOLD YOU I'M NOT BUYING WHAT YOU'RE OFFERING.>
<THEN YOU WILL RETURN TO TBILISI EMPTY-HANDED.>
<I WOULDN'T SAY THAT.>
DNA PATCH ESTABLISHED. TWO SECONDS AND OUR FLUID SENSORS WILL HAVE NEURAL ACCESS. HOLD THAT POSITION.
I KNOW HOW TO KISS, NATASHA.
SO DO I.
HER CHEMISTRY'S OFF. TONY, SHE'S HACKING YOUR BRAIN!!!

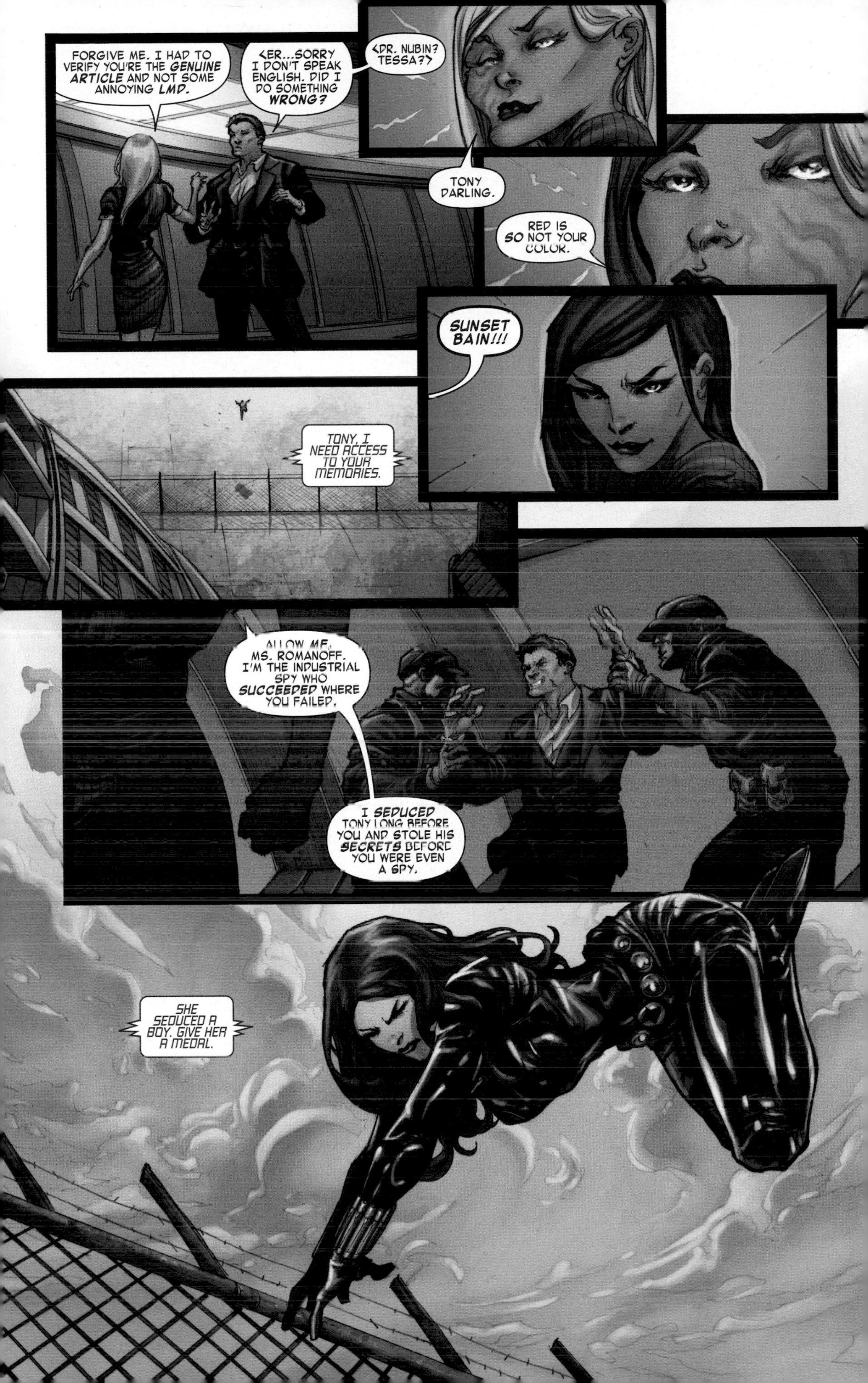
FORGIVE ME. I HAD TO VERIFY YOU'RE THE GENUINE ARTICLE AND NOT SOME ANNOYING LMD.
<ER...SORRY I DON'T SPEAK ENGLISH. DID I DO SOMETHING WRONG?
<DR. NUBIN? TESSA?>
TONY DARLING.
RED IS SO NOT YOUR COLOR.
SUNSET BAIN!!!
TONY, I NEED ACCESS TO YOUR MEMORIES.
ALLOW ME, MS. ROMANOFF. I'M THE INDUSTRIAL SPY WHO SUCCEEDED WHERE YOU FAILED.
I SEDUCED TONY LONG BEFORE YOU AND STOLE HIS SECRETS BEFORE YOU WERE EVEN A SPY.
SHE SEDUCED A BOY. GIVE HER A MEDAL.

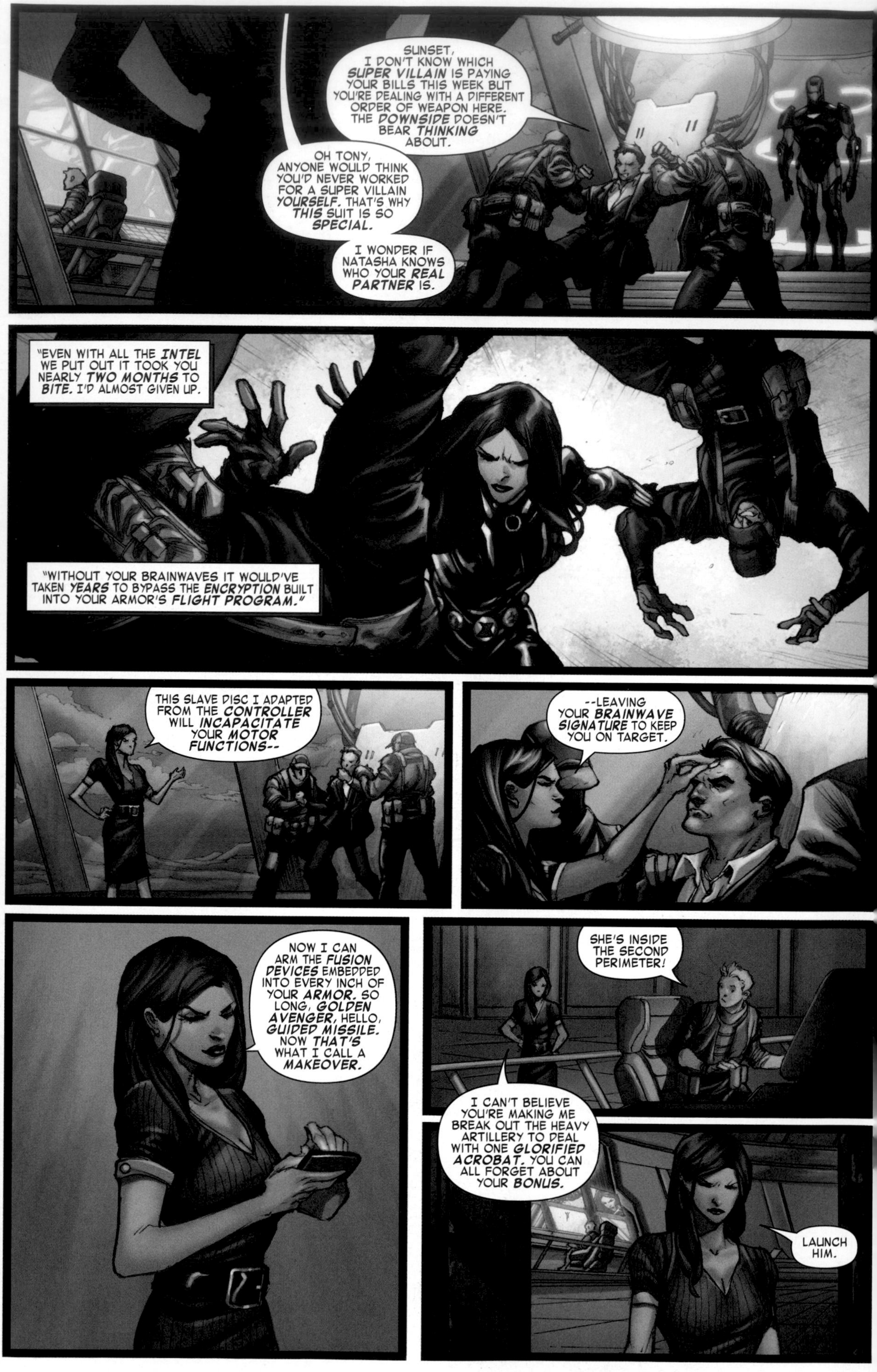
SUNSET, I DON'T KNOW WHICH SUPER VILLAIN IS PAYING YOUR BILLS THIS WEEK BUT YOU'RE DEALING WITH A DIFFERENT ORDER OF WEAPON HERE. THE DOWNSIDE DOESN'T BEAR THINKING ABOUT.
OH TONY, ANYONE WOULD THINK YOU'D NEVER WORKED FOR A SUPER VILLAIN YOURSELF. THAT'S WHY THIS SUIT IS SO SPECIAL.
I WONDER IF NATASHA KNOWS WHO YOUR REAL PARTNER IS.
"EVEN WITH ALL THE INTEL WE PUT OUT IT TOOK YOU NEARLY TWO MONTHS TO BITE. I'D ALMOST GIVEN UP.
"WITHOUT YOUR BRAINWAVES IT WOULD'VE TAKEN YEARS TO BYPASS THE ENCRYPTION BUILT INTO YOUR ARMOR'S FLIGHT PROGRAM."
THIS SLAVE DISC I ADAPTED FROM THE CONTROLLER WILL INCAPACITATE YOUR MOTOR FUNCTIONS--
--LEAVING YOUR BRAINWAVE SIGNATURE TO KEEP YOU ON TARGET.
NOW I CAN ARM THE FUSION DEVICES EMBEDDED INTO EVERY INCH OF YOUR ARMOR. SO LONG, GOLDEN AVENGER, HELLO, GUIDED MISSILE. NOW THAT'S WHAT I CALL A MAKEOVER.
SHE'S INSIDE THE SECOND PERIMETER!
I CAN'T BELIEVE YOU'RE MAKING ME BREAK OUT THE HEAVY ARTILLERY TO DEAL WITH ONE GLORIFIED ACROBAT. YOU CAN ALL FORGET ABOUT YOUR BONUS.
LAUNCH HIM.

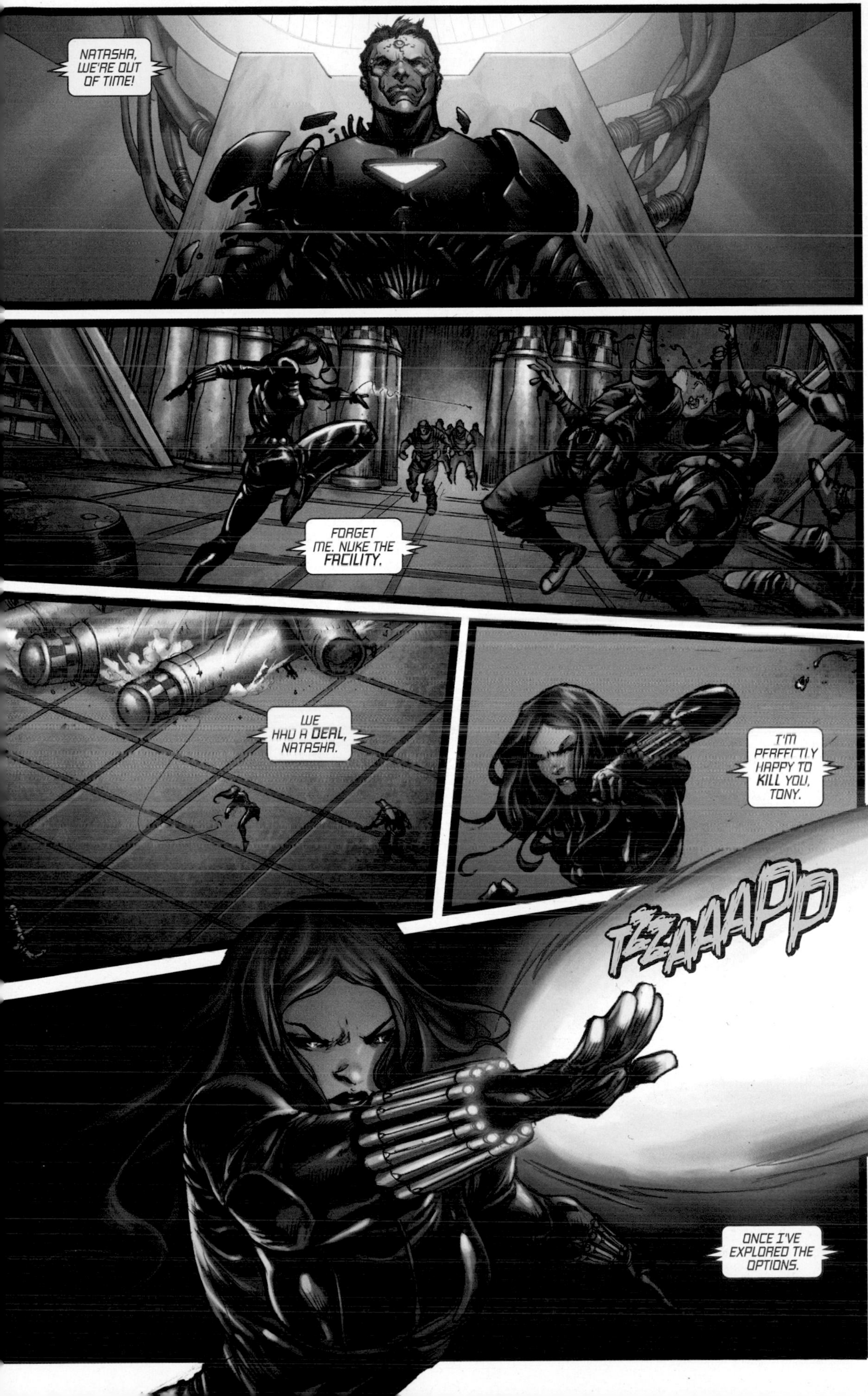
NATASHA, WE'RE OUT OF TIME!
FORGET ME. NUKE THE FACILITY.
WE HAD A DEAL, NATASHA.
I'M PERFECTLY HAPPY TO KILL YOU, TONY.
TZZAAAPP
ONCE I'VE EXPLORED THE OPTIONS.

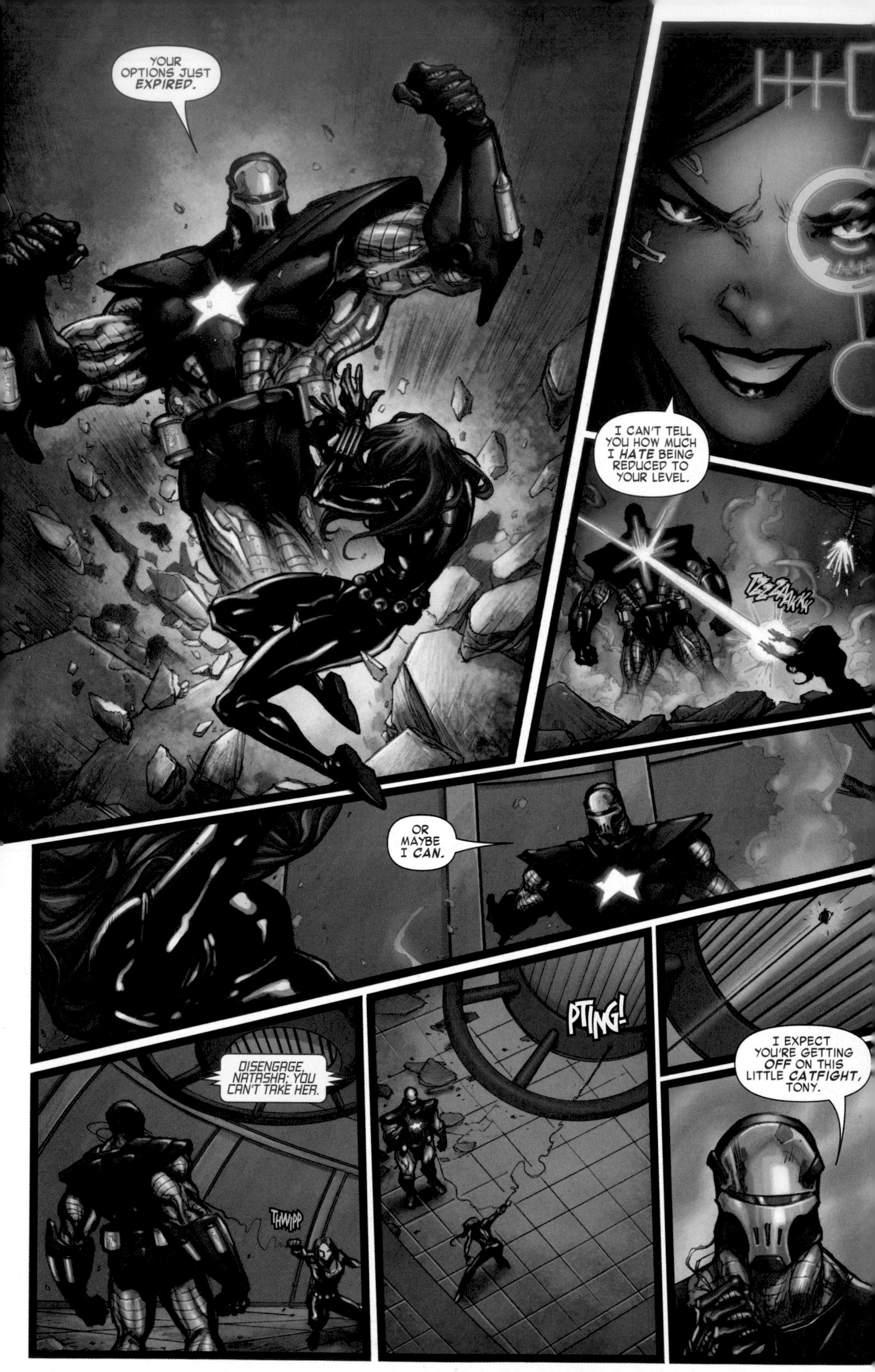

YOUR OPTIONS JUST *EXPIRED.*
I CAN'T TELL YOU HOW MUCH I *HATE* BEING REDUCED TO YOUR LEVEL.
TZZZAAKK
OR MAYBE I *CAN.*
PTING!
DISENGAGE, NATASHA; YOU CAN'T TAKE HER.
THWIPP
I EXPECT YOU'RE GETTING *OFF* ON THIS LITTLE *CATFIGHT,* TONY.

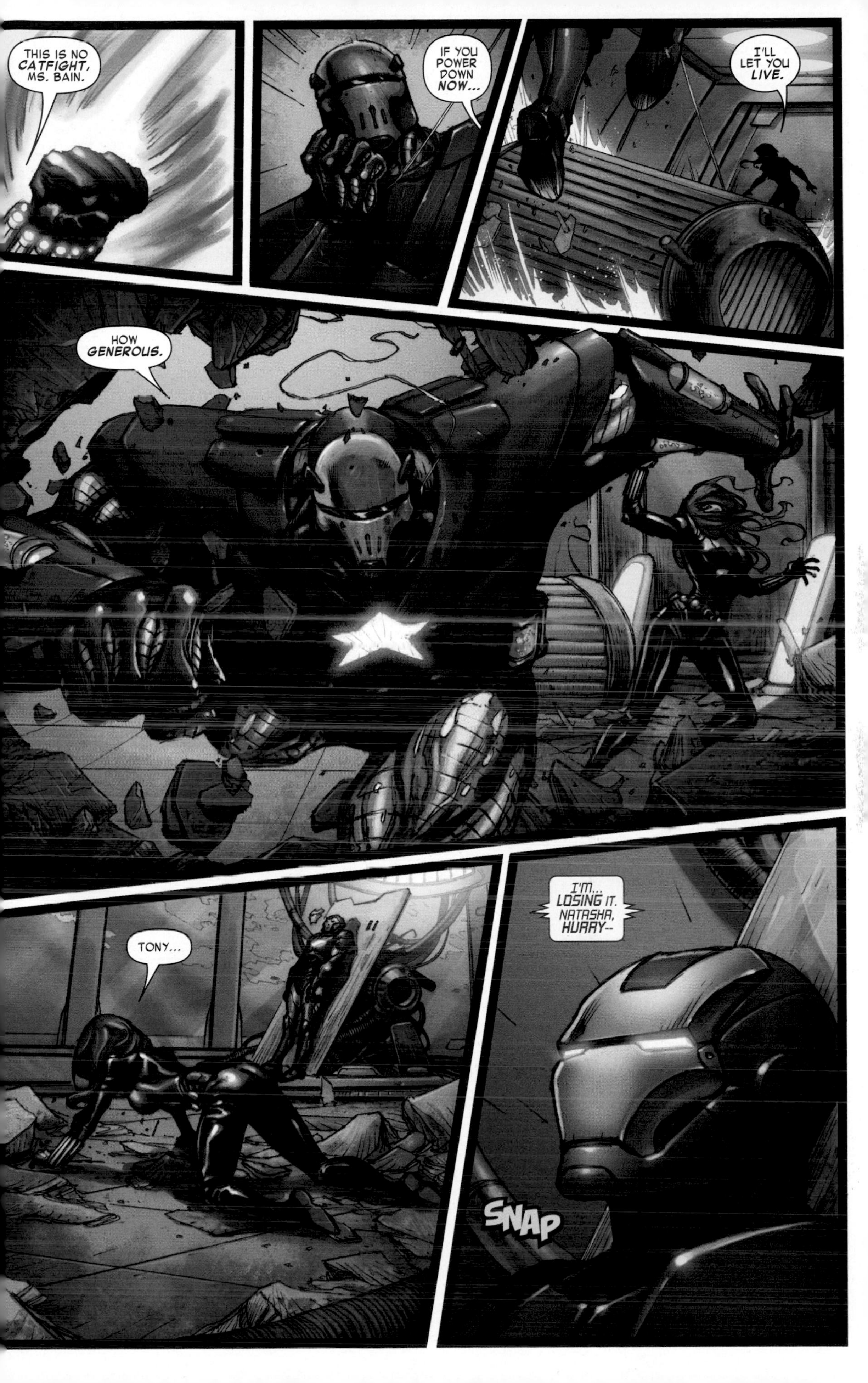

THIS IS NO CATFIGHT, MS. BAIN.
IF YOU POWER DOWN NOW...
I'LL LET YOU LIVE.
HOW GENEROUS.
TONY...
I'M... LOSING IT. NATASHA, HURRY--
SNAP

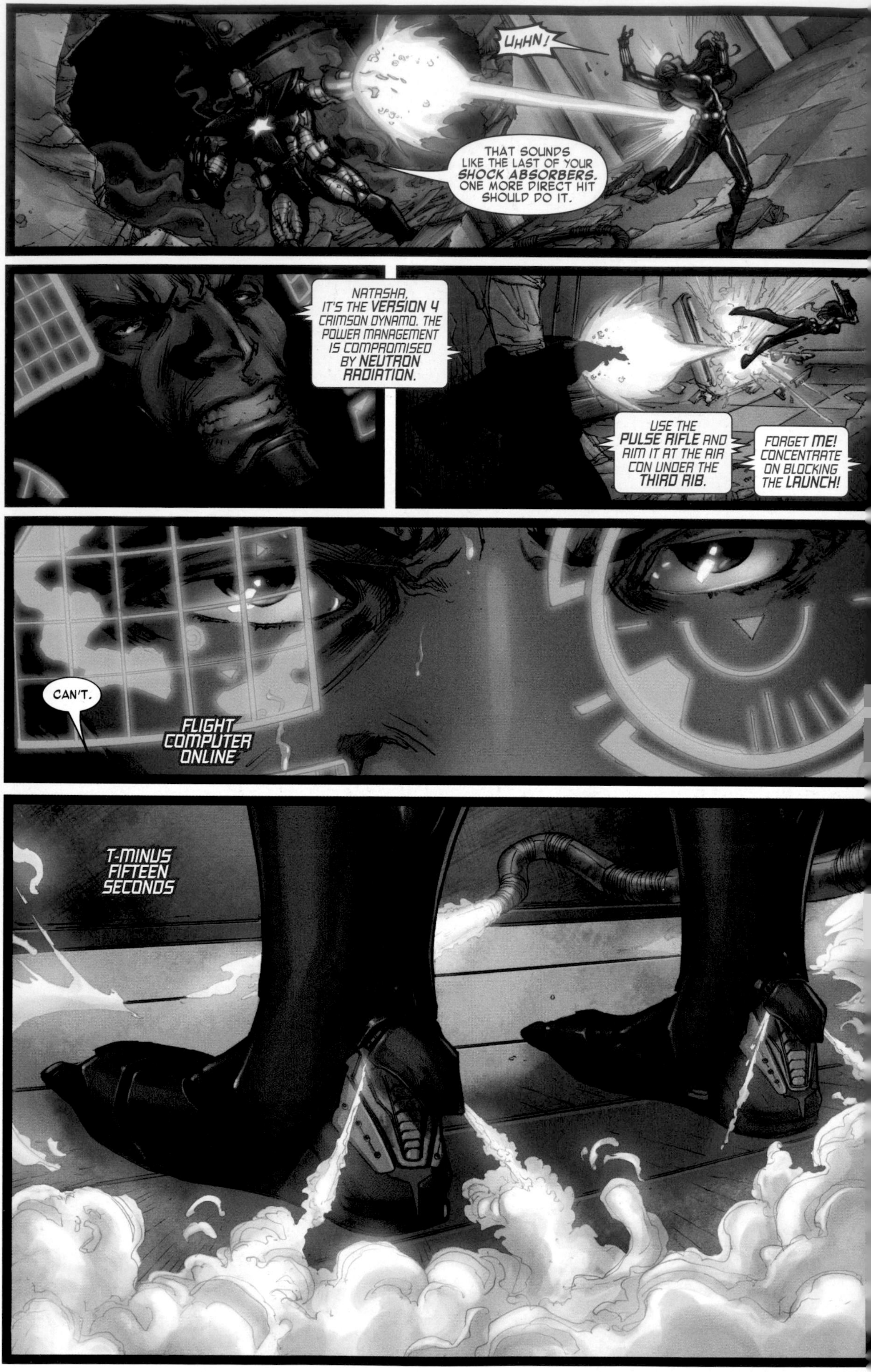
UHHN!
THAT SOUNDS LIKE THE LAST OF YOUR SHOCK ABSORBERS. ONE MORE DIRECT HIT SHOULD DO IT.
NATASHA, IT'S THE VERSION 4 CRIMSON DYNAMO. THE POWER MANAGEMENT IS COMPROMISED BY NEUTRON RADIATION.
USE THE PULSE RIFLE AND AIM IT AT THE AIR CON UNDER THE THIRD RIB.
FORGET ME! CONCENTRATE ON BLOCKING THE LAUNCH!
CAN'T.
FLIGHT COMPUTER ONLINE
T-MINUS FIFTEEN SECONDS

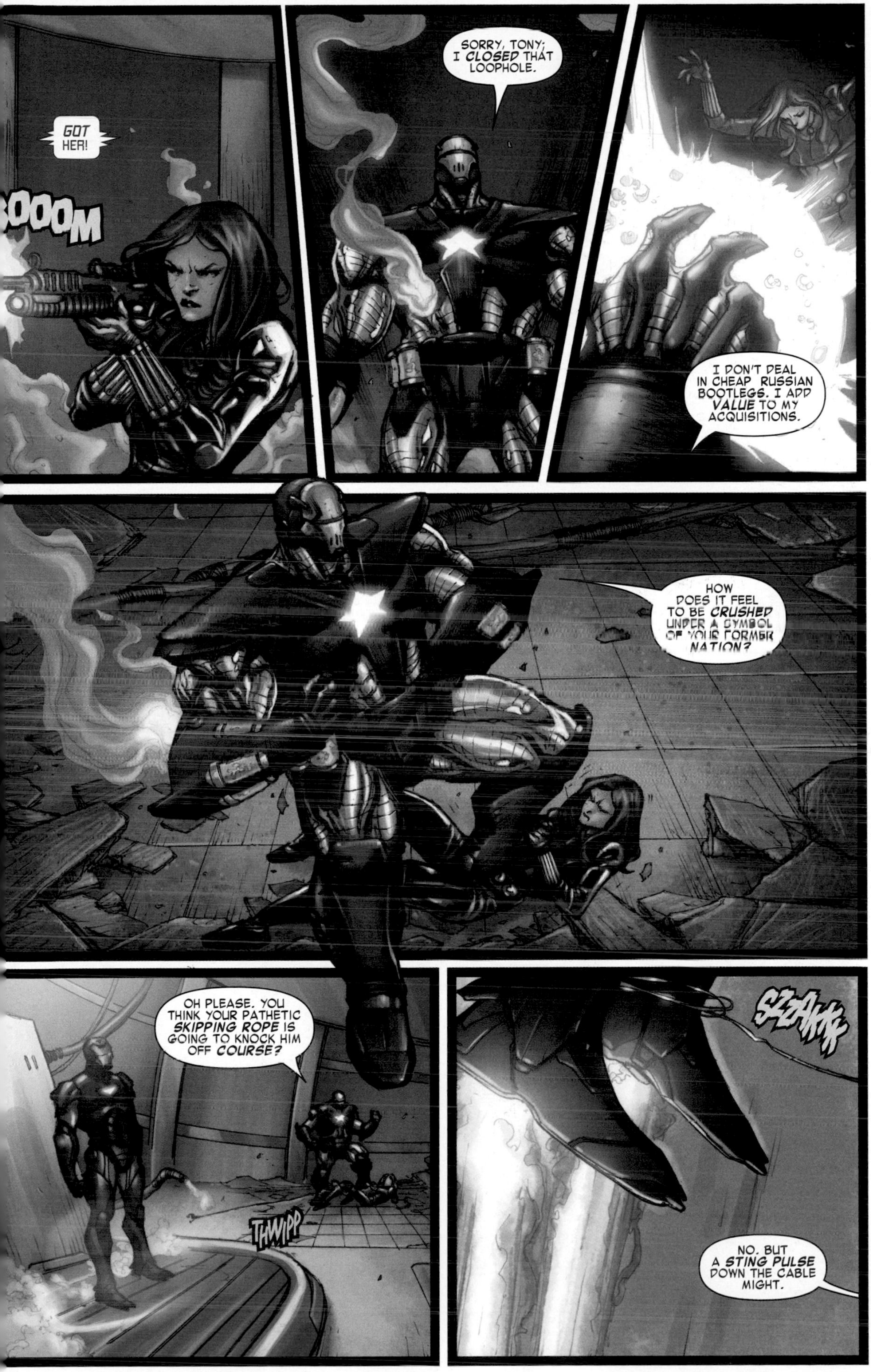
GOT HER!
BOOOM
SORRY, TONY; I CLOSED THAT LOOPHOLE.
I DON'T DEAL IN CHEAP RUSSIAN BOOTLEGS. I ADD VALUE TO MY ACQUISITIONS.
HOW DOES IT FEEL TO BE CRUSHED UNDER A SYMBOL OF YOUR FORMER NATION?
OH PLEASE. YOU THINK YOUR PATHETIC SKIPPING ROPE IS GOING TO KNOCK HIM OFF COURSE?
THWIPP
SZZAKKK
NO. BUT A STING PULSE DOWN THE CABLE MIGHT.

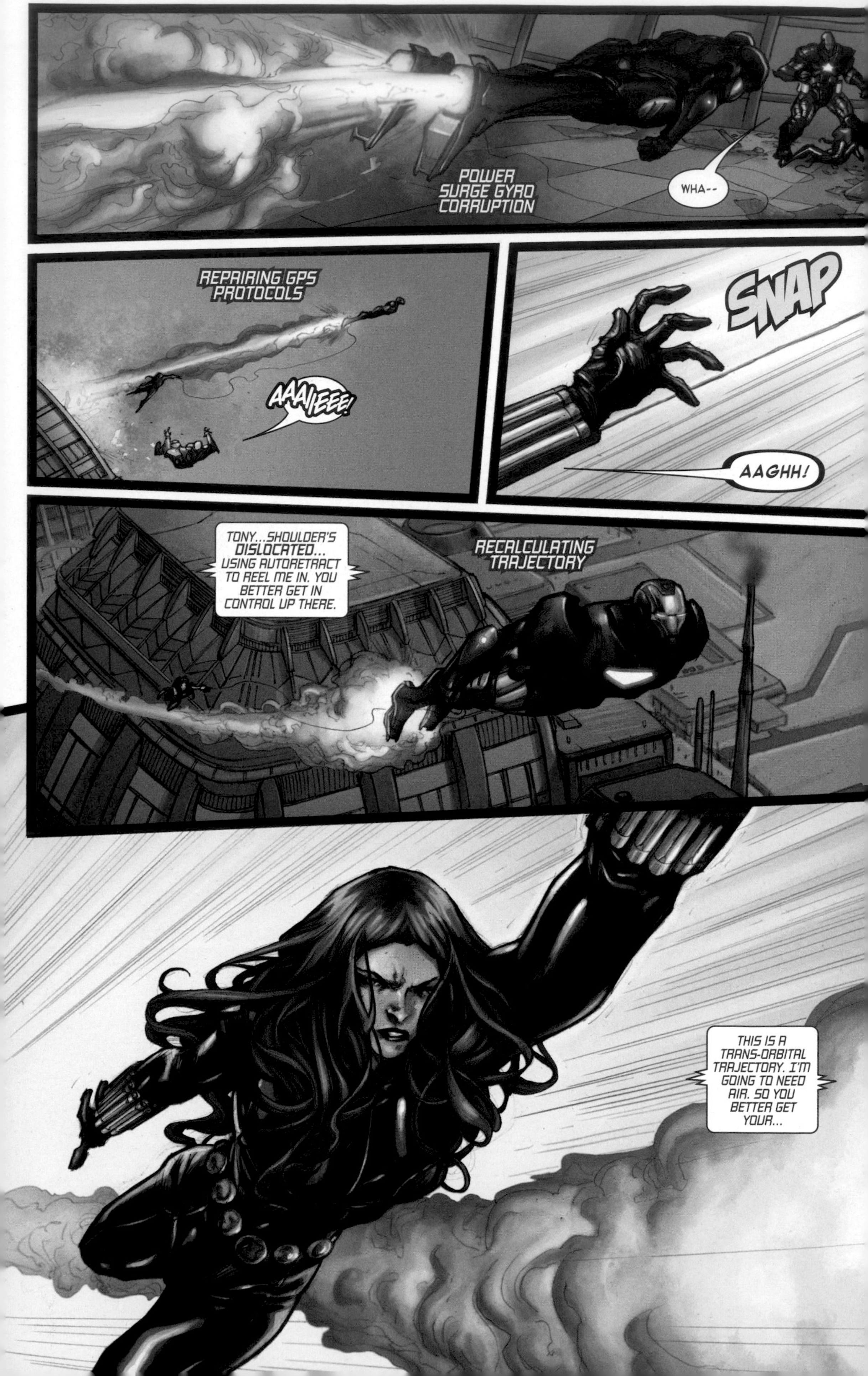
POWER SURGE GYRO CORRUPTION
WHA--
REPAIRING GPS PROTOCOLS
AAAIIEEE!
SNAP
AAGHH!
TONY...SHOULDER'S DISLOCATED... USING AUTORETRACT TO REEL ME IN. YOU BETTER GET IN CONTROL UP THERE.
RECALCULATING TRAJECTORY
THIS IS A TRANS-ORBITAL TRAJECTORY. I'M GOING TO NEED AIR. SO YOU BETTER GET YOUR...

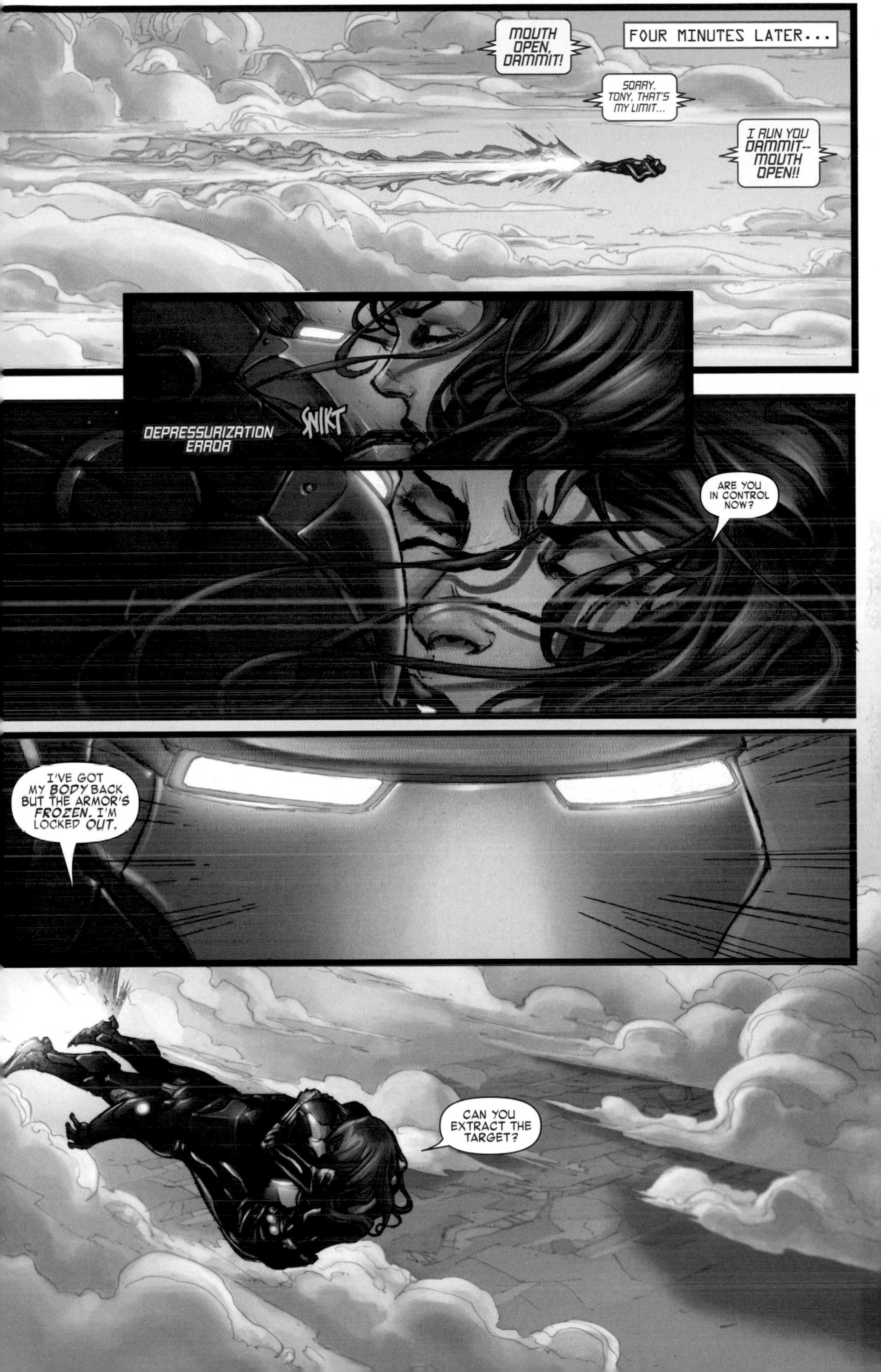
FOUR MINUTES LATER...
MOUTH OPEN, DAMMIT!
SORRY, TONY, THAT'S MY LIMIT...
I RUN YOU DAMMIT-- MOUTH OPEN!!
DEPRESSURIZATION ERROR
SNIKT
ARE YOU IN CONTROL NOW?
I'VE GOT MY BODY BACK BUT THE ARMOR'S FROZEN. I'M LOCKED OUT.
CAN YOU EXTRACT THE TARGET?

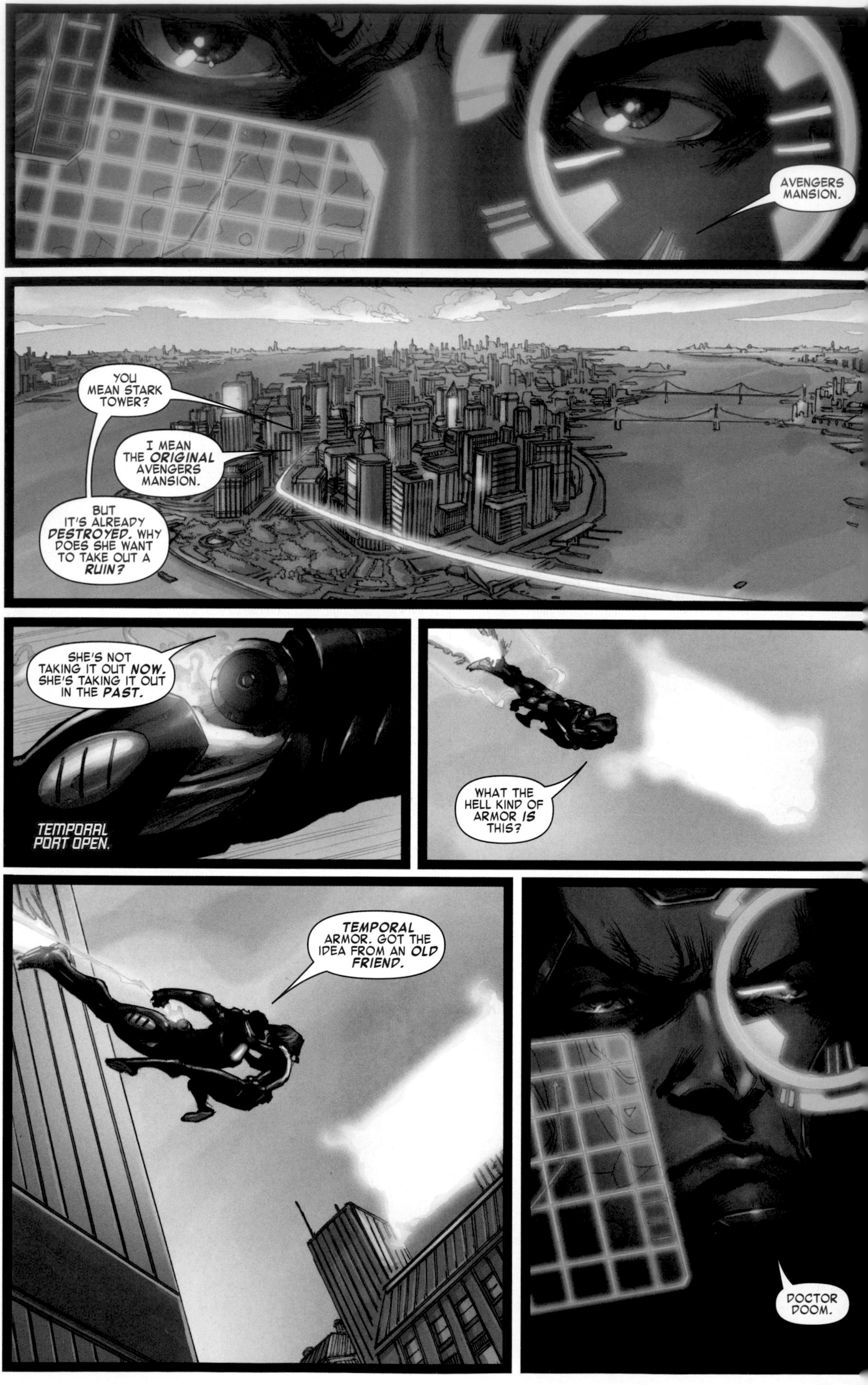
AVENGERS MANSION.
YOU MEAN STARK TOWER?
I MEAN THE ORIGINAL AVENGERS MANSION.
BUT IT'S ALREADY DESTROYED. WHY DOES SHE WANT TO TAKE OUT A RUIN?
SHE'S NOT TAKING IT OUT NOW. SHE'S TAKING IT OUT IN THE PAST.
TEMPORAL PORT OPEN.
WHAT THE HELL KIND OF ARMOR IS THIS?
TEMPORAL ARMOR. GOT THE IDEA FROM AN OLD FRIEND.
DOCTOR DOOM.

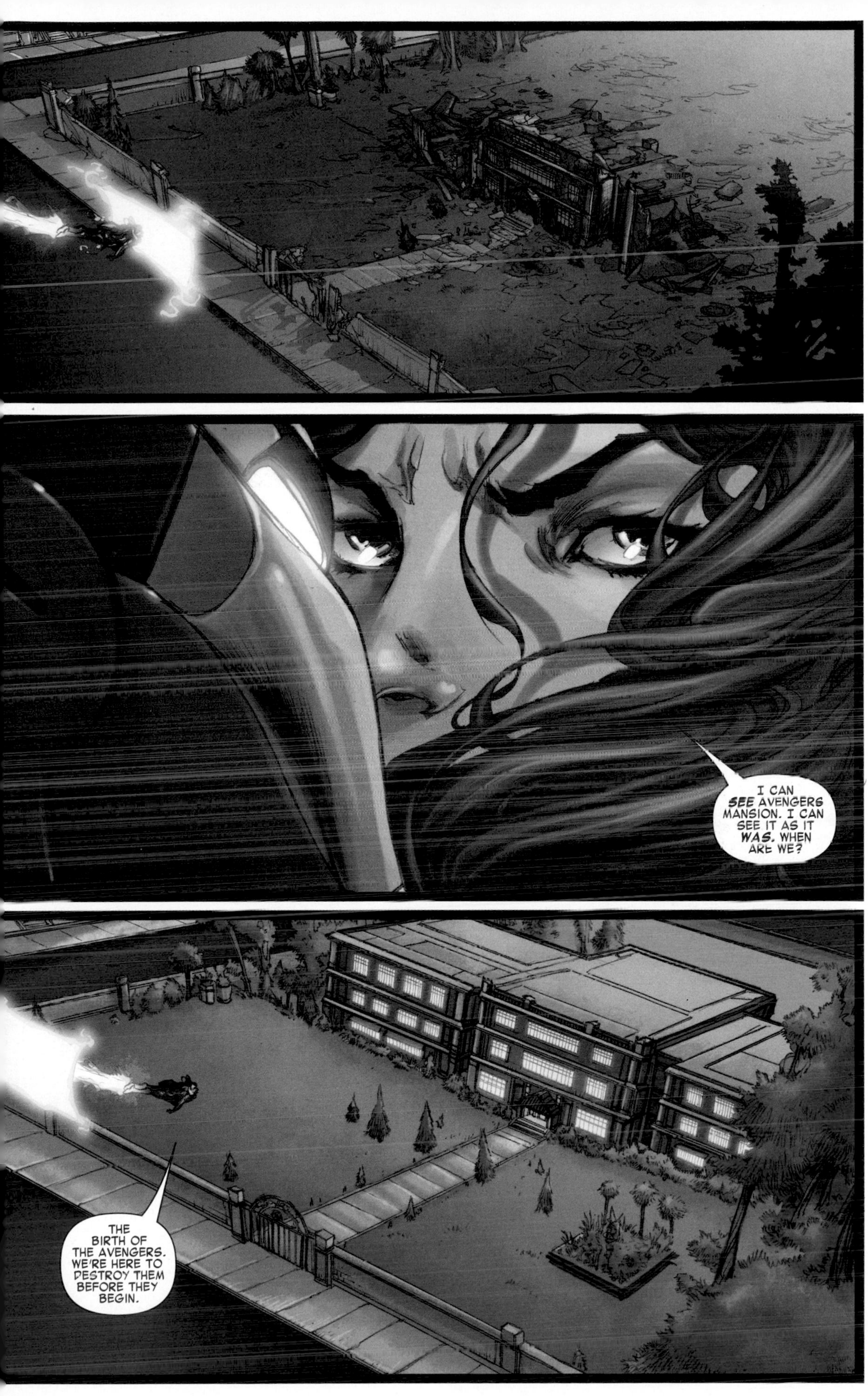
I CAN SEE AVENGERS MANSION. I CAN SEE IT AS IT WAS. WHEN ARE WE?
THE BIRTH OF THE AVENGERS. WE'RE HERE TO DESTROY THEM BEFORE THEY BEGIN.

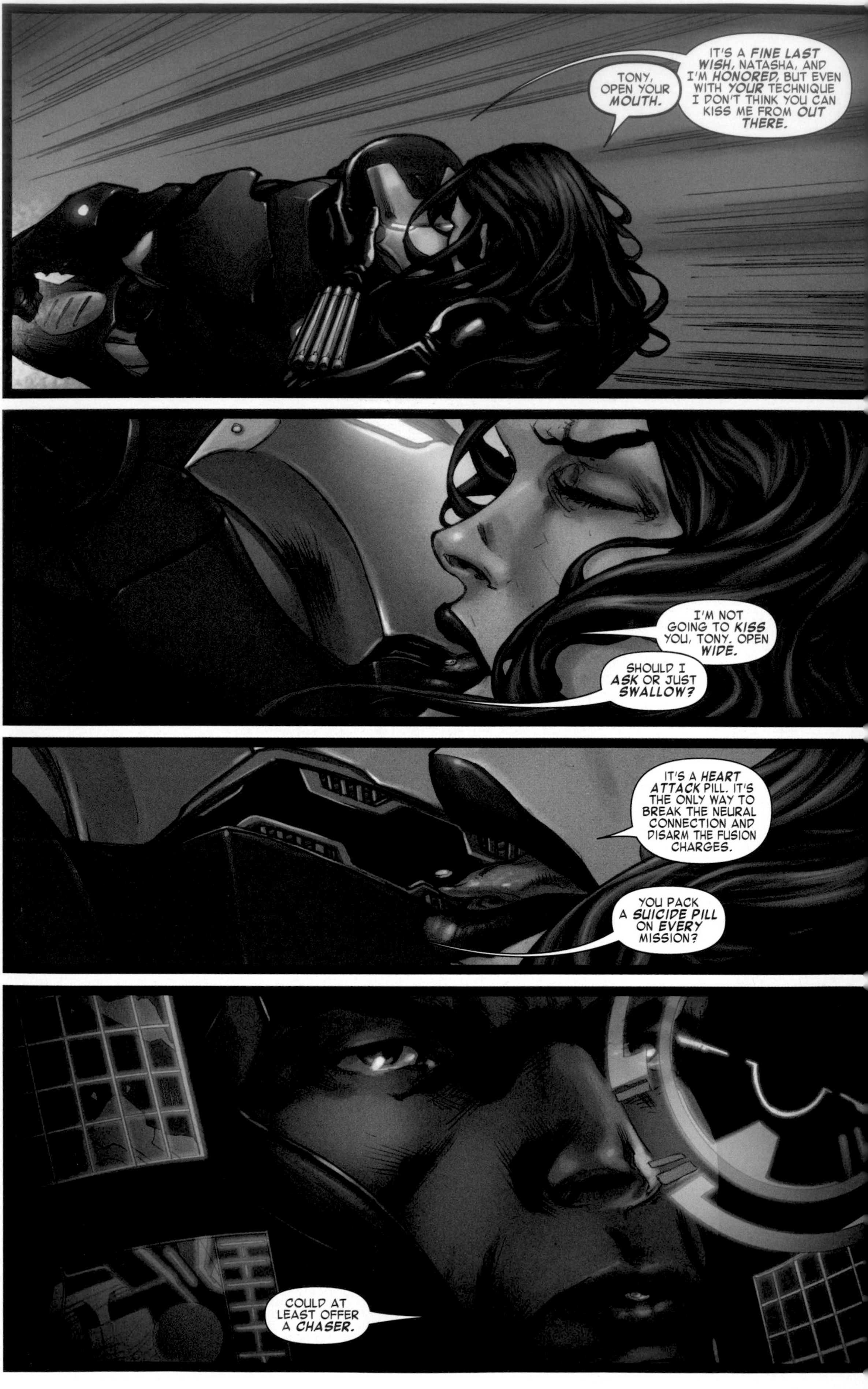
IT'S A FINE LAST WISH, NATASHA, AND I'M HONORED, BUT EVEN WITH YOUR TECHNIQUE I DON'T THINK YOU CAN KISS ME FROM OUT THERE.
TONY, OPEN YOUR MOUTH.
I'M NOT GOING TO KISS YOU, TONY. OPEN WIDE.
SHOULD I ASK OR JUST SWALLOW?
IT'S A HEART ATTACK PILL. IT'S THE ONLY WAY TO BREAK THE NEURAL CONNECTION AND DISARM THE FUSION CHARGES.
YOU PACK A SUICIDE PILL ON EVERY MISSION?
COULD AT LEAST OFFER A CHASER.

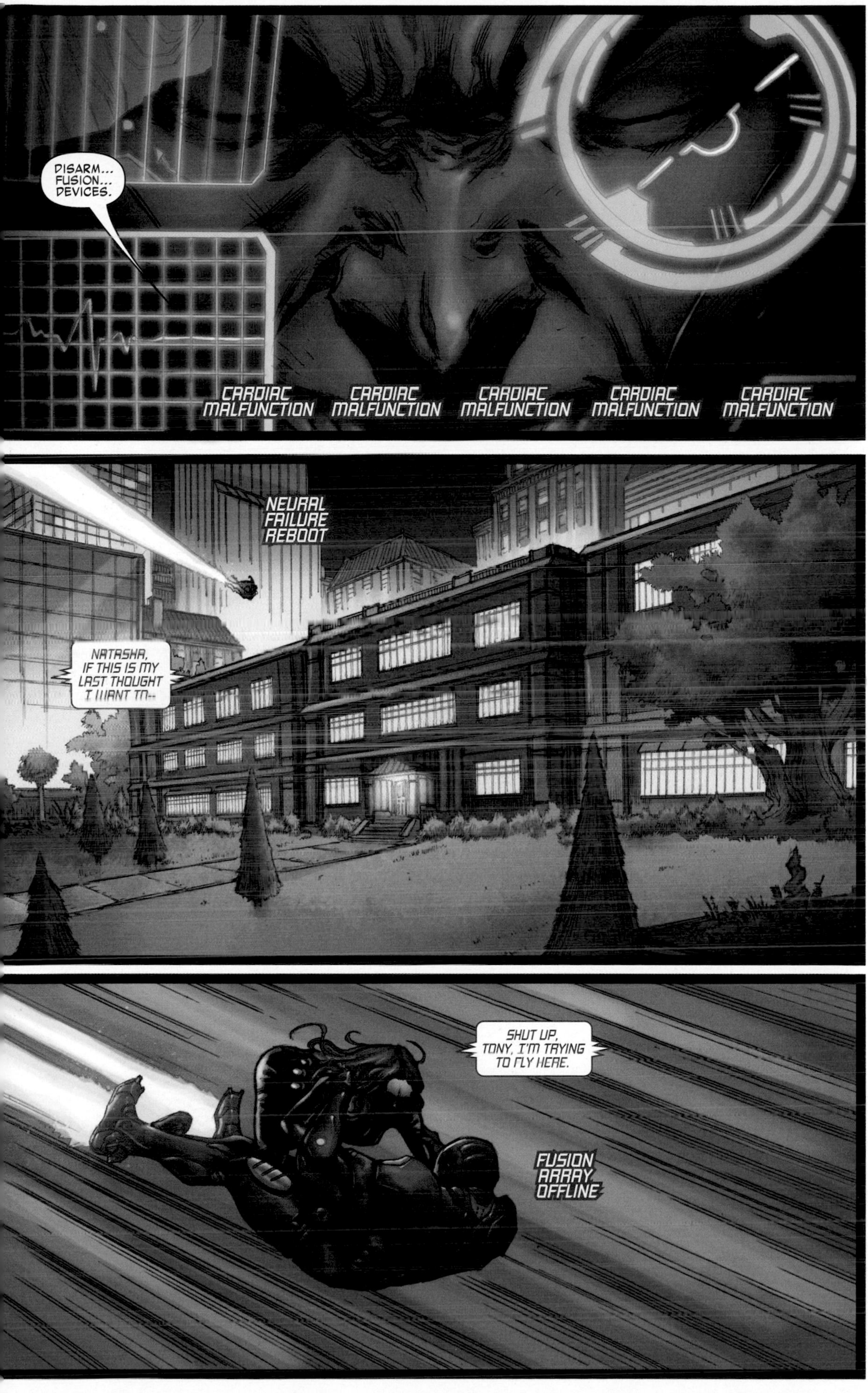
DISARM... FUSION... DEVICES.
CARDIAC MALFUNCTION
CARDIAC MALFUNCTION
CARDIAC MALFUNCTION
CARDIAC MALFUNCTION
CARDIAC MALFUNCTION
NEURAL FAILURE REBOOT
NATASHA, IF THIS IS MY LAST THOUGHT I WANT TO--
SHUT UP, TONY, I'M TRYING TO FLY HERE.
FUSION ARRAY OFFLINE

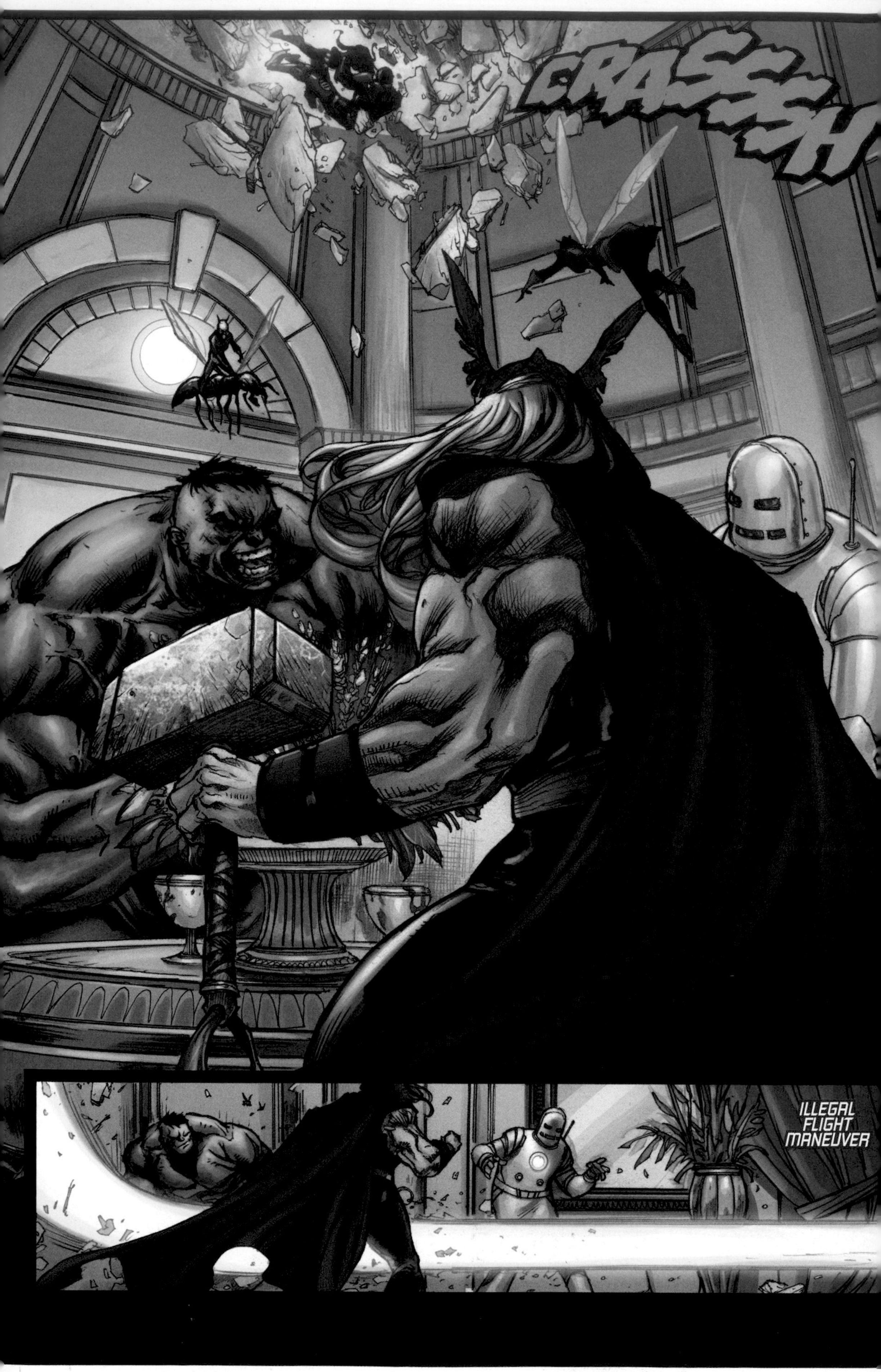
CRASSSH
ILLEGAL
FLIGHT
MANEUVER

TEMPORAL
PORT OPEN

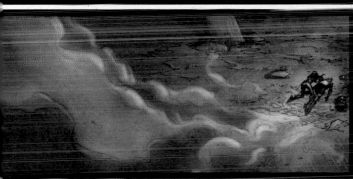

ZZZRAAKK!

OW!
WHAT THE
HELL!!

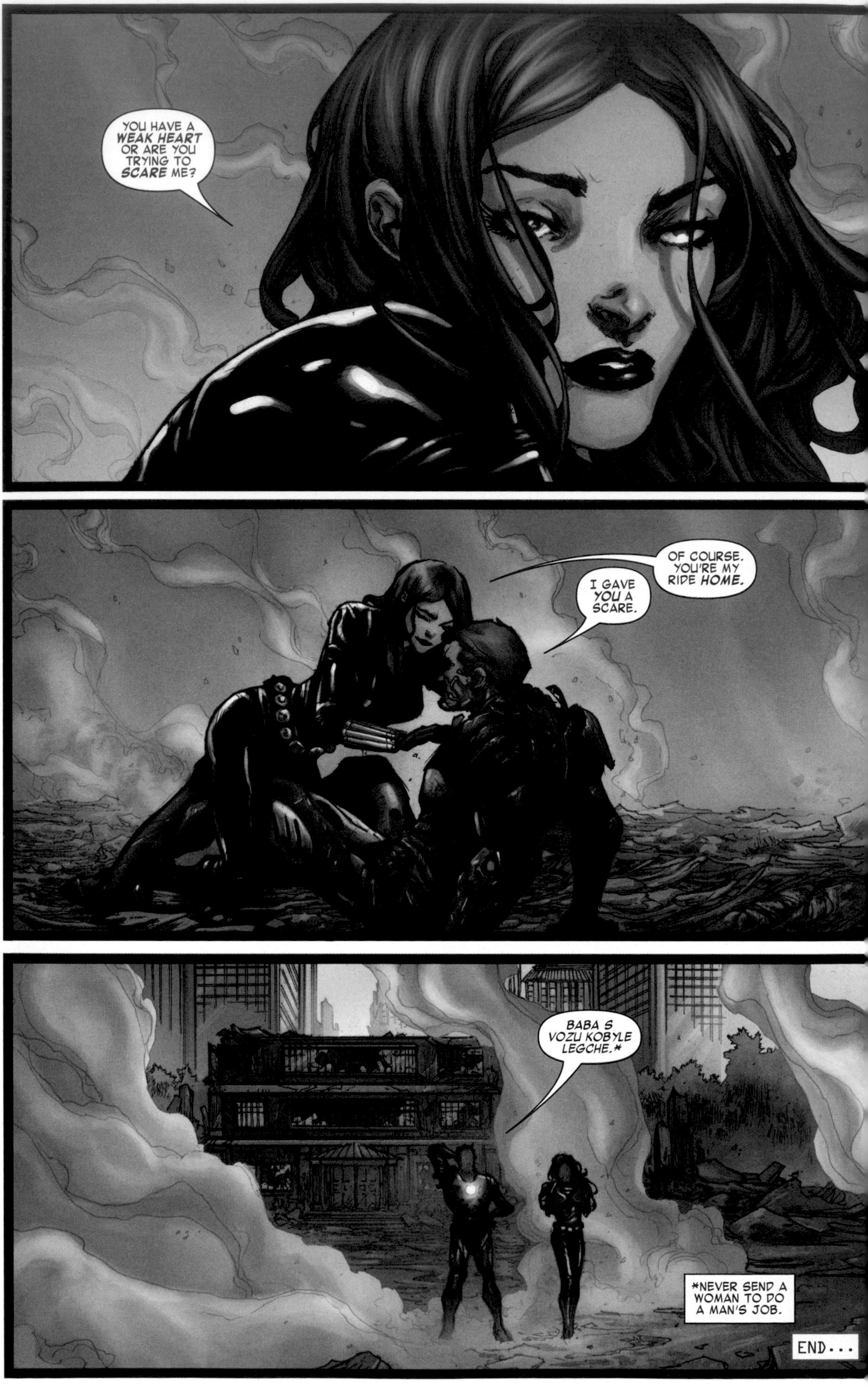
YOU HAVE A WEAK HEART OR ARE YOU TRYING TO SCARE ME?
I GAVE YOU A SCARE.
OF COURSE. YOU'RE MY RIDE HOME.
BABA S VOZU KOBYLE LEGCHE.*
*NEVER SEND A WOMAN TO DO A MAN'S JOB.
END...

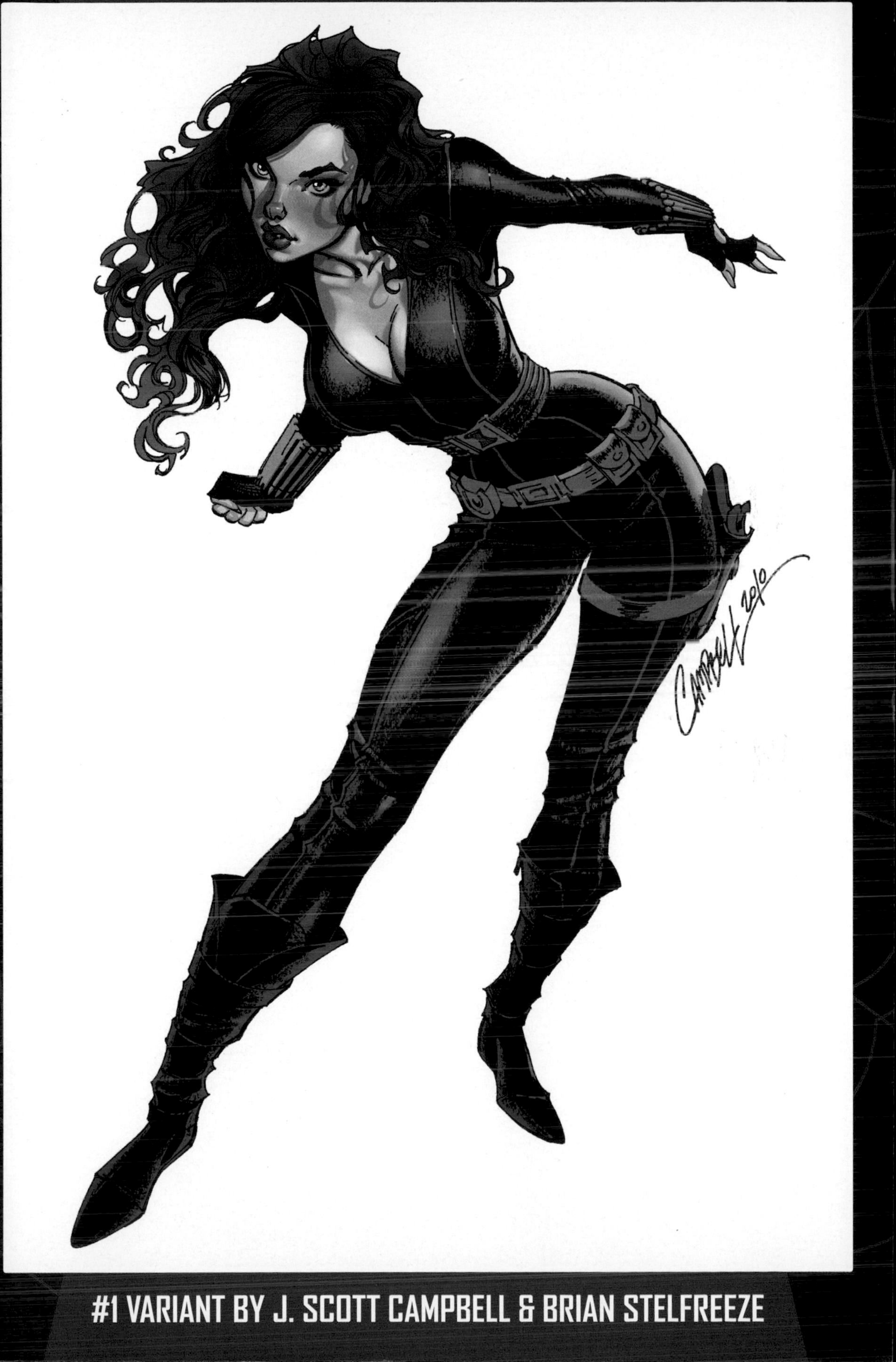

#1 VARIANT BY J. SCOTT CAMPBELL & BRIAN STELFREEZE

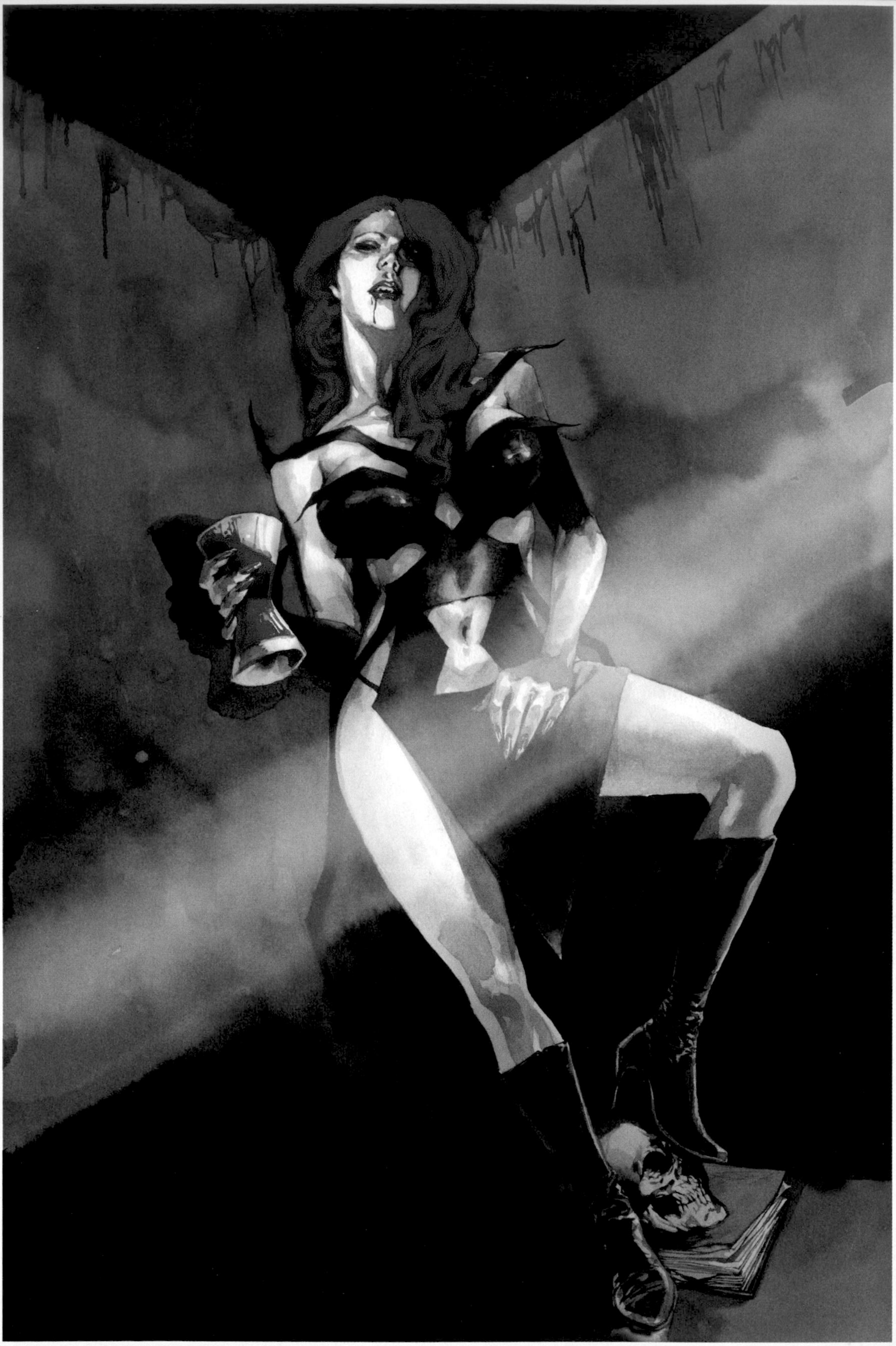

#7 VAMPIRE VARIANT BY STEPHANE PERGER